COLLECTIONS

OF

E NEW-YORK HISTORICAL SOCIETY

FOR THE YEAR

1901.

PUBLICATION FUND SERIES

NEW YORK:
PRINTED FOR THE SOCIETY.
MDCCCCII.

EXECUTIVE COMMITTEE.

FIRST CLASS—FOR ONE YEAR, ENDING 1903.

NICHOLAS FISH,　　　　　ISAAC J. GREENWOOD

CHARLES FREDERICK HOFFMAN, Jr.

SECOND CLASS—FOR TWO YEARS, ENDING 1904.

GEORGE W. VANDERBILT,　　　　CHARLES ISHAM,

FRANK TILFORD.

THIRD CLASS—FOR THREE YEARS, ENDING 1905.

JOHN A. WEEKES, Jr.,　　　J. PIERPONT MORGAN,

JOHN J. TUCKER.

FOURTH CLASS—FOR FOUR YEARS, ENDING 1906.

F. ROBERT SCHELL,　　　　DANIEL PARISH, Jr.,

FREDERIC WENDELL JACKSON.

JOHN J. TUCKER, *Chairman,*
DANIEL PARISH, Jr., *Secretary.*

[The President, Recording Secretary, Treasurer, and Librarian
are members of the Executive Committee.]

ABSTRACTS OF WILLS

ON FILE IN THE SURROGATE'S OFFICE,
CITY OF NEW YORK.

VOLUME· X.

OCTOBER 28, 1780—NOVEMBER 5, 1782.

In Memoriam

EUGENE AUGUSTUS HOFFMAN

President, 1901–1902

INTRODUCTION.

The copy of abstracts of wills in this volume was furnished by the Rev. John Keller, and contains abstracts of wills recorded in Liber 34 and part of Liber 35, in the Surrogate's office, this city. All the volumes of this series have been published by the Society, under the direction of the Librarian.

The expense of preparing and publishing this volume has been provided for by Mrs. Eugene A. Hoffman.

CONTENTS.

ABSTRACTS OF WILLS

ON FILE IN THE SURROGATE'S OFFICE,

CITY OF NEW YORK.

LIBER 34.

Page 1.—In the name of God, Amen. I, JOHN LEGGETT, of the West Farms, in the Borrough Town of Westchester, yeoman, being sensible of the mortality of my body, I direct all debts and funeral charges to be paid. I leave to my son Ebenezer all my right, title and interest in, and to a certain farm or Neck of land, called Cow Neck, in the Borough Town of Westchester, with all the meadows thereto belonging. Also a negro boy, Jim. I leave to my wife Mary, the use of my house and farm where I now live, and all my meadows lying in the West Farms, so long as she remains my widow and no longer. I leave to my wife all my movable estate except as here given. If she marries then I leave to my daughters, Mary and Martha, £100 each and the remainder of my movable estate to my daughters, Anna, Abigail, Mary, and Martha. After the death or marriage of my wife I leave to my son John the farm where I now live, with all the meadows that are in the West Farms, and all farming utensils, and my silver tankard and my negro boy Faith. I make my wife and my son Ebenezer and my friend, Stephen Hunt, executors.

Dated January 8, 1780. Witnesses, John Fowler, Thomas Lawrence, Daniel White, Physician. Proved, October 23, 1780, before Carey Ludlow, Esq.

Confirmed by His Excellency, James Robertson, Governor, October 23, 1780. Samuel Bayard jr., Secretary.

Page 3.—In the name of God, Amen. I, CHARLES WILLETT, of Flushing, in Queens County, on the Island of Nassau. My executors are to pay all debts and funeral charges. I leave to my wife Helena one half of all household goods and furniture, and a maintainance out of my house and land in Flushing, so long as she remains my widow. I leave to my daughter, Sarah Willett, £1000, and a cow and a horse, and her choice of two negro girls, and one half of the household furniture (except the tables and clock and desk). I leave to my son James one half of all my lands and meadows, which half is to be taken out of the farm which formerly belonged to Jeronemus Rapalye. I leave to my son Thomas one half of all my lands and meadows, which is to be the farm where I now live. I leave to my son James my desk, and one half of my negroes, and one third of my personal estate. I leave to my daughter Sarah one third of my personal estate. I leave to my wife three cows and one horse. I make Joseph Hewlett and Joseph Field, executors.

Dated June 15, 1767. Witnesses, Robert Morrell, Thomas Willett, Edward Willett. Proved, October 5, 1780, before John T. Troup, surrogate. Confirmed, October 24, 1780.

Page 4.—I, HANNAH BURR, of Cow Neck, in the town of Hempstead, in Queens County, widow, being sick and weak. Whereas an agreement of Partnership in Trade was made between me and my son James, that he should have one half of the profits, in consideration of his extraordinary trouble. In consideration of his agreeing to relinquish the same, I leave him all my farm and tract of land, and dwelling house and premises in Cow Neck, with about 2½ acres of land adjoining the land of Caleb Morrell, and the homestead with appurtenances. And my brothers, Samuel Mabbett and Joseph Mabbett (who have in themselves the legal title in Trust for me) are to execute a deed to my son James. I also leave to my son James £200, and he is to educate and bring up in a decent and becoming manner my three children, Jonathan, Susannah, and Joseph, during their minority. All the rest of my estate, of every description, I leave to all my children, James, Isaac, Jonathan, Susannah, and Joseph. My son James is to have at prime cost, my shop goods and merchandise, for his advancement in trade. I make my friends, Robert Mitchell and Joseph Pearsall, and my son James, executors.

Dated September 25, 1780. Witnesses, Daniel Kissam, Attorney at Law, Joseph Mabbett, John Burtis. Proved, October 9, 1780.

Page 6.—In the name of God, Amen. I, DAVID STUART, Serjeant in the Grenadier Company of His Majesty's 22d Regiment, and acting Quartermaster in the second Batalion of British Grenadiers. I leave to my wife, Mary Stuart, otherwise Smith, all my estate, real and personal, and all arrears of pay, and she is to pay all debts. And she shall pay to my only son, James Stuart, aged nine years, one half of what I shall die possessed of. I make my wife executor.

Dated October 10, 1780. Witnesses, Alexander Stuart, Serjeant 22d R'g't, David White, Serjeant 64th R'g't, George Thompson, Serjeant 63d R'g't of Grenadiers. Proved, November 6, 1780.

Page 7.—In the name of God, Amen. I, NATHANIEL PROVOST, of Newtown, in Queens County. All debts to be paid by my executors, as soon as they can obtain an indemnifying release from my mortgage against my estate. My executors are to sell whatever may be unnecessary to keep on the place, to best advantage. I leave to my wife during her widowhood, the house and land where I now live, with the furniture,

for her maintainance and to bring up my children. I
leave to my son John, when he is 21, all my real estate, and what is my personal estate out of doors for
his inheritance, and Right of First born, and he is to
pay to his sister Elizabeth £15, and to his brothers,
Robert and Nathaniel, £15 each. My wife is to live
on my estate for life if she chooses to do so. I make
my uncle, Nathaniel Moore, Captain Cornelius Rapalyea, and Jacobus Ricker, executors.

Dated May 12, 1780. Witnesses, John Keams, William Hallett, Nathaniel Moore. Proved, June 10, 1780.

Page 9.—In the name of God, Amen. I, Daniel
Rapalye Sr., of Newtown in Queens County, yeoman,
being in reasonable health, my executors are to pay
all debts. I leave to my son Joris £5 for his Birth
right. I leave to my son Cornelius the piece of fresh
meadow that lyes near where William Betts now lives,
being 3¾ acres. Bounded north by road, east by Joseph Burroughs, south by the creek, west by William
Betts. Which is to be valued at £80, and he is to have
enough more to make him equal with the rest of his
brothers and sisters. I leave to my son Martin my
farm where I now live, with the meadow thereto belonging, being about 150 acres, bounded northwest
by Joseph Lawrence and Richard Berrian, southwest
by Richard Berrian, Benjamin Cornish, John Moore,
jr., the estate of Lambert Moore, and estate of Samuel Waldron, south by the estate of Samuel Fish, William Betts and Joseph Burroughs, east by highway
that leads from Newtown to John Fish's mill, north
by Daniel Rapalyea, Esq. Also a piece of salt meadow joining to Robert Coe's land. And the whole to be
valued at £1920. And he is to pay to his brothers and
sisters enough to make them equal with himself. I
leave to my children, Joris, Sarah, wife of Isaac Bogart, Jannettie, wife of Hendrick Ryher, and Neeltie,
wife of Jeremiah Remsen, all the rest of my estate.
I make my three sons executors.

Dated April 12, 1776. Witnesses, Isaac Rapalye, Jacob Rapalye, Samuel Moore, 3d. Proved, November 26, 1776. Confirmed, November 7, 1780.

Page 11.—In the name of God, Amen. I, JACOB BLACKWELL, of Queens County, on Nassau or Long Island, being at this time in perfect health, August 29, 1779. I leave to my sons, James and Jacob, my Island known by the name of Blackwell's Island, to them and their heirs and assigns forever. And they are to pay half the legacies. I leave to my sons, Samuel and Josiah, the farm on Nassau, or Long Island, whereon I now dwell, and they are to pay one half of the legacies. I leave to my wife Lydia the choice of any room in my house, and the use of one third of my farm and Island during her life or widowhood. Also a negro wench Belinda, and one third of household furniture. I leave to my sons, Joseph and Robert, each £10. I leave to my daughter, Lydia Blackwell, £300, and a negro girl, Sylva, and one third of household furniture. To my daughter, Mary Blackwell, £300, and a negro girl and one third of household furniture. I order that a tract of land, of 8 acres, on York island, near Harlem, and the rest of my negroes, to be sold, and the proceeds used to pay debts and legacies. All the stock and farming utensils are to remain on the farm. My executors are to enclose one quarter of an acre of land, where the burying place now is, the same to be reserved for ever as a family burying place. Whereas I have in the hands of Mr. Jacob Hallett, of the Jerseys, about £200, it is to be applied towards debts and legacies. I make my sons, Robert and Jacob, executors.

Witnesses, Jacob Hallett, Jr., Richard Betts, Ferryman, Hendrick Suydam, miller. Proved, November 13, 1780.

Page 13.—I, HENRY FRANKLIN, of New York, this 26 day of the 5th month 1780, being in health. My executors are to pay all debts and funeral charges. I leave to my wife Mary all household goods, plate and furniture, and £50 yearly while she remains my widow. If she marries, she is to have one ninth of the personal property and the use of one ninth of the real estate, except a certain tract of land given to my five sons, and six farms in the Town of Dartmouth. My executors are to sell all real estate, except as here given, and the interest is to be paid to my wife, for bringing up and educating my children. Of the remainder I leave one ninth to each of my children, Henry, Matthew, Richard, William, Samuel, Phebe, Sarah, and Philadelphia, when of age. Now as touching the six lots or farms, in the township of Dartmouth, on the west bank of the North river I bequeath them to to my three daughters. And as touching a tract of land, granted by Governor Tryon, by Patent to me and Frederick Rhinelander and others, being about six miles northwest of Onion river, in Charlotte County, my part containing about 40,000 acres, I leave the same to my five sons, when my youngest son Samuel is of age, which will be on the first day of the 3d month, 1805, but one eleventh of the profits is to be for my wife. My executors are to be guardians of my children. My five sons are to be put to trades or business, among Friends, if it can be. I make my wife and my esteemed friends, James Mott, William Rhinelander, and William Rickman executors, and they are to have five per cent on all monies, above the debts.

Witnesses, Samuel Mabbett, Joseph Hanford, Isaac Burr. Proved, November 13, 1780. (The witnesses are all merchants of New York, and all of the People called Quakers.)

Page 16.—In the name of God, Amen. I, BLANCHE BEAU, of New York, spinster, being in an infirm state of health. I leave all my real and personal estate to the use of my sister, Elizabeth Beau, during her life, and to the use of my brother, Renne Beau, during his life; and my brother, Renne Beau, is to be supported during his natural life in a Christian like, decent and handsome manner. After the death of my sister, my negro woman and her children are to be free. After the death of my brother and sister, I leave to my friend, Jane Smith, widow (late Jane Papoon), and her two sisters, Mary and Elizabeth Papoon, all my real estate during their lives. After the death of my brother and sister, I leave all my personal estate to my God children, Blanche Dominic, Phebe Totten, Magdalene Flandereau, and Garret Richard, and to the two God children of my said sister, viz., Isaac Totten, and Ann Dominic, and to my worthy friends, Elizabeth, wife of John Lasshan, Mary, wife of James Wilmot, Catharine Pino, Jane Harrison, daughter of Morly Harrison, Christina Theobald, and Mary Kelliker. After the death of Jane Smith, and Mary and Elizabeth Papoon, my executors are to sell all my real estate and pay the proceeds to my said God children. I make my sister Elizabeth, William Ustick, David Seabury, and George Dominic, executors.

Dated February 28, 1780. Witnesses, Simeon Lugrin, school master, John Barrow, baker, Bartholomew Crannell, Esq. Proved, November 6, 1780.

[NOTE.—The newspaper of this date says: "Miss Blanche Beau, who from her earliest days till a few months before her death taught one of the most serviceable schools in this city, died October 12, 1780, aged 60."—W. S. P.]

Page 19.—October 5, 1780. The following is the last will and testament of LEWIS DEBOYES. After all reasonable charges are paid, I leave to my sister, Elizabeth Deboyes, my interest wholly, except my wearing apparell. I leave to my brother John, my wearing clothes, chest and tools. The above is the true and last will of Lewis Deboyes. The estate of Lewis Deboyes to be left in the care of Col. Benjamin Simmonds, of Staten

Island, and he is to demand all notes, bonds, and book debts.

Witnesses, Stephen Farrand, Jacob Loder, Henry Hennion. Proved, November 13, 1780.

Page 20.—In the name of God, Amen. I, JOSEPH CONKLIN, being weak and sick. I leave to my cousin, Jeremiah Havens, all my movable estate, after paying all debts, and I make him executor. I leave to my negro wench, Merria, her time. I also give to Merria, her daughter, Cloe, during her life.

Dated September 30, 1780. Witnesses, David Howell, John Havens, Joseph Clarke, doctor. Proved in Suffolk County before Nathan Woodhull, surrogate. November 17, 1780.

[NOTE.—The testator probably lived on Shelter Island, or on Hog Neck, in the town of Southampton. The will presents a curious instance of a mother holding a daughter as a slave.—W. S. P.]

Page 21.—In the name of God, Amen. I, GEORGE PETTINER, Lieutenant in His Majesty's 6th Regiment, at present in New York. I leave to my wife, Anna Frances, the use of all my estate for life, for maintaining and educating my daughter, Frances Kean Pettiner, and after my wife's decease I leave all to my said daughter. I make my wife executor.

Dated December 23, 1778. Witnesses, Terrence Kevin, Esq., Notary Public, I. Randel, Richard Fletcher. Proved, November 27, 1780.

Page 22.—In the name of God, Amen. I, SAMUEL SACKET, of Jamaica, in Queens County, Gentleman, being sick. I leave to my wife Mary the use of all household furniture, lands, negroes, horse and chair, two best cows, with pasturing and firewood for two fires, if she lives in the country. If she chooses to live in the city, I leave her the use of the back part of my house in New York, in Queen street, with the back

room, two chambers and loft and kitchen. If she choose
to live in the country, I leave her £50 a year and one
fifth of the income of estate. I leave to my oldest son,
Samuel, £700. To my son Richard £500. To my son
Augustus £500, when of age. My executors are to allow to my wife £50 for each of my children, yearly,
so long as they live with her, as compensation for their
meat, drink, washing, clothing and education. And
when they are of suitable age, they are to be put to
callings, as my executors may think most suitable.
My executors are to sell all stock and farming utensils.
After the death of my wife, I leave all to my children,
Samuel, Richard, Augustus, and Sophia. I make my
relation, Captain Thomas Laurence, of Newtown, and
my friends, James Desbrosses, of New York, and
Christopher Smith and Cary Ludlow, of Jamaica, executors.

. Dated September 26, 1780. Witnesses, Jacob
Sharpe, Charles Welling, Samuel Welling. Proved,
October 25, 1780.

[NOTE.—Mr. Samuel Sackett died at Jamaica, September 30, 1780.]

Page 25.—I, SAMUEL JACKSON, SR., of Jerusalem, in
the town of Hempstead, in Queens County, July 26,
1778, being weak and infirm. I leave to my wife Mary
£500, and a horse and riding chair and negro girl, and
£40 yearly so long as she remains my widow. And
the use of half my dwelling house. Her horse is to be
kept with grass, hay, and grain, and she is to have
firewood, cut and carted to the door. I leave to my
daughter Ruth £300. To my daughter Mary £250.
To my daughter Jemima £150. To my daughters, Le-
titicia and Martha, £346 between them. I leave to
my wife and my daughters, Ruth and Mary, all household goods, including the cloths, linnen and woolen.
And my wife shall make the yarn, not made, into cloth,
and the cloth, not made, into clothes for my children.
My daughters, Ruth and Mary, are to live with my

wife or their brothers, Townsend and Thomas Jackson, so long as they are unmarried. I leave to my grandson, Samuel Jackson, one horse, value £20, and a saddle and bridle, when he is sixteen. I leave to my son Richard over and above what I have already given him, one half of the land which I purchased of Joseph Lockwood and of Thomas and Elnathan Hanford, at or near Cold Spring, in Oyster Bay, to be taken off the north side. I leave to my sons, Townsend and Thomas, all the rest of my estate, lands, and movables, except so much as may be sold to pay debts. I make my sons, Townsend and Thomas, and my nephew, George Hewlett, executors.

Witnesses, William Jones, Richard Jackson, Jacob Jackson.

Codicil. February 17, 1780. Revokes the gift of land made to his son Richard, and leaves the same to his grandson, Samuel Jackson, son of said Richard. And he acquits his son Richard from all due from him for money advanced. Also leaves to his wife Mary another cow and the privilege of a garden. I leave to my daughter Ruth a cow. My daughter Mary being since married, I leave her a part of the household goods immediately. I leave to each of my daughters £50, and to Mary £10 more.

Witnesses, John Jackson Jr., Jacob Jackson, Samuel Jones. Proved, November 29, 1780.

Page 28.—In the name of God, Amen. I, JAMES BUVELOT, of New York, being in perfect health. All debts to be paid. I leave to my wife Mary the rest of my dwelling house and lot lying in Hanover Square, in the East Ward of New York, during her widowhood, and then to my nephew, John Buvelot, and my niece, Margaret Bassett. I leave to my wife Mary the dwelling house and lot in Beekman street, where I now live, and all the rest of my estate. I make my wife and my friends, John Aymar and Simeon Lugrin, late of New York, but now of Jamaica, executors.

Dated August 4, 1777. Witnesses, Joseph Bell, Elizabeth Van Dyck, widow, John Woods. Proved, December 4, 1780.

Page 30.—In the name of God, Amen. I, JOHN FIELD, of Flushing, in Queens County, being in perfect health. My executors are to sell all my estate at public vendue, and pay the proceeds to my four brothers, Benjamin, Gilbert, Charles, and James. I make my brothers, Benjamin and Gilbert, and my friend, John Rodman, executors.

Dated April 1, 1773. Witnesses, John Fowler, Quaker, John Carl, Freelove Carl. Proved, October 31, 1780.

Page 31.—In the name of God, Amen. I, TERRENCE McDERMOTT, Ensign in His Majesty's 35th Regiment, and eldest son and heir of Owen McDermott, late of County Roscommon (Ireland). I leave to my wife Elizabeth £500, and all household furniture and personalities, of whatever kind, and £100 stirling yearly. In the event my wife is now with child, if it be a son, he shall have all the remainder of my estate. If a daughter, then £2000 when of age or married. All the remainder of my estate I leave to my brother Patrick, in case I have no more children. I make Christopher French, late Lieutenant Colonel, 52nd Regiment, and Hon. Hugh Wallace, of New York, Lawrence Parsons, major of 7th Regiment, Patrick McDermott, and my wife Elizabeth, executors.

Dated October 27, 1778. Witnesses, F. Rush Clark, John West, David Campbell. Proved, December 18, 1780.

Page 32.—In the name of God, Amen. I, FRANCES VAN CORTLANDT, of the Little or Lower Yonkers, in Westchester County, being in good health. My Body to be decently buried near my deceased husband in our Family vault, at discretion of my executors. All debts and funeral expenses to be paid. I leave to my two daughters, Anne Van Horne, and Eve White, £1000 each, before any division of my estate between them and their brothers, to whom my deceased husband hath devised the most considerable part of all his real estate, and left it to me to make further provision for my two daughters, out of the estate I expected to receive or have from my father and mother, both deceased. I leave to my daughter, Anne Van Horne, the choice of my negro girls. I leave to my daughter Eve a negro girl named Susan. I leave to my son Frederick a negro wench Hester and a negro boy Pero. I leave to my son James a negro man, John, who now lives with him. All the rest of my estate, real and personal, I leave to my five children, James, Augustus, Frederick, Eve, and Anne. My executors may sell all real estate. I make my sons, James and Frederick, executors.

Dated March 2, 1771, in the 11 year of Kinge George III. Witnesses, Pelatiah Haus, John Cozine, Jr., Esq., John Noble. Proved, December 28, 1780. Confirmed, January 5, 1781.

[NOTE.—Frances Van Cortlandt was the daughter of Augustus Jay and his wife, Anna Maria Bayard. She married Frederick Van Cortlandt, January 19, 1724. He died February 12, 1749, and she died August 2, 1780, aged 79. The estate, of which Van Cortlandt Park is a part, descended to his son, James Van Cortlandt, who died April 1, 1781. Owing to entailment and want of issue, it went to his uncle, Augustus Van Cortlandt, who died in 1823. From him it descended to his grandson, Augustus White, son of Henry White, and his daughter, Anna Van Cortlandt. He took the name of Van Cortlandt. In default of issue the estate went to his nephew, Augustus Bibby, son of his sister, Augusta Van Cortlandt, who married Dr. E. N. Bibby. Augustus Bibby also took the name of Van Cortlandt, and his son, Augustus Van Cortlandt, and his sons are the present representatives of this ancient and honored family. The daughter Eve, mentioned in the will, married Henry White. The daughter Anne married, first, Nathaniel Marston, Jr.; second, Augustus Van Horne. —W. S. P.]

Page 34.—In the name of God, Amen. I, Jacob Rapelje, of Newtown, in Queens County, on Nassau Island, being in reasonable health. I leave to my wife Catrina the use of all estate during her widowhood. I leave to my son Peter £5 for his birth right. After my wife's decease or marriage I leave to my sons, Peter, George, and Jacob, £50 each, being for outsets. I leave to my son Peter my negro boy Joe. To my son George a negro boy Sam. To my daughter Sarah a negro girl. To my son Jacob a negro girl, and to my daughter Catrina a negro girl. After all debts are paid I leave all my estate to all my children, Angenietie, wife of Martin Schenck, Peter, George, Sarah, Jacob, and Catrina. After my wife's decease or marriage, all my estate to be put up to sale to the highest bidder. I make my sons, Peter and George, and my son in law, Martin Schenck, executors.

Dated January. 6, 1775. Witnesses, Jonh. Laurence, Edmund Pinfold, John Laurence. Proved, November 20, 1780.

Page 36.—In the name of God, Amen. I, Charles Nicoll, of New York, merchant, for the settlement of my temporal affairs do make this my last will and testament. I leave to my nephew, Charles Nicoll Taylor, and to my two nieces, Ann, wife of Evert Bancker, Jr., grocer, and Sarah, wife of Matthew Nicoll, all my real estate, consisting of the lot of land on which stood my late dwelling house near White Hall, in New York, and also one lot in said city which I purchased of Anthony A. Rutgers. Also one thousand acres of land in Tryon County, on the north side of the Mohawk river, being part of a large tract granted to John Glen and ninety-three others, by Letters Patent, April 12, 1770.

I leave to my nephew, Charles Nicoll Taylor, my negro lad named Edinborough, but commonly called Burrough, and my gold watch and wearing apparell, and all linnens and woolen. Of all the rest of my personal estate I leave to my brother, Edward Nicoll, one third. To my brother John one third, and to Charles Nicoll Taylor and my two said nieces, one third. I make my brother Edward, and my nephew, Charles Nicoll Taylor, and Evert Bancker, Jr., executors.

Dated December 4, 1780. Witnesses, John Kelly, Notary Public, Joseph Allicocke, grocer, Terrence Reilly. Proved, December 18, 1780.

Page 37.—In the name of God, Amen. I, ZOPHOR ROGERS, of Hunttington, Suffolk County, being weak in body. November 2, 1780. I leave to my wife Deborah four cows. I leave to my wife and my four daughters (*not named*) all the rest of my movable estate. I leave to my wife the use of the best room, and chamber and small cellar, during her widowhood. I leave to my three sons, Zophor, Joel, and Moses, all my lands and meadows, and all my rights in commonage. I make my wife Deborah, Austin Jarvis, and Melancthon Bryan, executors.

Witnesses, Henry Jarvis, Stephen Rogers, Daniel Jarvis. Proved, November 24, 1780.

Page 38.—In the name of God, Amen. I, SOLOMON FOWLER, of East Chester, yeoman, being in good health. After all debts are paid I leave all my estate of lands and goods to my wife Sarah and my child Rachel. If my daughter dies under age, then all to my wife. I make my wife and my brother-in-law, Thomas Hunt, executors.

Dated April 28, 1763. Witnesses, John Bartow, Basil Bartow, Aaron Quinby. Proved, December 18, 1780.

[NOTE.—" Captain Solomon Fowler was killed in attack on the rebels at Horse Neck, May 22, 1780."

Page 40.—In the name of God, Amen. I, JANNETJE GOELET, of New York, widow, being in perfect health. My executors are to pay all debts. I leave to my grandson, John Goelet, son of my son, Francis Goelet, deceased, Twenty shillings. I leave to my daughter, Mary Goelet, all my furniture, plate, and wearing apparell. Whereas my son Francis had the sum of £100 before his decease, my other children, Peter, Mary, Jane Zabriskie, and Catharine shall have the like sum of £100. All the rest of estate I leave to my said children and the heirs of my son Francis. I make my son Peter, and my son-in-law, John Zabriskie, Jr., executors.

Dated February 20, 1770. Witnesses, Henry Remsen, Jr., Edmund Seaman, merchant, David Seabury, merchant. Proved, December 18, 1780.

Page 41.—In the name of God, Amen. I, MARY GOELET, late of New York, shopkeeper, and at present of Bergen County, New Jersey, spinster, being in good health. I leave to my sister Jane, wife of John Zabriskie, Jr., of Bergen County, £100. I leave to my Godson, James Goelet, son of my late brother, Francis Goelet, £50. To my Goddaughter, Jane Goelet, daughter of my brother, Peter Goelet, £50. To my nephew, John Zabriskie the 3d, son of my sister Jane, £50, to be paid to his mother. I leave to my sister, Catharine Goelet, now a single woman, all the rest of my estate, real and personal, and make her executor. I have set my hand and seal in New York, September 3, 1773.

Witnesses, John Q. Myers, William Wentworth, John McKesson. Proved, December 18, 1780, upon oath of Peter Goelet.

Page 43.—In the name of God, Amen. I, JOHN TAYLOR, of New York, mariner, for the settlement of my temporal affairs. I leave to my son, Charles Nicoll Taylor, one thousand acres of land which was conveyed to me by my brother-in-law, Charles Nicoll, by Deeds of Lease and Release, February 6–7, 1775, being part of a certain large tract granted by Letters Patent, April 12, 1770, to Henry Glen and the said Charles Nicoll and ninety-two others, situate in Tryon County, on the north side of Mohawks river, and designated on a map of partition as the East half of Lot twenty-six and the West half of Lot seventy-three. I leave to my said son, Charles Nicoll Taylor, my negro man and a small feather bed that I used to carry to sea with me. I leave to my friend and brother-in-law, Charles Nicoll, my large silver tankard, which I formerly had from him. I leave to my daughter Sarah all the rest of my plate and household furniture, which I think equal in value to what I have already given to my daughter Anne, wife of Evert Bancker, Jr. I leave to my sister, Sarah Barns, £15. My executors are to sell my house, tenement and lot in John street, in which I now live, and the proceeds to my son and daughters. I make my brother-in-law, Charles Nicoll, and my brother, Willett Taylor, and my son-in-law, Evert Bancker, Jr., executors.

Dated April 21, 1777. Witnesses, Samuel Bard, Physician, Louis Foavere, Physician, Mary Creighton. Proved, May 3, 1777. Confirmed, December 4, 1780.

Page 45.—In the name of God, Amen. I, WHITE-HEAD HICKS, of Flushing, in Queens County, being in a low state of health. All debts to be paid. I leave to my son John all that farm or Plantation whereon I now reside, situate at Bayside, in Flushing, with all appurtenances, and he is to pay to my son Thomas £500. I leave to my sons, John, Thomas, and Elias, all my lands in Cumberland County or elsewhere. I leave all my plate, slaves, household furniture, live stock, farming utensils, and personal estate to my wife Charlotte, and my daughter Margaret, and my three sons. I make my wife and Henry Brevoort, and Hon. William Smith, Esq., Chief Justice of the Province of New York, and David Colden, Esq., of Flushing, executors.

Dated October 1, 1780. Witnesses, Joseph Laurence, Thomas Willett, Scott Hicks. Proved, November 18, 1780.

[NOTE.—Hon. Whitehead Hicks, Judge of the Supreme Court, and Mayor of New York, 1766–1776, died at Flushing, October 3, 1780.—W. S. P.]

Page 46.—I, Matthew Franklin, of Flushing, in Queens County, yeoman, this 2 day of the 8 month called August, 1779, being well in body and am desirous to set my house in order. My executors to pay all debts. I leave to Sarah Franklin, daughter of Thomas Franklin, and granddaughter of my brother, Henry Franklin, £50. I leave to Richard Titus, son of James Titus, of Westbury, £50. My executors are to put at interest £150, the interest to be applied to the use of providing poor Negro children books, and also towards paying their schooling, them that their parents did belong among the People called Quakers. I leave to my friend, Matthew Farrington, of Flushing, all my wearing apparell. My executors may sell all houses and lands. Whereas I have purchased of Matthew Farrington his dwelling house and all the land on which he now lives, containing sixteen acres, upon condition that he shall have the use during the life of him and his wife Hannah. After their death my executors are to sell the same, and from the proceeds take the amount due me on bond, and pay the rest to the heirs of Matthew Farrington. After all lands are sold and legacies paid, I leave all the rest to Henry Franklin and Elizabeth Hull, children of my brother, Henry Franklin, and to Walter, John, Samuel, James, Sarah Curser, and Mary Whister, the children of my brother, Thomas Franklin. And to Samuel Bowne, James Bowne, Mary Farrington, Sarah Titus, Abigail Embree, and Willett Bowne, children of my sister, Sarah Bowne. I make my trusty kinsmen and friends, John Farrington, James Bowne, and John Field, all of Flushing, executors.

Witnesses, Ebenezer Beamun, Hannah Beamun, Charity Doty. Proved, November 30, 1780.

Page 48.—In the name of God, Amen. I, NICLASE WILLIAMSON, of the township of Gravesend, Kings County, being sick, knowing that it behooveth every man to settle his worldly affairs in such a manner that no strife or Debate may arise about the same. I direct all debts to be paid. I leave to my wife Eida the use of all my estate, real and personal, during the time she remains my widow. I leave to my son, Rem Williamson, after the death or marriage of my wife, all my real and personal estate in Gravesend or elsewhere. And he is to pay £100 to his brother William, and to his brother Coert £100, to the children of his brother Stephen £100, and £100 to the two daughters of his brother Jacobus, viz., Lucretia and Eida. And £100 to each of his brothers, Garrett, Jeremias, and John, and to his sister Eva, wife of Peter Prine, and to his sister Majaca, wife of Jacobus Rider, and to his sisters, Janettie, wife of Peter Vanderbilt, and Antie, wife of Jost Stilwell. I make my son Rem executor.

Dated September 27, 1776. Witnesses, Nicholas Cowenhoven, Peter Cavilier, of New York, Innkeeper, Garret Williamson, of Kings County, Innkeeper. Proved, December 18, 1780.

Page 50.—In the name of God, Amen. I, HENDRICK BRINKERHOFF, of Newtown, in Queens County, on Nassau Island, being in good health. All debts to be paid. I leave to my wife Lammetie the use of all my estate during her widowhood for the support and bringing up of my children. I leave to my oldest son, Joris, for his birthright £30. All the rest I leave to my wife and children, Joris, Daniel, Abraham, Tunis, and Isaac, and my daughter, Alke Brinkerhoff, and my grandson Hendrick, son of my son Johannis, deceased. Some of my children have received an outset out of my estate, and my grandson hath received the outset which I gave to his father, and my other children must receive proportionately. I make my brother-in-law, Daniel Rapelja, and my cousin, Abraham Brinkerhoff, and my son Joris and my son Daniel, executors.

Dated June 10, 1766. Witnesses, Abraham Brinkerhoff, Samuel Waldron, Jr., Jacob Palmer. Proved, June 24, 1777.

Page 53.—In the name of God, Amen. I, ABRAHAM BRINKERHOFF, SR., of Newtown, Queens County, yeoman, being sick. I leave to my wife Elizabeth £800 and a negro woman, and a negro boy, and all my plate marked E. B. H., and my best bed and the furniture thereto belonging, and her cupboard and linnen, and my riding chair and best horse, and my large tea kettle, silver teapot, and case of silver handled knives and forks, to her and her heirs and assigns. I leave to my nephew, Abraham Brinkerhoff Rapalye, son of my sister Elizabeth, my silver tankard and £200, and a new riding saddle when of age. I leave to my nephew, Abraham Polhemus, son of my sister Anne, all my wearing apparell. My executors are to sell all the rest of my estate, and I leave the proceeds to the children of my sister, Anne Polhemus, viz., Abraham, Allette, Theodorus, Charity, Jacob, and George. And to the children of my sister, Elizabeth Rapalye, viz., Jeromus, Catharine, Abraham Brinkerhoff, Allette and Richard. And to Hendrick Brinkerhoff, son of my sister Sarah, and to the children of my sister, Polly Bloodgood, viz., Abraham, Allette, and Elizabeth. My executors are to pay to my sister Katharine an equal share. I leave to my cousin (nephew), Abraham Polhemus, son of my sister Anne, besides his share, my Large Dutch Bible and my gun. I make my cousin, Samuel Waldron, Isaac Brinkerhoff, and George Brinkerhoff, Jr., executors.

Dated June 27, 1780. Witnesses, Elathan Levrick, David Van Wickel, Mary Bloodgood, widow. Proved, October 7, 1780.

Page 55.—In the name of God, Amen. I, John Christofer De Huyn, Major General of the forces of his Serene Highness, the Land Grave of Hesse Cassell, at present serving in North America, being sick and weak. I leave to my daughter, Sophie De Huyn, all my money and stock in the public funds of Great Britain, and all my personal estate. I make my friends, John George Lorentz and Justin Henry Motz, both Counsellors of war of his Serene Highness, executors.

Dated June 23, 1780. Witnesses, David Campbell, Notary Public, Charles Schmedtz, Paymaster General of the Hessians, Philip Ludewiz, Paymaster and Quartermaster and Major of Regiment Prince Hered. Proved, January 9, 1781.

Page 57.—I, Peter Middleton, in the city of New York, Physician, do, this First day of November, 1780, make this my last will and Testament. My executors are to call in all open accounts and book debts, and sell all household furniture and effects, and pay all debts, funeral expenses and legacies. I leave to my daughter, Susanah Margaret Middleton, my gold watch and seals, my three silver waiters, my Pearl broach, and all my rings (except two), and all my paintings and iron chest to preserve papers. Whatever Books of History or Entertainment my executors may think proper are to be selected for my daughter. I leave to my pupil, John B. Middleton, all my wearing apparell except my large camblet cloak. And I leave him all my arms, medicines, shop furniture, instruments, medical books, and manuscripts. Also all my land lying on the Unadilla branch of the Susquehannah river, in what is called Col. Craghans Purchase, amounting to five thousand acres. Also one fifth of my personal estate and twenty-five Guineas to purchase him present necessaries. I leave to my daughter in law (stepdaughter), Anne Burges, £300 Stirling as a merited gratuity for her good behavior and kind attentions to me and to my dead daughter Susan. I also leave her

twenty-five Guineas for mourning. I leave to Margaret
Burges, now Mrs. Smythies, twenty-five Guineas for
mourning. I leave to my esteemed sister-in-law, Mrs.
Jane Harrison, my gold broach, set with red and white
stones. I leave to the Hon. Andrew Elliot, Esq., my
large camblet cloak and my Scots Peeble ring. I leave
to Goldstraw Banzar, Esq., my Cornelian seal ring.
To Robert Auchmuty, Esq., my gold mason's jewell
and my apron. I leave to my daughter all the income
of my estate, houses and lands, and four fifths of all my
personal estate. If my daughter die without heirs,
what is left to her is to go to John B. Middleton, or his
oldest male descendant of the name of Middleton. And
in default of heirs to him, then to my nearest male
heirs bearing the name of Middleton. He leaves to his
daughter certain negroes. I make my much esteemed
friends, Hon. Andrew Elliot, Esq., Robert Auchmuty,
Esq., and Goldstraw Banzar, Esq., executors.

Witnesses, Lambert Moore, George Webster, John.
King, Jr.

Codicil. My daughter is to remain under the care
of Anne Burges until my executors think it necessary
to remove her. And whereas I have lately had two
gold watches bequeathed to me, I leave the best, with
the trinkets and seals, to my daughter, and the other
to Anne Burges, if they both come safe here. I leave
to Mr. William Smythies ten Guineas, and to his son
Carleton five Guineas. I leave to my old friend, Dr.
John Bard, my Stots Horn Snishing mill. And I leave
mourning rings to Dr. [Jonathan] Mallet, and to Dr.
Samuel Bard, and to Dr. Michalis and Dr. Bayley, for
their kind attentions during my painful and lingering
illness. I leave to my good friend, Anthony Van Dam,
Esq., my gold-headed cane. I leave to William Seton
my Grand Master's mason jewel. And I also make
them executors with the others.

Dated December 14, 1780. Witnesses, George Webster, grocer, Samuel Bard, James Wells, Jr. Proved,
January 15, 1781.

[Note.—Dr. Peter Middleton, who was for thirty years a noted physician in New York, died January 9, 1781.]

Page 60.—In the name of God, Amen. I, JACOBUS LAURENCE, of Hempstead, in Queens County, being now well in health. I leave to my granddaughter, Sarah Archibald, the best bed and furniture, and two pair of sheets, two pair pillow cases, one set of white curtains, one chest of drawers, two round tables, six red-painted chairs, six silver teaspoons, and one gold ring, all of which was designed to be given to my late daughter Polly. I also leave her all my late daughter's wearing apparell. All the rest of my estate I leave to my son, Benjamin Laurence. And he is to pay to my grandson, John Laurence, £100 when of age, and to my grandson, John Archibald, £50 when of age, and to my granddaughter, Sarah Archibald, £10 when eighteen, and he is to provide her sufficient support and apparell until of age or married, and she is to have one Quarter's schooling at his expense. And he is also to furnish my grandson, John Archibald, sufficient support and apparell, and also to give him as much schooling as he conveniently can until he is 16, and then be put to a trade. My executors may purchase a piece of woodland for my son, and they may dispose of my young negroes. I make my son Benjamin, and my friends, Silvanus Bidell and Samuel Clowes, executors.

Dated February 25, 1778. Witnesses, Samuel Langdon, Adam Seabury, Practitioner of Physic, Richard Rhoades. Proved, December 9, 1780.

Page 62.—In the name of God, Amen. I, TIMOTHY HUDSON, of Wading River, in the town of Southold, Suffolk County, yeoman, being weak in body. My Body being dead, to be decently buried. I leave to my granddaughter, Mary Hegges (Hedges?), now living with me, all my movable estate, and the use of lands and dwelling houses for three years, and then I give all my lands to my eldest son, Frederick Hudson. I make my friend, James Sill, and my granddaughter, Mary Hegges, executors.

Dated November 13, 1780. Witnesses, Wessell Sill, Zadock Reeve, Saul Glover. Proved, December 20, 1780, before Nathan Woodhill, Esq.

[NOTE.—The farm of Timothy Hudson, inherited by his son, Col. Frederick Hudson, was the place, in late years, owned by Sylvester Miller. The famous Indian preacher, Paul Coffee, lived in the family of Col. Hudson when a boy.—W. S. P.]

Page 63.—In the name of God, Amen. I, JOHN TALMAN, of Flushing, in Queens County. I leave to my wife Phebe the use and profits of my farm called the Homestead, and my lot of land and salt meadow lying by the land of Joseph Laurence, and the use of all my personal estate, for the term of seven years, in order to bring up and educate my children. But my executors may sell the same, if most to the advantage of my children, at public vendue. My executors are to sell one half of a lot of land and one half of a stone house standing on said lot, in New York, which I have in partnership with John Latham. My executors are also to sell at public vendue two lots of land, one of which I purchased of John Rapalye, called fifty acres, and the other, bought of John Field, called thirty acres. They may also sell all estate except what is left to my wife, and the money is to be paid to my wife and children, as follows: To my wife Phebe, £200, and my best bed with its furniture, and my riding chairs, and the best of my negro women, which she is to choose for herself. And the use of as much Plate as she will choose, during her life and no longer, and then all the plate is to go to my daughter, and all the beds. I leave to my son Isaac five shillings, as I have given him his portion before. I leave to my son Samuel £200, as I have before given him considerable. To my son

Thomas £400. To my son John £400. To my son
Peter £400. To my son William £400. To my daughters, Sarah and Elizabeth, £250 each. To my daughter
Phebe £200. To my daughter Ann £250. To be paid
to my sons when twenty-one, and to my daughters when
eighteen. All the rest I leave to my wife and children
except my son Isaac. My young sons are to be put to
learn good trades. I make my wife and my brother-in-
law, William Thorne, and my friend, Richard Thorne,
both of Great Neck, executors.

Dated October 7, 1777. Witnesses, Whitehead Hicks,
Judge of Supreme Court, Samuel Latham, John Field,
Quaker. Proved, March 9, 1778. Confirmed, January
25, 1781.

Page 66.—In the name of God, Amen. September
6, 1780. I, PHILIP WOOLLEY, of Great Neck, Queens
County, Long Island, being sick. I leave to my
brother, Thomas Woolley, all that sum of money which
he owes me, provided he brings no account against my
estate. I leave to my brother Henry £25. To my sister, Elizabeth Van Astron, widow, £25. To Jane
Campbell, £6. I leave to my brothers, John, Benjamin,
and Samuel, all the remainder of my estate. I make
my true and faithful friends, William Thorne and
George Hewlett, both of Great Neck, executors. Witnesses, Thomas Tredwell, Daniel Morow, Peter Bonnet. Proved, October 16, 1780.

Page 68.—In the name of God, Amen. I, JOSEPH
HEWLETT, of Great Neck, in the Town of Hempstead,
Queens County, farmer, being sick. I direct all debts
to be paid. I leave to my wife Deborah £500, and all
household and kitchen furniture, and all my negroes
except Price, and one of my best horses, and my riding
chair. And all my hogs and half my cows. I leave to
my son, Laurence Hewlett, all my homestead farms
and lands and real estate at Great Neck, and a yoke of
oxen and cart, and my negro Price, and two horses,

and my boat and rigging, and all farming utensils. I
leave to my daughter Elizabeth one half the money due
me on bonds, and the use of the other half for life, and
then to her children. Also my silver bowl. I leave to
my two grandchildren, Joseph and James Davenport,
my two house lots on Minnifords Island, in Westchester County. I leave to my daughter Elizabeth the rest
of my cows and all my sheep. I make William Thorne
and Daniel Kissam, of Hempstead, and Frederick De
Voe, of Westchester County, executors.

Dated September 28, 1777. Witnesses, John Tredwell, John Touffey, George Hewlett, John Willett.

Codicil. The £500 left to my wife Deborah is to be
taken out of my cash or bonds at her choice. October
1, 1777. Witnesses, John Woolley, Jr., Philip Woolley,
John Willett. Proved, November 17, 1777. Confirmed,
January 25, 1781.

Page 71.—I, WILLIAM JONES, of Oyster Bay, in
Queens County, June 12, 1778, being weak and infirm.
I leave to my wife Phebe one half of all household
goods, including linnen and woolens, and my riding
chair and horse, and my negro wench Judy. I leave
to my wife Phebe, during her widowhood, and to my
sons, Walter and John, the use of all the rest of my
movable estate, and all my lands and meadows, in the
Southern part of Oyster Bay, West Neck, where I now
dwell, with all the improvements, bounded on the north
on the east side of the highway which leads from the
meadows of said West Neck, at, or near, the middle of
said West Neck, to the Great Plains, by the tenth Great
Lot of upland, in the Second Division of said West
Neck lands. And on the east by the eastermost limits
of said West Neck, until it comes to the lands which
my son Samuel has purchased of my son David, on the
said West Neck. Also the use of all the remainder of
my Plain lands, which I Purchased of Richard Ebson,
on Hempstead Plains. After the death or marriage of
my wife Phebe, I leave all the rest of my household

goods, and my female negroes, to my daughters, Elizabeth, Margaret, Phebe, and Sarah. And I leave all my live stock and male negroes, and all the rest of my lands, meadows, and plains, to my sons, John and Walter. And they are to pay to my sons, Richard and Jackson Hallet Jones, £600 between them. And they are to be at the expense of learning my two sons some useful trades. And they are to pay to my son Thomas £150, for the use of my son Gilbert, and they are to pay to my son William £100 for the use of my daughter Freelove and her children. And they are to pay to my daughters, Elizabeth, Margaret, Phebe, and Sarah, £400. Of these sums, one half is to be paid in one year, and one half after the death of my wife. From the rest of my estate I leave to my wife the use of £600 for life, and then to my sons, John and Walter. I leave to my sons, Richard and Jackson Hallet Jones, £600, and the expense of teaching them useful trades. All the rest of my lands in Oyster Bay, West Neck, and my plains in Bethpage Purchase of plains, I leave to my sons, Richard and Jackson Hallet Jones, and to my grandsons, William, son of my son David, and William, son of my son Samuel, except the use of the 17th and 18th Lots in the 4th Division of West Neck lands, with the improvements, which I leave to my wife Phebe during widowhood, and then to my said sons and grandsons. My daughters, Margaret and Sarah, are to live with my sons, John and Walter, and my wife while unmarried. I leave all my beaches and marshes to all my sons. I make my wife Phebe, and my sons, Samuel, William, John, and Walter, executors.

Witnesses, Richard Jackson, Silas Smith, saddler, Jacob Jackson.

Codicil. I leave to my daughter Elizabeth £20, and to my daughters, Margaret, Phebe, and Sarah, £68 each, and to my son Richard £12, over and above what is left to them. My son Richard is to be put to the trade of a Silver Smith, and my son, Jackson Hallet

Jones, is to be left one year to learn the Latin Tongue, and then put to a Doctor of Physick to learn the art and trade thereof.

Dated January 24, 1779. Witnesses, Benjamin Seaman, Nicholas Herring, Ann Herring. Proved, January 17, 1781.

Page 76.—In the name of God, Amen. I, JOHN TREDWELL, of Great Neck, in Hempstead, Queens County, farmer. All debts to be paid. I leave to my wife Margaret £300 as soon as convenient after my decease. And one half my plate, and a negro woman, and horse and riding chairs and two beds, one to be her choice and the other at the discretion of my executors. And the use of one half my dwelling house, with kitchen and cellar room, and suitable furniture for the same during her widowhood. My farm and lands, and stocks and negroes, are to be kept in the hands of my executors until my youngest child is of age, for maintaining and educating my wife and children. And my executors and my son Thomas are to manage to the best advantage. And my executors are to make satisfaction to my son Thomas according to his care and attention, and the remainder to the rest of my children, Phebe, Benjamin, Sarah, Elizabeth, and Richard. When my youngest child is of age, my executors are to sell all my stock, negroes, and personal property, and from the proceeds and money in my possession they are to pay to my sons, Benjamin and Richard, £700 each. To my daughters, Sarah and Elizabeth, £200 each, to make them equal with my daughter Phebe, to whom I have advanced that sum. All my farm, lands and tenements on Great Neck, where I now live, I leave to my sons, Thomas and John. All the rest of my personal estate to all my children. I make my brother, Benjamin Tredwell, and my brother-in-law, William Thorne, and my wife, executors.

Dated December 1, 1779. Witnesses, Daniel Kissam,

Philip Woolly, Samuel Woolly. Proved, February 4, 1780.

Page 79.—In the name of God, Amen. I, MARY TYSON, of Richmond County, widow of Barnet Tyson. I leave to my youngest daughter, Mary, wife of William Lake, my bed and chest. All the rest I leave to my three daughters, Sarah, wife of Benjamin Pratt; Martha, wife of Aaron Depeaw, and Mary, wife of William Lake. I make my son-in-law, William Lake, executor.

Dated May 5, 1779. Witnesses, James Guyon, Joseph Guyon, Isaac Doty. Proved, January 22, 1781, before Benjamin Seaman.

Page 81.—In the name of God, Amen. September 1, 1780. I, EASTER LATOURRETTE, of Staten Island, being sick. All my movable estate to be sold in three months, and the proceeds and money in hand to be put at interest, and I leave one half of the interest to my executors for their service and trouble, and the interest on the other half to be added to the stock. I leave to my grandson, John Parker, when of age, £25, and one fourth of the remainder. To my grandson, Benjamin Parker, one third. To my grandson Ephraim one half of the sum that then shall be, and the other half to my granddaughter, Easter Parker, when of age. I make David Latourrette and Jonathan Lewis, Sr., executors.

Witnesses, Henry Latourrette, John Vanderbilt. Proved, January 19, 1781.

Page 83.—In the name of God, Amen. April 30, 1780. I, JOHN BEDEL, of Richmond County, Esq., being very sick but having my usual senses. All debts to be paid. I leave to my wife Hannah £200, and my negro wench Tenah, and two beds with their furniture, and as much other household goods as shall be sufficient for her to keep house with, and my riding chair and horse, and two cows. I leave to my daughter Hannah, wife of Abraham Cole, £300. To my granddaughter, Charity Bogart, £250, when of age, and a negro girl, and a cupboard commonly called her mother's cupboard, and a bed. I leave to my son, Israel, £1000, including £600 already advanced, and a negro boy. I leave to my son John the Plantation he now lives on at Smoaking Point, being all the lands and meadows I purchased of Anthony Waters. I leave to my son Cornelius the Plantation I now live on, with houses, buildings, and mills. Reserving to the use of his mother, during her widowhood, the room next to the kitchen and the back bedroom, with the use of the kitchen and cellar and firewood at the door, for her own use. And my son Cornelius shall provide hay and pasture, and the privilege of one hog to run with his own, and grain and fruit. And he shall furnish her yearly twenty bushels of wheat, ten of Rye, and ten of Corn. All the rest of my estate to be sold, and I leave all to my sons, John, Israel, and Cornelius, and my daughter Hannah, wife of Abraham Cole. I make my sons, John and Israel, executors.

Witnesses, James Whiteman, Surgeon of 22d Regiment, Catharine Bedell, Benjamin Seaman. Proved, January 26, 1781.

Page 85.—In the name of God, Amen. I, DANIEL LAKE, of Staten Island. All my estate, real and personal, to be sold in four or five months. From the proceeds, I leave one half to my wife Margretha and my daughter Alleday, and one half to my son William. I make my father-in-law, Harmanis Gerritson, and my brother, William Lake, executors.

Dated December 1, 1780. Witnesses, Christian Jacobson, Christian Smith, Thomas Dagity. Proved, January 23, 1781.

Page 87.—In the name of God, Amen. September 11, 1753. I, AUGUSTIN BRYAN, being very sick. All my

meadows, lands, stock, buildings and farming utensils,
and one negro man, are to be sold by way of public
vendue, and all debts paid. I leave to my son Melancthon £60 when of age, and all my wearing apparell. I leave to my wife Deborah all household
goods and a negro girl, and an equal proportion of my
whole estate. All the rest I leave to my wife and my
three sons and six daughters. My wife is to have the
use of all the estate for the good and comfortable support of my children until they are of age (*names not
given*). I make my wife Deborah, Epenetus Bryan,
and David Resco, executors.

Witnesses, Ann Wicks, John Bunce, Samuel Allen.
Proved in Suffolk County, January 16, 1781.

[NOTE.—The testator lived in the town of Huntington.]

Page 88.—In the name of God, Amen. I, PETER
POILLON, of Richmond County, being very weak. I
leave to my wife Margerett my best bed and a cupboard and looking glass, and all other household furniture and other things that was given her by her
father, and all the hanging pictures about my house,
and all silver spoons and China ware, and my riding
chair and sorrel horse branded D, and four cows and
£400. And the use of all lands till my eldest son,
Abraham, is of eighteen years of age. And my wife
is to maintain, educate, and support my three sons,
Abraham, John, and Peter, in decent cloathes and
proper education. I leave to my son Abraham all my
wearing apparell, and my riding saddle and long gun.
I leave to my son John my silver-hilted sword, pistols
and holsters, and my carbine with all accoutrements.
I leave to my son Peter my silver shoe, knee, and stock
buckles, and a pair of gold sleeve buttons. All the rest
of personal property to be sold, and all debts paid.
My wife is to have the charge of all my negroes until
my son Abraham is eighteen years old. I leave all my
real estate to my three sons, and my executors are to

make a just and equal division among them without favor or affection. I make my trusty friend, John Micheau, and my two brothers-in-law, Peter Rezeau and William Lake, executors.

Dated October 3, 1780. Witnesses, Paul Micheau, James Poillon, Jr., Amos Rook. Proved, January 22, 1781.

Page 91.—In the name of God, Amen. March 2, 1758. I, ALEXANDER BRYAN, of the town of Hunttington in Suffolk County, on Nassau Island, being in reasonable health. All debts are to be paid by my two sons, Augustine and Epenetus Bryan. I leave to my grandson, Ebenezer Bryan, my silver tankard. To my son Augustine two silver spoons. To my son Epenetus two silver spoons and my wearing apparell. To my daughter,Ann, wife of Simon Fleet, two spoons and all household goods. To my son Epenetus all my shop. I leave to my grandson, Ebenezer Bryan, all that piece of land lying on the west side of Crab Meadow Neck commonly called Whitehead's Cove. Bounded west by the bank, north by the highway to the landing at the widow Bunce's, east by Eatons Neck path, south by the Cordwood path, with all appurtenances. Also my orchard, joining to Whitehead's Cove. Bounded north by the cordwood path, south by land his father bought of John Skidmore, and partly by land he bought of John Smith, east by Eatons Neck path and containing ten acres. And my fresh meadow, all lying on the east side of the road at Crab meadow, opposite from the widow Skidmore's land. Also a hundred right in the Old Purchase of this Town, and a hundred right in the Crab meadow Purchase. I leave to my son Augustine all the point of land lying at Crab meadow that I bought of John and Daniel Ingersoll. Also one lot of meadow opposite to his dwelling house, and one third of a piece of land lying on Crab meadow Neck, including sixty acres that was measured to him by Solomon Ketcham, joining to the southeast side of the highway that runs across the Neck, and also joining to James Smith's land. Also a piece of land joining to the highway that leads from Crab meadow to Town. Also a piece of land lying on the Plains near Whitman's Hollow, being fifteen acres. Also one half of a hundred right of Commonage in the Old Purchase, and a hundred and three-quarters right in the Eastern Purchase. I leave to my son Epenetus a small lot of upland at Cow Harbor, about one acre, with all the buildings. Also my mill, with all utensils and privileges. And the western half of an acre of meadow. And all that piece of land I bought of Jeremiah Smith, commonly called the Long Hill. Also all that piece of land lying on the north side of the highway that leads to Crab meadow joining to the east side of Eatons Neck path, and joining to the south side of the Cordwood path. The said piece of land, bought of Jeremiah Smith, is bounded north by the highway to Crab meadow, east by highway leading to the Long Hill, south and west by another highway that comes from the Long Hill. Also five acres joining the east side of Long Hill path. And a lot of meadow, both fresh and salt and sedge, at Crab meadow, adjoining to the land and meadow of Moses Veal. Also two lots of meadow lying on the east side of Crab meadow gut, or inlet, between the meadow of widow Skidmore and the meadow of Simon Fleet. Also a hundred and three-quarters right in the Eastern Purchase, and one half of a hundred right in the Old Purchase. I appoint Joseph Lewis, Samuel Allen, and Samuel Ketcham, all of Huntington, executors.

Witnesses, Zebediah Bunce, Jesse Bunce, William Nichols.

Codicil. I leave to my daughter-in-law, Phebe Bryan, now the widow of my son, Alexander Bryan, deceased, the use of one third of all the lands which I left to my grandson, Ebenezer Bryan.

Dated April 14, 1758 (same witnesses). Proved, January 1, 1781.

Page 94.—In the name of God, Amen. I, ELIZABETH COLVILL, of New Town, in Queens County, on Nassau Island. All such debts as I shall justly owe at the time of my decease, and my funeral charges and expenses, be in the first place paid by my executors. I leave to the children of my son, Thomas Colvill, deceased, one equal third part (the whole in equal parts to be divided) of all my personal estate, to be equally divided between them, share and share alike, and to survive among the children of the said Thomas Colvill, in case any of them die before the age of twenty-one years. To the children of my son, William Colvill, of the City of London, mariner, one third part of all my said personal estate, to be equally divided between them, share and share alike, and to survive among the children of the said William Colvill, in case any of them die before the age of twenty-one years. To the children of my daughter Hannah, the wife of the Reverend David Griffith, the remaining third part of all my said personal estate to be equally divided between them, share and share alike, and to survive among the children of the said Hannah, in case any of them die before the age of twenty-one years. Provided always, and the true intended meaning of this my Will is, That whereas I am held and firmly bound, in a certain Bond or Obligation, for the Payment of the Sum of £100, lawful money of New York, with interest for the same, to Richard Charlton, deceased, as a Security for & with the said Griffith, if therefore the said David Griffith, his Heirs, Executors or Administrators shall not pay or Cause to be paid to the Executors or Administrators of the said Richard Charlton the said Sum of £100 with the Interest due thereon, Then and in such Case I do will and order that so much be deducted out of the share of the children of my said daughter Hannah as shall be equivalent to the principal and interest of the said Bond till the Payment thereof. All my household furniture, stock in trade and other moveable effects to be sold at Public vendue or otherwise (except

my wearing apparel and household linen, which I do
hereby give and bequeath unto my said daughter Hannah), and the monies arising from such sale together
with such sum as I shall die possessed of, to put out
at interest, for the use of the said children of my sons,
Thomas and William, and daughter Hannah, when they
shall severally attain the age of twenty-one years. And
I do hereby will and order that such part shares and
proportions as is hereinbefore given and bequeathed
to the children of my said sons, Thomas and William,
and the children of my said daughter Hannah, be paid
upon the said children severally arriving at the age of
twenty-one years, and not before, except to the children of my said son Thomas, who are to receive the
interest, or a part thereof, or their third part share or
proportion, if my executors think they stand in need
thereof, for their education or maintenance, in such
moderate or reasonable sums as my executors shall
think necessary. I make my loving brothers, Henry
Roome, of the City of New York, merchant, and William Grigg, of the same city, silversmith, executors.

Dated December 19, 1778. Witnesses, Thomas W.
W. Beavans, James Bonney. Proved, August 14,
1780.

Page 97.—In the name of God, Amen. I, ADAM
LAWRENCE, Esq., High Sheriff of Queens County, Long
Island, and Province of New York. I leave to my
three daughters, Deborah Van Wyck, Sarah Hewlett,
and Catharine Platt, £100 each; unto my two granddaughters, Elizabeth and Deborah Lawrence (daughters of my late son George, deceased), the sum of £50
each; to my grandson, Philip Lawrence (son of my said
son George), the sum of £160, to be paid him by my
eldest son, Doctor Daniel Lawrence, as soon as he shall
be in possession of that part of my real estate hereinafter devised him. To my son Stephen a negro boy
named Aaron. All the rest and residue of my personal
estate I leave to my sons, Joseph and Clarke, to be

shared equally between them. I give and devise unto
my sons, Doctor Daniel Lawrence and Stephen Lawrence, all that tract of land being on the east side of
the road leading from the Great Plains to Captain
Samuel Cornell, on which I now live, bounded on the
west by the road above mentioned; northerly the lands
of the Adriance's and of Mr. Cha. Crommelin; easterly
by the land of said Crommelin; southerly by the Great
Plains; together with plain lands adjoining the same,
and including my rights in the said unlocated Great
Plains, to be divided between them according to the
quantity and quality of the land. I also leave to my
said sons, Doctor Daniel Lawrence and Stephen Lawrence, a piece of woodland bounded on the south and
west by the lands of John Hegeman and Philip S. Platt,
on the north by the lands of Philip S. Platt and on the
east by the land of Daniel Duryea, and the east of my
son, George Lawrence, deceased, containing about 20
acres, to be equally divided, the west part of which
division with the improvements including the last
mentioned "lott" of woodland I leave to my son, Doctor Daniel Lawrence, and the eastern part, including
the woodland adjoining Cha. Crommelin, I leave to my
said son, Stephen Lawrence. Unto my son Clarke a
piece or parcel of land situate, lying and being directly
in the front of the house of Albert and Jacob Adriance,
containing about 40 acres; a piece of woodland lying
on the hills of the northwest of the Adriance's house
above mentioned, bounded easterly and northerly by
the lands of Obadiah Cornell, westerly by the lands of
Thos. Forster and Thos. Mitchell, and southerly with
the hills, containing 20 odd acres. I make my son-in-
law, James Hewlett, and my sons, Stephen and Clarke,
executors. I likewise impower them to receive from
my son, Doctor Daniel Lawrence, the sum of £160,
which I hereby order him to pay them for the legacy
of my grandson, Philip Lawrence, and before mentioned in his bequest. I devise they will put out on
interest in good security the sum of £150, and also

the two legacies of £50 each, bequeathed my two granddaughters, Elizabeth and Deborah Lawrence, for their several uses.

Dated March 6, 1768. Witnesses, Joseph Young, Gabriel G. Ludlow, George D. Ludlow. Proved, July 19, 1780.

Page 99.—In the name of God, Amen. I, THOMAS ROSE, give, devise, and dispose of my worldly estate in the following manner and form. I give to my true and beloved wife, Deborah Rose, all my estate, both real and personal, for the use and design of paying all my just debts and bringing up of my family so long as she remains my widow. I give unto my son William the sum of £100, to be paid to him when he comes to the age of twenty-one, and I further order that he be learnt some suitable trade such as he shall choose and my executors think proper. To my three daughters, named Ruth, Sarah, and Charity, £30, to be paid to each of them when they come of age or marry, and I further order that so long as they remain single that they shall have the liberty of a home or Residence in my house with " disturbance or controul," and further if they or either of them should be unable to maintain themselves that they be provided with whatever is necessary for their comfortable support. To my son John all the rest of my estate, both real and personal. I make my loving wife, my brother, Nathan Rose, and friend, Isaac Overton, executors.

Dated March 15, 1780. Witnesses, Jesse Rose, yeoman, Ruth Helme, John Leeke. Proved, January 23, 1781.

Page 102.—In the name of God, Amen. I, ISRAEL SMITH, of Brookhaven, in the County of Suffolk, and Province of New York, yeoman, give and bequeath all my estate, both real and personal, to the Trustees of the Town of Brookhaven, and their successors forever, upon trust and confidence, and to the intent and pur-

pose that they shall after my decease rent and hire to
any person or persons at their will and pleasure all
my lands, tenements, heridataments, money, and other
moveable estate during the time the same shall be
legally charged, and incumbered with the lawful maintenance and dower of my best beloved wife Mahittable,
in case she shall survive me; and it is my will that the
Trustees aforesaid and their successors do pay them
themselves out of the hires of said estate, and also pay
all other charges for putting this my last will and
testament in execution; and that they out of the same
pay all my just debts, and that the remainder of the
rents and hires of said estate be yearly paid by the said
Trustees into the hands of the regular minister and
other ruling officers for the time being of the Baptist
Church of Christ in Corum which now doth hold water
baptism to be rightly administered by Immersion only,
upon trust and confidence that they will use and appropriate the same to such use and uses as shall be
judged by the major part of the regular members of
said Church to be most for the Glory of God in promoting the best interests and lasting good of said
Church of Christ, more especially in preaching the
Gospel of Christ in that part of Brookhaven called
Corum, which doth now hold and profess to believe that
water Baptism is administered according to Scripture,
by Immersion only, of which Church I am a member.
And in case that at any time there should happen to
be neither minister nor other ruling officers to said
Church, or in case said Church be divided or broken
to pieces, then it is my will and pleasure that the
Trustees aforesaid and their successors in either or
both these cases do and shall appropriate the rents and
hire aforesaid to such use and uses, purpose and purposes, as they shall judge best and most likely to answer my design and intent in promoting the Cause of
Religion and good Estate of the Church aforesaid,
more especially in preaching the Gospel of Christ. And
it is my will and I order that the Trustees of Brook-

haven do (at such time as the Incumbrances and Dower aforesaid shall cease) will and truly sell all the estate aforesaid, and put the monies thence arising to interest on good and real security and appropriate the interest yearly, according to the above directions concerning rents and hires and for the same purposes aforesaid. I do appoint and constitute the Trustees of Brookhaven aforesaid and their successors forever to be executors of this my last will and testament, and I do by these presents give, grant, will and transfer to my executors full power and authority to grant alien bargains, sell, convey and assure all or any part or parcel of said estate to any person or persons in fee simple by all and every such lawful ways and means in the law as my said executors or their Council learned in the law shall seem fit or necessary; and to do all and every other act or acts, thing or things, necessary to be done in the executing this my last will and testament. In Testimony whereof I have hereunto set my hand and affixed my Seal, the Twenty-first day of May in the year of Our Lord Christ one thousand seven hundred and seventy-four, 1774.

Dated May 21, 1774. Witnesses (In the presence of the said Testator and in the presence of each other afterlining these words twice, viz.: more especially in preaching the Gospel of Christ), William Dayton, James Bishop, yeoman, Ebenezer Dayton. Proved, October 7, 1780.

Page 104.—In the name of God, Amen. I, HANNAH SMITH, of the Township of Hempsted, in Queens County, on the Island of Nassau, and in the Province of New York. My executors to pay and discharge all my just debts and funeral expenses. I leave to my loving sister, Sarah Barton, the sum of £200 during her natural life, and at her decease to decend or fall to her children in manner following: that is to say, unto John Barton £100, unto Elijah Barton £50, to my niece, Elizabeth Ludlow, £50. I leave to my loving sister, Phebe Pine, £150; to my loving sister, Elizabeth Peters, £150. My will is that my sisters, Phebe Pine and Sarah Barton, may have each one of them a bed and covering. To my nieces, Meriam Smith, Phebe Smith, Sarah Smith, and Elizabeth Cornwell, £10 each. All the residue and remainder of my estate to my above mentioned legaties, to be equally divided amongst them. My sisters to have my linen and wearing apparal. I make my brother-in-law, John Peters, and my nephew, John Barton, executors.

Dated August 22, 1780. Witnesses, James Smith, Charles Peters, yeoman, James Cornwell, yeoman. Proved, January 13, 1781.

Page 105.—In the name of God, Amen. I, EPENETUS PLATT, of Hempsted, in Queens County, and in the Province of New York, yeoman. My executors are to sell part of my personal estate such as they shall think most proper and sufficient to pay all my just debts and funeral expenses, and also the sum of £265 which I leave to my daughter Mary, which sum is equivalent to what I have already advanced to my daughter Sarah. I give equally between my two daughters, Mary and Sarah, one hundred acres of land laying on the east of my farm, running a north and south line through the same, to be equally divided between them, and also all the remainder of my personal estate (excepting my negro man Rodger, my desk and my watch, which I give to my son Epenetus) to be equally divided between my said daughters, and when my said son shall arrive to the age of twenty-one years, which legacies to my two daughters, or the profits therefrom, shall be left in the hands of my executors, for the bringing up and educating my said son in the study of either Law or " Physick," which he may choose, until he arrives at the age of twenty-one years. To my son Epenetus all the residue of my real estate, to be managed and improved to the best advantage by my executors until he shall arrive to the age of twenty-one years, for maintaining and educating my said son as aforesaid. I make my brother, Phillip Smith Platt, Uriah Platt, my son-in-law, Thomas Applebee, executors (and my daughter, Mary Platt, executrix).

Dated November 27, 1775. Witnesses, Isaac Smith, yeoman, Samuel Denton, James Cornwell, yeoman. Proved, March 1, 1777.

Page 107.—Be it known unto all men by these Presents that JAMES SMITH, SR., of Hempsted, in Queens County, on the Island of Nassau, and in the Province of New York, yeoman, being this twenty-sixth day of April, 1765, well in health of body and of sound mind and memory. I leave to my loving and well-beloved wife, Sarah Smith, all my moveable estate excepting such as I shall hereinafter dispose of, which my said wife shall make use of at her own discretion for her comfort and maintenance during her natural life, and after her death the remainder which my said wife hath not made use of be equally divided between my two daughters, Sarah Birdsall and Martha Sering, and to be at their own disposal. To my son James the one half of all my land whereon my son now liveth, situate between the road that leads from Hempsted Town to Washborns Neck and the road that leads from the said Town to Coes Neck, which said land comes to a point on the north, and is bounded on the south by the land of Joseph Rainder, Cornelius Vanostran, and also the half of the dwelling house which I do give to my son James to possess during his natural life, and after his death the said half of land and dwelling-house with the whole of the barn shall be equally divided amongst the three sons of my son James, namely, James, Daniel, and Stephen. To my son Obadiah the other half part of the above described land and dwelling-house with the apperternances. He shall not sell nor dispose of the aforesaid house and land without the " Councell and Consent and Good Liking of my executors." To my sons, Joshua and Edmund, all my whole farm or land with the houses lying and being at south, at a place called Merock, and to extend northward from the house as far as my land goes to be equally divided between them. Also, the half of eleven and a half acres of land; also, a piece of woodland containing about twenty-two acres which lies above Merock; also, all the swamp or land that is lying on the east side of the main Brook in the east meadow swamp that was included in my survey. To my son Silvanus all the land and houses and grist mill that I purchased of Thomas Frost and Nathaniel Oakley, lying and being in the South Woods, also the swamp ground that lyeth on the west side of the main Brook. To my five sons my two lots of salt meadow, the one in Great Mearock, and the other upon Little Mearock on the south side within the bounds of Hempsted, equally to be divided. In case any son or sons shall refuse to pay testator's just debts, the executors are directed to sell so much of the salt meadow as shall pay such one's part and proportion of said debts and to be deducted out of his or their parts and portion, and to give a good title for the same. To my sons all my rights of undivided lands and meadows within the Patent and Township of Hempsted to be equally divided, excepting what I have already above disposed of. To my son Joshua one negro man slave named Lew; to my son Silvanus one negro man slave named Bill; to my son Edmund one negro man slave named Tim; to my son Obadiah one negro man slave named Charles; to my daughter, Sarah Birdsall, one negro woman named Sib; to my daughter, Martha Sering, one negro woman slave named Jude, and be at their disposal. To my wife, Sarah Smith, the use and privilege of the east room and leanto, wherein I now dwell, during her natural life. I make my sons, Joshua, Silvanus, and Edmund, executors.

Witnesses, Henry Smith, John Haviland, yeoman, Richard Ellison, Jr., yeoman. Proved, May 4, 1776.

Page 110.—The thirtieth day of the eighth month, 1765. I, RICHARD MOTT, of Hempsted, Queens County, on Nassau Island. Give to well-beloved wife, Phoebe Mott, two cows, best bed and furniture, one hog, all my Puter, and all my Grain and Indian corn to be at her disposal. All the rest of my household goods, a Loom and Tackling, as long as she remains my widow, and no longer. All my stock of cattle, my "mear," sheep, swine, and farming utensils, to be sold by executors. Empower them to pay debts and funeral charges, and to use residue for bringing up my children. To my wife use of house and land, while my widow, in lieu of her thirds and dowry. At her marriage or death then to be sold and proceeds to be given to my children as followeth: the child that my wife is now like to have, I give the sum of £10; the remainder to my daughter Amy and my son James, James to have £20 more than Amy. If either of my children should die before they come of lawful age, or without lawful issue, then his, her, or their part to be divided among the survivors. I make my brother, John Mott, and Edmon Smith, executors.

Witnesses, James Rainer, James Smith, yeoman, Samuel Mott. Proved, March 25, 1776.

Page 111.—In the name of God, Amen. I, WILLIAM COLVILLE, now of the City of New York, mariner. All debts to be paid. I leave to my loving friend, Margaret Neal, the wife of James Neal, mariner, all my estate, real and personal, and make the said Margaret Neal my executrix, and utterly disallow and unmake former wills.

Dated November 22, 1780, and in the Twentieth year of His Majesty's reign. Witnesses, Elias Pelletreau, Sophia Rusler, D. Grim. Proved, March 5, 1781.

Page 112.—In the name of God, Amen. I, JACOBUS CORNEL, of the new Lotts, in the Township of Flatbush, in King's County, yeoman. All just and lawful debts and funeral charges to be paid out of my estate. I leave to my son, Gileyam Cornel, my grey stallion, and my largest gun; to my son, John Cornel, my four years old grey mare, and my smallest gun; to my loving wife Maragrietje the use and benefits of my dwelling house, barn, orchard, meadows, etc., and real estate whatsoever and wheresoever, with the sole use and benefit of the rest and residue of my personal estate, for her maintenance and support while my widow, and for the support of my children. At her remarriage I bequeath £20, my cupboard with the linen and woolen cloth therein, and also one of my bedsteads, she to have her choice. To my daughter Cornelia £50 at her marriage. After my wife ceases to be my widow, unto my two sons, Gileyam Cornel and John Cornel, my dwelling house, barn, etc., and all real, moveable and personal estate, equally, except I give to my son Gileyam £5 for his birthright before division is made. Sons to pay daughter Cornelia one half of £150 one year after they have full possession of the real estate, should she be of lawful age of 21 years, or otherways when she shall arrive at such age. Heirs are to pay the other legacies hereinbefore given. I make my sons, Gileyam, John, his brother, Johannes Cornel, and brother-in-law, Michael Stryker, executors.

Dated September 29, 1767. Witnesses, Jacob Wyckoff, gentleman, John Wyckoff, Johannis Lott, Jr., yeoman. Proved, February 23, 1780.

Page 114.—In the name of God, Amen. I, DANIEL WINANT, of Richmond County. I leave to my eldest son, Daniel, five shillings; to Catharine Wiser, my youngest daughter, all my money and goods and chattels (except Bonds); to Elizabeth Winant, my granddaughter, £5, to be paid out of the Bonds when the money is called in; to Ann Winant, my granddaughter, £10 out of said Bonds; to my granddaughter, Mary Winant, the daughter of Catharine Wiser, £10 out of said Bonds; to my daughter, Catharine Wiser, two

equal shares out of said Bonds, with my grandchildren,
viz.: Daniel Butler, John Butler, Peter Butler, Catharine Butler, Christian Butler, Rachel Butler, Mary
Macmoe, Daniel Winant, George Winant, Moses
Winant, Zedekiah Winant, Rebeckah Winant, Elizabeth Winant, Martha Winant, Peter Winant, Cornelius
Winant, George Winant, Isaac Winant, Jane Winant,
Andeziah Winant, Mary Winant, each one equal share
out of said Bonds. I make John Mersereau, Esq., and
my daughter, Catharine Wiser, executors.

Dated November 19, 1780. Witnesses, Gilbert Totten, farmer, Jacob Rickhow, farmer, Isaac Doty.
Proved, March 7, 1781.

Page 116.—In the name of God, Amen. I, THOMAS
EVERIT, of Brooklyn Ferry, butcher. All just debts
and funeral expenses to be paid. I leave to my wife
Catharine all my real and personal estate, to be sold
by her, three months after my decease, to the best advantage, and the monies arising therefrom to be retained by her, together with all furniture. After her
decease to be distributed among her children as she
shall think proper. She is to take son Richard Everitt
into her entire charge, to maintain him out of the profits of the estate until his majority. I make my wife
executrix.

Dated July 26, 1780. Witnesses, John Doughty,
George Powers, butcher, John Hicks, taylor. ("I appoint my brother-in-law, Hendrick Whihkoff, and
Abraham Burtis, my son-in-law, to be assistance to my
wife Catharine.") Proved, March 5, 1781.

Page 117.—In the name of God, Amen. I, DANIEL
DeVoo, of the Borough of West Chester, yeoman. All
just debts and funeral charges to be paid and satisfied.
I will that my dear wife Letty have the use of the
profits of all my estate, real and personal, during her
widowhood; at her remarriage what the law directs.
To Abraham De Voo, the eldest son of my eldest son

Daniel, deceased, I leave £5 currency; to Daniel De Voo, another of his sons, £10, to be paid at the majority of each. One half share of the land that properly did belong to my father, now belonging to my brother John and me, I give unto my two sons, Peter and Isaac, at the decease of my wife " or at her intermarriage." They shall pay unto my son John £100 currency as soon as they shall take the land in possession, but in case either Peter or Isaac should die without issue before they possess the land it shall belong to the survivor, and in case of both their deaths without issue then it shall belong to my son John and my grandchild, William Whore. One half of the land known by the name of the " Gore," now belonging to my brother John and me, which we purchased of Lewis Morris, Esq., to be sold to the highest bidder amongst my three sons, John, Peter, and Isaac, at the decease or intermarriage of my wife, and the proceeds to be equally divided amongst my five daughters, Rachel, Letty, Elizabeth, Margaret, and Laney. To my daughter Laney one milch cow and my large Dutch Bible, at her majority or marriage. My grandson, William Whore, to be paid £50 by executors at his majority, and that he have ten quarters schooling. My wearing apparel to son or sons remaining with him at his decease. After debts, funeral expenses and legacies are paid, the remainder of my estate to be equally divided among my five daughters; in case any should die without issue before said divisions, then their shares shall be equally divided among the survivors or their children. I make my two sons, Peter and Isaac De Voo, and my son-in-law, Benjamin Archer, executors.

Dated April 3, 1777. Witnesses, Jacob Collard, John Byvanck, Robert Gilmore, schoolmaster. Proved, March 12, 1781.

[The will is signed Daniel De Voe.]

Page 119.—In the name of God, Amen. I, MATHIAS SWAME, of Staten Island. I leave to my sons, John,

Simon, Matise, and Benjamin, all the piece of meadow called the Bock Meadow, to be equally divided, situate on Carl's Neck. The remainder of my lands and meadows shall be sold, and all my moveable estate, at the discretion of executors. After debts and funeral expenses are paid the remainder of the estate is to be equally divided amongst five sons; one share to be equally divided between my grandchildren, heirs of my daughter Hester, deceased. If either of these children should die before they come of age the survivor is to have their share; if both should die before they come of age then that one part is to be divided equally amongst my five sons. I make my sons, Simon Swame and Matise Swame, executors.

Dated December 20, 1780. (Before signing and sealing I order that my son John should have £50 over and above the other legatees.) Witnesses, Abraham Egberts, cordwainer, Israel Britten, Richard Conner. Proved, March 12, 1781.

Page 121.—In the name of God, Amen. I, DANIEL STILES, at present of the Township of Jamaica, Nassau Island, but late of the City of New York, merchant. After my debts and funeral expenses are paid, give all my estate, real and personal, to my beloved wife, Mary Stiles, for life, and after her death I devise the same to my grandson, William Brownjohn, the son of Doctor William Brownjohn, of the City of New York. In case my said grandson, William Brownjohn, should die under age, and without lawful issue, my said estate shall be equally divided between my brothers, Richard Stiles and Coopland Stiles, both of the Island of Bermuda, gentlemen, and between my sisters, Mary Dickerson, Elizabeth Conyard, and Susannah Salter, all of the Island of Bermuda aforesaid as Tenants in Common and not as Jointenants. Whereas my daughter, Deborah Brownjohn, the wife of Doctor William Brownjohn aforesaid, is of insane mind and understanding, and altogether incapable of taking care of herself, I hereby commit the Custody and Charge of her to my executors, and an annual charge of £100, current money, be made against the estate during her natural life for her support and maintenance, and that she be treated with Tenderness and Humanity. I make my wife, Mary Stiles, executrix, and my friends, the Hon. Hugh Wallis and John Lake, of the City of New York, merchants, executors.

Dated September 30, 1780. Witnesses, Rudolphus Ritzema, Esq., Richard Betts, one of the Captains of Militia for the County of Richmond, Stephen Higbie, labourer of said County. Proved, January 21, 1781.

Page 123.—In the name of God, Amen. I, ROELOF LOTT, of New Lots, in the Township of Flatbush, in Kings County, yeoman. All debts and funeral charges to be paid out of my moveable estate. I leave to Elizabeth, my beloved wife, all my real and personal estate for maintenance and support of herself during widowhood, and for maintenance, support and education of my children; on remarriage or death of my wife the whole personal and real estate to be sold at public vendue or otherwise; I authorize executors to give deeds in fee simple for real estate. All money arising from sale, from bonds, bill or otherwise, or by " Wills," I will and dispose of as followeth: Unto my wife Elizabeth £100 if she shall happen to remarry; to my son Michael £20, ten pounds thereof in consideration of his birthright; to my son Hendrick £10 of like money; the overplus I give unto all my sons and my daughter, equally divided, Viz.: Michael Lott, Hendrick Lott, Joris Lott, John Lott, and Rebecca Lott. Executors are to sell my negro slaves at their discretion for the advantage of my wife and children, and buy others in their Room if profitable. If my wife ceases to be my widow before children come to lawful age then executors shall use sufficient money from estate for maintenance of children. I make my wife Elizabeth, my brother, Johannes Lott, my brother-in-law, John Stryker, and cousin, Johannes Lott, Jr., or any two of them, as executors.

Dated October 18, 1780. Witnesses, Stephen Ryder, yeoman, Derick Remsen, Johannes Lott, yeoman. Proved, March 26, 1781.

Page 125.—In the name of God, Amen. I, JAMES VAN CORTLANDT, late of Yonkers, in West Chester County, but now residing in the City of New York. All just debts and funeral charges to be paid. I leave to my dearly beloved wife Elizabeth for life such part of my goods and chattels as she shall think necessary to keep for her own convenience, and the interest of all my estate; also the use, rents, profits and income of all my lands and real estate until the sale hereinafter directed, if she shall so long live with full power and authority to devise and bequeath by her last will and testament, or otherwise dispose of, so much of my personal estate and proceeds of sale thereof, and from sale of lands and real estate, at her will and discretion, as shall with her own estate real and personal, to which I am not entitled, make up one equal half in value of both estates together, and the rest, residue, reversive and remainder of my real estate and personal, subject nevertheless to sale or appropriation hereinafter mentioned, and the monies to arise from such sale thereof (exclusive of such part thereof as my said wife hath hereby power to dispose of as aforesaid), from and immediately after her death, I give and bequeath unto and among my brothers, Augustus Van Cortlandt and Frederick Van Cortlandt, and to my sisters, Anne Van Horne, wife of Augustus Van Horne, and Eve White, wife of Henry White, Esq., to be equally divided as Tenants in Common, all such part of my personal estate, goods and chattels as my said wife shall not want for her own use, I direct and order to be sold by my executors, and the proceeds to be put at interest by them for the benefit of my wife.

My executors are to sell all my lands, houses and real estate, and to execute good and sufficient deeds of Conveyance in fee simple and put the proceeds (if the sale is made during the lifetime of my wife) at interest, and to pay the same to her, Except that my House and Lott and Water Lott west of the Broadway are not to be sold till after my wife's death. And as to such parts of my real estate as shall happen not to be sold during her lifetime, such part and proportion aforesaid of the moneys that shall arise from the sale thereof afterwards shall nevertheless be and remain subject to her disposal as aforesaid, in the same manner as if such Estate had been sold before her death. As to such part and proportion of my estate undisposed of by will and testament, and otherwise by my wife, from and immediately after her death, I give and devise to my said brothers and sisters above named to be equally divided among them. In case of the death of any or either of these brothers and sisters during the lifetime of myself or wife, then the share and shares of the deceased in my estate, real and personal, and proceeds of sales, I give to the respective child or children of the deceased who shall be living at the time of their parent's death respectively, and to be equally divided among them as Tenants in Common. I make my wife, Elizabeth Van Cortlandt, executrix, and my brothers, Augustus Van Cortlandt and Frederick Van Cortlandt, and brother-in-law, Augustus Van Horne, executors.

Dated March 23, 1781. Witnesses, Benjamin Kissam, Samuel Nicoll, physician, Philip Kearney. Proved, April 9, 1781.

Page 127.—In the name of God, Amen. I, SAMUEL SMITH, of the County of Richmond, on Staten Island, yeoman, will and positively order all debts to be paid, and give to my well-beloved wife, Elizabeth Smith, my sons, Samuel Isaac Smith and Gilbert Smith, all my estate. And as to the place whereon I now live at ye

Morning Star on the North side of Staten Island is on
redemption of mortgage, it shall be sold and the price
equally divided amongst them also. I reserve for my
loving wife out of the Movables towards her part of
the same, two feather beds and the appurtenances, two
cows, one looking-glass and ten silver spoons which
shall not be sold. I make my wife executrix, and John
Simonson, of the north side of Staten Island, and William Talman, of Queens County, Nassau Island, executors. I do also (since the above) order that the estate
whereon I live shall not be sold, but shall be left for
my wife and children for their maintenance and learning, and to put them out to Trades, and also to be further kept till the said Redemption is paid, or they see
a prospect of selling it advantageously. Also that the
cows, two beds, be valued to the full worth and to be
deducted out of the estate toward her part of the same.
I order the ten spoons to be valued and kept for my
two sons and also the estate on Long Island that is
between me and my two brothers, Gilbert Smith and
Talman Smith, my part to be sold and proceeds put
at interest for the benefit of my said sons, and when
my oldest son comes to age the money to be divided
and the said son to receive his part and the younger
one part, to be kept on interest till he comes to age,
and then to be given to him. If either of them die before he comes to age his part of the estate to be given
to his brother, and if they both die before they come
to age their estate to fall to my brother Talman
Smith's children, to be divided among them. If my
said widow shall die before my children come to age,
her part of said estate to be divided between them. I
do also order my negro woman to be sold as my executors shall see most profitable for my heirs, by private
sale or by vendue with the rest of the moveables, and
the provisions that shall be in the house at my decease
shall be kept for the use of my family.

Dated January 22, 1781, and in the twenty-first year
of His Majesty's reign. Witnesses, Garret Elless (El-

lis), yeoman, Garet Post, Jr., James Pritchard (schoolmaster). Proved, March 30, 1781.

Page 129.—In the name of God, Amen. I, ABRAHAM SPEARS, of Staten Island, give to my son Abraham Spears my silver watch and my gold seal ring. To my wife, Anna Spears, £25 to be paid her upon demand; also the whole of her effects that she brought with her into my house and all the " Difficiencys " of the same shall be justly made up to her, that being an agreement made between us before our marriage was instituted; also the rest of my whole real and personal estate I do bequeath amongst all my children, share and share alike, that is, Abraham, John, Hendrick, Gitty and Monos, and Closon, with this Proviso that Monos, Closon and Hendrick to be maintained and educated out of my estate till they be fit to go to their trades or occupations, and all my debts and funeral expenses paid, then to be divided as above said. I make my son-in-law, Danl. Corson and my sons Abraham and John Spears, executors, and overseers of this will to take and perform or see the same perform'd according to my true intent and meaning.

Dated October 17, 1780. Witnesses, Daniel Salter, yeoman, Moses Clendenney, blacksmith, William Evan Hughs. Proved, March 30, 1781.

Page 131.—Know all men by these presents that I, PETER COLYER, of the Township of Huntington, in the County of Suffolk, on Nassau Island, in the Colony of New York, housewright. My will and desire is that all my lands and buildings together with my stock and carpenters tools and farming " utentials " shall be sold to pay all my just and lawful debts; if in case when my estate is turned into money that there is not money sufficient with what is due to me to pay my debts, then my executors shall sell so many of my household goods as shall be needful to pay all my debts as above said. When my debts are paid, my wife Hannah shall have all the remainder of my estate to be or to remain to her and her heirs forever. I make my friends, James Rushmore, of the Township, County and Province aforesaid, and William Seamen, of Oyster Bay Township, in Queens County, executors.

Dated August 5, 1775. Witnesses, John Colyer, Jesse Willmoth (Willmarth), Nathan Willmarth, of Huntington, carpenter. Proved, February 5, 1781.

Page 132.—In the name of God, Amen. I, EDWARD TITUS, in New Town, Queens County, Nassau Island, in the Colony of New York, yeoman, this thirty-first day of October, 1779. All just debts and funeral charges shall be paid by my executors. I leave to my beloved wife, Elizabeth Titus, my best bed and furniture, and the third of my lands that is reserved for my son, James Titus, during the time she is my widow; to my daughter, Susannah Furman, the lot lying the east side of Jonath or Furmans woodland, containing by estimation twenty acres as the fence now stands, and likewise the lot of land that lay joining to Benjamin Moores land; to my daughter " Abicail " Wiggins the lot of land joining the highway and Schencks land, containing by estimation twenty acres, as the fence now stands; to my daughter, Hannah Titus, the lot of land joining to Schencks woods, lying between my daughter Susannah and Abigails lots, containing by estimation twenty acres, as the fence formerly stood; to my daughter, Ama Titus, twenty acres of land adjoining to Thomas North's woodland, late of New York, deceased, and Edalls woods; to my daughter, Susannah Furman, two acres of land joining to Christopher Ramsen's and Thomas Betts's land; to my daughter, Hannah Titus, three acres of land joining to my daughter Susannah's lot running a south line to Thomas Betts's land; to my daughter, Ama Titus, three acres of land joining to my daughter Hannah's lot, running a south line to Thomas Betts's land; to my son, James Titus, all the rest of my lands, buildings, meadow land and woodland; to my granddaughter, Abigail Ramsen, £50 to be paid her by my son, James Titus, when she is of age. It is my will and I do order that in case any of my children die before they are of age that it shall be equally divided between the rest of my children, except my daughter, Abigail Wiggins. In case my son die at a non age that his estate shall pay yearly to my daughter, Abigail Wiggens, £10 during her life by the survivors that enjoy the estate. When my son James comes of age that he shall pay £10 to each of my daughters then living. I make my beloved wife, Elizabeth Titus, my daughter, Susannah Furman, and my son-in-law, Jonathan Furman, executors.

Witnesses, Jean Whipple, Samuel Waldron, yeoman, James Harper, yeoman. Proved, February 27, 1781.

Page 134.—I, DANIEL BRUSH, of the Township of Huntington, in Suffolk County, in the Province of New York, and Island of Nassau, being this twenty-sixth day of March, 1774, well in health of Body and of sound mind and memory am therefore willing to set my house in order before my final change doth come. My executors to pay all just debts, also sell my lands and buildings and all my moveable estate, except that it be judged best for my wife to reserve some of my moveable estate for her use, if so, I desire it may be allowed her. My executors shall take "Cear" of the money's arising from the sale of my estate, and to see that my wife shall have a comfortable support therefrom during her natural life. My will is further that my wife shall have full power to dispose of one third of all that shall be left at her decease; the other two thirds of what remains after her death to be equally divided among all my brother, Jonathan Brush's sons, except five shillings, good current money of New York, which I give to my brother, Ruben Brush, or to his heir. I make my cousin, Daniel Brush, son of my brother, Jonathan Brush, and my cousin, Jaccamiah Brush, executors.

Witnesses, Joseph White, Sarah Platt, John Witson, yeoman, being one of the people called Quakers did solemnly, sincerely, and truly declare and affirm. Proved, March 9, 1781.

Page 136.—In the name of God, Amen. I, JOSEPH LATTEN, of Oyster Bay, in Queens County, on Nassau Island, in the Colony of New York, yeoman. Executors to pay all just debts and funeral charges out of my moveable estate. All my moveable estate (except such part as I shall hereafter dispose of) and all my farm or plantation of land which I have on Oak Neck, so called, except my salt meadow and Crickthatch which I reserve for my son William, my executors are to sell after my decease for certain purposes and uses hereafter to be named. Now as touching my moveable estate I give to my son William my "worken oxen" my three negro men, Tim, Frederick, and James, always reserving so much of my negro James' time for my loving wife Mary as to cut her fire wood, and cart it home, and make "syder" as much as she may have occasion of, for her "one" use. I also give to my son William all my farming tools and utensils. To my loving wife Mary a good "Cheer" horse, my riding "Chear," one good "milks" Cow, my negro wench Lediah together with all my household furniture, of all kinds. To my granddaughter, Sarah Lawrence, eldest daughter of my daughter, Phebe Lawrence, my negro girl Ame, and if my granddaughter should not live, in that case, I give my negro girl Ame to my granddaughter, Zipahrah Lawrence, second daughter of my daughter, Phebe Lawrence, always provided my son-in-law, William Lawrence, keeps and supports her, "ye said garl Ame" till my granddaughters be of full age or happens to marry. To my granddaughter, Ann Thorn, wife of "Charls" Thorn,

my negro girl Judah. To my granddaughter, Etha-
lindiah Latten, daughter of my son, William Latten,
my negro girl " Charroty." One half of the remainder
of my Stock of Cattle, horses, sheep, hogs and all kinds
of stock whatsoever I give to my son William; " ye "
other half to be sold and retained in my executors
hands for certain purposes as I shall hereafter order
and direct. The whole residue of my estate, except my
farm or plantation which I have on " Ock Neech " I
give " oncontrolable " use of, to my son William, all
my houses, barns, orchards, wood and " Cleard " lands
of all kinds and nature whatsoever, which I have in
the Township of Oyster Bay, I give to my said son
for life, providing my loving wife shall have ye privilege of the west end of my house, a privilege in the
kitchen and cellar for her use during her natural life,
as also a garden and privilege of keeping poultry both
" Gees and Dunghill Fowls." My son William is to
keep and support a horse and cow, both summer and
winter, for my wife Mary, fit for her use, free and
clear, apples for her use summer and winter out of
my orchard, and apples for cider for her " one " use.
Immediately after my son William Latten's decease,
I devise and give to my grandsons lawfully begotten
by my son William all my lands, houses, barns, orchards, woods and cleared lands, and meadow free and
clear to them, always excepting ye farm I have on
Oak Neck, before devised to my executors for certain
purposes to be directed hereafter. I also provide that
my wife Mary shall have her firewood of my land during her life free and clear of any charge. My executors are to sell my moveable estate that is not before
given away, and my farm at Oak Neck, and pay to
my loving wife £100 out of the first money raised
from my moveable estate, and if there should not be
sufficient money raised out of the moveable estate I
order and direct that the £100 be made up out of ye
money I have at interest at my decease. My executors are to put the money arising from ye farm or

plantation I have at Oak Neck, and money arising
from my moveable estate, and what money I have
at interest at my decease, except ye £100 given to my
wife, at interest and pay the money arising for interest yearly to my wife during her life, and at her decease my executors are to retain in their hands £250
and put the same at interest for my daughter, Ethalindah Frost, wife of William Frost. At ye decease of my daughter, Ethalindah Frost, I give the
said £200 to my granddaughter, Sarah Lawrence,
eldest daughter to my daughter, Phebe Lawrence, providing my said granddaughter, Sarah Lawrence, lives
to be of full age, otherwise if she should not live to
be of full age nor happen to marry, I will the said
£250 to my granddaughter, Zepahrah Lawrence, second daughter of my daughter, Phebe Lawrence. My
executors are to take and put at interest £200 for my
granddaughter, Mary Coles, wife of "Jurden" Coles,
till she shall have heir or heirs to live to be of four
years of age, then I order the £200 last mentioned to
be paid to Mary Coles for her use, and if it should so
happen that my said granddaughter should not have
heir or heirs at the time of her two children which
she had by her former husband, Thorn Carpenter,
comes to be of full age, "to say Hannah and Thorn
Carpenter," then my executors to pay to them ye last
mentioned £200. The remaining moneys I will to my
grandchildren, the children of my son William, of my
daughter, Hannah Kirbee, of my daughter, Ethalindah Frost, and of my daughter, Phebe Lawrence, when
the said grandchildren shall arrive at full age or happen to marry. Should my daughter Ethalindah live
to have children, or a child, alive at the decease of
my wife Mary, or should have a child any time before
my granddaughter, Sarah Lawrence, shall arrive at
full age or happen to marry, then I give the aforesaid £250 to my daughter, Ethalindah Frost, free
and clear. I do declare the foregoing legacies given
to my loving wife in full lieu of dower and if my

wife Mary does not accept the same in full lieu of her dower and discharge my full estate from every charge or further claim on receiving ye foregoing legacies and privileges and give a "Quitance" to any further demands, then the foregoing privileges alloted for her, my said wife, I then devise and give each and every privilege to my son William and every legacy to him, my son William, and to his one use free and clear. I make my son William, my loving friend, Nathaniel Coles, and my loving friend, Pryer Towsend, executors.

(*Signed* JOSEPH LATTIN.)

Dated August, 24, 1775. Witnesses, Penn Frost, William Roe, yeoman, Wright Crofts, yeoman. Proved, May 20, 1778.

Page 140.—In the name of God, Amen. I, CATHARINE BOELEN, of the City of New York, will and order that all my real and personal estate, viz.: the part of the estate left to me by my late Father's will, shall be sold and the monies therefrom arising together with what cash there may be for divers good causes and considerations "me thearunto" moving be disposed of in the manner following: To my brother, Jacob Boelen, silversmith, of the City of New York, £150; to Mary Boelen, the wife of the said Jacob Boelen, £5; to Christian Frederic Oerter, of Bethlehem, £10; to my aunt, Catharine Van Winkler, widow of Henry Van Winkler, of Bergen, £20; to my cousin, Catharine Brower, wife of Hanis Brower, of Bergen, £5; to the Reverend Gustavus Shewkirk £10; for the use of the "Bretherns" Chapel in Fair Street, of the City of New York, £20; to Agnes Breasted, wife of Simon Breasted of New York, £10; to Cornelia Allen, widow, of New York, £10; to Martha Van Derlipp, of New York, £5. I give and bequeath all the residue of my estate that is left after the said respective legacies have been paid to Henry Boelen, son of my brother, Jacob Boelen, silversmith, of the City of New

York, and to Henry and Joseph Oerter, sons of Christian Fred. Oerter, of "Bethlem," and to Ann and Catharine Oerter, daughters of the said Christian Fred. Oerter to be divided amongst them equally. In case of the death of Henry Boelen, son of my brother, Jacob Boelen, before he is of age, then his share to go to the said children of the said Christian Fred. Oerter or the survivors of them. I make my brother, Jacob Boelen, silversmith, of City of New York, Christian Frederic Oerter, of Bethlehem, and his son, Henry Oerter, executors.

Dated January 7, 1778. Witnesses, John Houseman, painter and glazier, Dav. Thompson, cordwainer, Simon Breasted, cooper. Proved, April 9, 1781.

Page 142.—In the name of God, Amen. I, RICHARD STILLWELL, of the Township of Gravesend, in Kings County, (September 29, 1780). Lawful debts and funeral charges to be paid. I leave to my beloved wife, Ann Stillwell, all my lands and tenements as long as she remains my widow, but if in case she marry again it is then my will that she have £1,000 and a negro girl in lieu of her dower right; to my two sons, Richard and Jaques, all my real estate as follows: to my elder son, Richard, the old farm I live on; to my younger son, Jaques, all my farm and plantation I purchased of Cornelius Van Siclen; to my eldest daughter, Ida, the sum of £1,000 and a negro girl; to my younger daughter, "Motye," £1,000 and a negro girl. It is my will that my daughters, Ida and Motye, have their money or legacies at the expiration of five years after my decease out of my moveable estate, and further, that if any loss or losses be on my estate that my wife and children, names above mentioned, "Loose" in proportion to their legacies, or what I have given them, and if there be any overplus to go to my two sons, Richard and Jaques, equally. I make my trusty and well-beloved friends, Isaac Cortleyou, Richard Stillwell, and Rutgert Stillwell, executors.

Witnesses, Derick Lake, yeoman, Abraham Emans, yeoman, Daniel Lake, yeoman. Proved, April 12, 1781.

Page 143.—In the name of God, Amen. "This eight Intwen day" of August in the year of our Lord, 1780, I, WILLHALMUS RYDER, of Gravesend, in Kings County, in the Province of New York. It is my will that my loving wife, Gartie Ryder, shall remain in full possession of all my real and personal estate as long as she shall remain my widow; that my son, John Ryder, shall have out of my estate before any division that lot of land lying to the north of said Town, bounded south by a road, west by a road, north by Samuel and "Cornelious Strykor," east by the "Hears" of Abraham Emans and by Cornelius Emans. I leave to my four sons, John, Fernandus, Willhalmus, and Steven Ryder, the residue of my estate, lands and tenements, goods and chattels. To my six daughters, Mary, Alltey, Eleny, Ida, Elizabeth, and Geartie, each £50, to be paid after my wife's decease or remarriage. It is my will that my four daughters, Elena, Ida, Elizabeth, and Geartie, shall have £25 out of my estate before any division be made, for a setting out. I make my wife, Gartie Ryder, Fernandus Van Sickle, and my son, John Ryder, executors.

Dated August 18, 1780. Witnesses, John Buyce, yeoman, Richard Stillwell, Jr., yeoman, Richard Stillwell. Proved, April 25, 1781.

Page 145.—In the name of God, Amen. This one and twentieth Day of February in the year of our Lord Christ, 1769, I, CORNELIOUS STRYKOR, of Gravesend, in Kings County, in the Province of New York. After my lawful debts and funeral charges are paid by my executors my loving wife Rebecca shall remain in full possession of all my real and personal estate as long as she shall remain my widow, and if she should remarry she is to have £100 in lieu of her dower, to be paid by my two sons, Samuel and Cornelious. Also my negro wench named Anna, to do and dispose of at her will and pleasure. Also the best "Bead" in the house with its furniture, and the best "Cobbord." To my son Garrot £350 to be paid by his brothers, Samuel and Cornelious, and a negro girl named Sale; to my daughter Hanna, the wife of Michal Strykor, the sum of £250, to be paid by her two brothers. To my daughter Hanna a negro girl named Mot. All the remainder of my estate, real and personal, to my two sons, Samuel and Cornelious, part and part alike, except a negro boy, named Harry, I give to my son Cornelius; a negro girl named "Maree" I give to my son Samuel. It is my will that my son Cornelious shall have that part of my homestead whereon my house and barn now stand the "Bretel" of three home lots next to the Town Street, to be taken of that side which joins the widow Van Sicklen and Rutgert Van Brunts land. And it is my will that if any of my children should die without issue that their part should go to the rest of my children, part and part alike. I make my three sons, Garrot, Samuel, and Cornelious Strykor, executors.

Witnesses, Anne Stillwell, (widow), Jeremiah Stillwell, Richard Stillwell. Proved, April 12, 1781.

Page 147.—In the name of God, Amen. I, GEORGE CODMUS, of Pamapough, in the County of Bergen, in the Eastern division of the Province of New Jersey, yeoman. All just debts and funeral charges to be paid. I leave to my oldest son, George Codmus, all my farm consisting of about three hundred and forty acres, now in the possession of my tenant, Barent Waldron, situate at Tappan, formerly in Orange Co., in the Province of New York, but now in said County of Bergen. To hold the said farm to my son, George Codmus, subject to the payment of such "Legacy's" as is hereinafter charged thereon, and I give to my son George my negro man called Tom. To my sons, Dirck

Codmus and Casper Codmus, my dwelling house, farm and lands, and salt meadows, situate at Pamapough aforesaid in the Precinct or Corporation of Bergen aforesaid, and at Bergen Point, and also all my salt meadow situate in the said eastern division of New Jersey, on the west side of Newark Bay, together with all my farming utensils belonging to the said farm, to be entered upon and taken possession of by my said two last-mentioned sons when Casper, the youngest of them, shall attain the age of twenty-one years, subject to the payment of such legacies as are hereinafter charged in their respective shares of the said farm. I leave to my son Dirck my negro " Tite "; to my son Casper my negro girl " Marss." I leave to my daughter Jannete, the wife of Jacob Vrelandt, £300 to be paid to her by my son George within three years next after a peace shall take place between Great Britain and America, or the present war between them shall be discontinued, which shall first happen, the payment of which sum I expressly charge on my real estate devised to my son George. I leave to my daughter " Janneke " my negro girl Sarah, now in her possession; to my daughter Jannetje, the wife of Garret Vrelandt, £300 to be paid to her by my son Dirck, within one year after he attains the age of twenty-one years; to my daughter Jannetje my negro wench Peg now in her possession; to my daughter, Matje Codmus, the like sum of £300 to be paid by my son Casper within one year after he attains the age of twenty-one years; to my daughter Matje my negro girl Susan. To my dearly beloved wife Janneke, to her own use, the sum of £100 out of my personal estate, and two cows of her own choice, my negro girl Phill, and all my household furniture she brought to me in her marriage. So long as she remains my widow, my wife Janneke may have the use, possession, and profits of my said dwelling house, farm and meadows, and farming utensils given to my sons, Dirck and Casper, and my daughter Matje, until the said

Casper shall attain the age of twenty-one years, and then, £30 annually during her widowhood, £15 to be paid by my son George, the remaining £15 by my sons Dirck and Casper. I do declare that the bequests and provisions herein made to, and for my said wife, are and shall be in full lieu and bars of her dower in my estate. I give to my daughter Matje £50 out of the residue of my personal estate to be paid to her within six months after her marriage or when she is twenty-one years of age, which shall first happen. All the rest of my estate I give to all my children, equally to be divided among them. In case any or either of my three sons shall happen to die under the age of twenty-one years, and without leaving any lawful issue, then I leave all the estate, real and personal, given to such son or sons so dying, unto and among all my other surviving children. In case my daughter Matje shall happen to die under the age of twenty-one years, and unmarried, then I give her legacies to my other daughters. I make my wife Janneke, my son George, my son-in-law, Jacob Vrelandt, and Garret Vrelandt, executors and executrix.

Dated June 27, 1779. Witnesses, Tobias Stoutenburgh, of the City of New York, baker, Samuel Bard, Benjamin Kissam. Proved, April 10, 1781.

Page 150.—In the name of God, Amen. The fourth day of April, 1781. I, JEREMIAH SIMONSON, of the County of Richmond, and Colony of New York, will and direct that all my just debts and funeral charges shall be paid in such manner as shall be hereafter directed. I leave to my nephew, Isaac Simonson, the son of my brother Isaac, deceased, all my land and meadows with houses and all the improvements thereon which was "separated and divided" to me in the division between me and my brother Frederick, deceased, with my waggon, two horses, a plow, two harrows, all the "geers" and all my farming utensils, he paying and discharging all my just debts which

I do owe on my own account, and exclusive of any debts of my aforesaid brother, and my funeral charges. Whereas my brother Frederick by his last will and testament duly executed, bearing date, the 25 April, 1777, did give and devise to me all his plantation lands, meadows, mesuages and ferry, subjecting the same to the payment of his just debts, funeral charges and certain legacies specified in said will, as by said will may more fully appear. My will is that all that part of my estate willed to me by my brother, as aforesaid, shall be sold by my executors and the monies arising therefrom, and all my other moveable estate not before disposed of, I give and dispose of in the following manner, if any there be after paying the debts and legacies as aforesaid, to wit: One fourth part thereof to the children of my brother Simon, deceased; one fourth part to my nephew, Gozen Simonson; one fourth part to the children of my brother Jehonas, deceased; the remaining fourth part to the children of my brother Ram, deceased. I make my friend, Haremonas Garrison, my nephew, Gozen Simonson, and my nephew, Jehonas Simonson, the son of my brother Simon, executors.

Witnesses, Benjamin Seaman, Surrogate, Cornelius Corson, yeoman, Joseph Lake, yeoman. Proved, April 16, 1781.

Page 152.—In the name of God, Amen. The twenty-sixth of November, 1776, I, HANNAH CORNELL, of "Hemsted," in Queens County, Long Island. All just debts and funeral charges to be paid. I leave to my granddaughter, Hannah Cornell, £40; to my granddaughter, Hannah Cornell, three table-spoons and three tea-spoons and one piece of "Hucker Back"; to my grandson, Henry Cornell, £10; to my grandson, Barak Cornell, £10; to my grandson, Joshua Cornell, £10; to my grandson, John Cornell, £10; to my granddaughter, Mary Cornell, £10; to my granddaughter, Hannah Brucks, £20 and one bed and bedsted that I do sleep on, and one " pece " of Hucker Back; to my granddaughter, Abigil Sands, one bed and bedsted, is below, with a sale Tick, and £20, and one pece of Hucker Back; to my granddaughters, Hannah Brucks and Abigil Sands, equal alike three silver table-spoons and three tea-spoons between both. I do give my negro Pompe his liberty if he can pay my son, Barak Cornell, or his heirs, the sum of £4 per year for eighteen years. I give my negro Beller her liberty if she can pay my son Barak, or his heirs, the sum of £3 per year for eighteen years. When my negro girl called Jennea comes to be eighteen years old I give her liberty if she can pay my son Barak the sum of £3 per year for eighteen years. I give my negro boy Charles, when he is with age, his liberty if he can pay my son Barak the sum of £4 per year for eighteen years. I leave to my son Barak all the remainder of my moveable estate, and make him my sole executor.

Witnesses, Thomas Fowler, yeoman, Margrit Fowler, spinster, Deborah Cornell. Proved, March 11, 1777.

Page 153.—In the name of God, Amen. I, JESSE SMITH, of New York, mariner. First, after all my just debts be paid I give to my loving son Jesse all my houses and lands. If he, the said Jesse Smith, does not live to the age of twenty-one years, I then give it to my loving wife Charity, and my loving daughter, Hannah Smith, equally to be divided. I also leave to my wife Charity one third of my money, negroes, and moveable estate of whatsoever kind it be; to my son, Jesse Smith, one third of the same; to my loving daughter, Hannah Smith, one third of the same, at the age of twenty-one years, but if she should marry before she arrives at the age of twenty-one years, then she is to be paid the one half of her legacy. I also order that my wife receive the income of all my estate for her and my children's maintenance until they come of age. I make my loving wife Charity, my loving brother Aron, and my loving friend, John Lawrence, executors.

Dated November 15, 1771. Witnesses, John Lawrence, merchant, Quaker, Joseph Lawrence, Mary Harkur. Proved, April 23, 1781.

Page 155.—These presents witnesseth this sixth day of the ninth month, in the year of Christ, 1775, that I, SAMUEL MOTT, of Hempsted, in Queens County, on Nassau Island, carpenter. My executors are to sell all my moveable estate, except such things as I shall hereafter give away, and pay all my just debts and funeral charges, and if any remain from the sale thereof I give to my son John. I leave to the children of my son Richard, that is " Amay " and James, and to such a child, or children, as his widow is now like to have, twenty-five acres of land to be taken of the south end of my farm where I now live. But if either of them should die without lawful issue before they are of lawful age, then his, her, or their part, or parts, shall go and pass to the surviving children of said Richard, and if they should all die without lawful issue, or before they are of lawful age, then the land given them I leave to my two sons, Samuel and John, but the use of twenty-five acres, as also the use of all my farm and houses where I now live, I leave to my wife and daughter Hannah as long as they remain unmarried, and after the death or marriage of my wife and daughter Hannah the other part of my plantation, where I now live, not given away, I give to my son John. To my son Samuel all my lands that I purchased of Edwin Tatesson. To my two sons, Samuel and John, all rights in the undivided lands. To my son Jehu £2 and all my stays, gears and wearing apparel, and the use of one bed and bedding as long as my executors think proper. I give to my wife the use of two cows, my riding " chear " and my best horse or mare, two hogs, my cow bell, and all my household goods that is not given away (except one bed and furniture which

I give to my daughter Hannah), and also one cow, as long as she remains my widow, and after her marriage or death, if any of those things yet remain, then I order them to be sold and the money that arises therefrom shall be for the support of my daughter Hannah, my executors to let her have it as they see proper as long as she remains unmarried, and if any yet remain after her death or marriage it shall be equally divided between my two sons, Samuel and John. To my wife at her disposal all my grain in the ground. I make my brother, Jehu Mott, and Gideon Seaman, executors.

Witnesses, Elizabeth Rainner (Reynor), Andrew Allan, yeoman, Jacob Dosesee. Proved, April 23, 1781.

Page 157.—In the name of God, Amen. I, WILLIAM CORNELL, of Hempsted, in Queens County, yeoman. I leave to my son William my negro boy named Cesar, and another of my negro boys named Charles; to my son John, and to my son Timothy, I give another of my negro boys named Fortune, to be and remain to them respectively. I give unto my daughter Susannah my silver teapot; half a dozen silver teaspoons to my daughter Ann; half a dozen more of the same lot I give to my daughter Elizabeth. I will and require that all, and singular, my messuages, dwelling houses, lands, meadows, tenements and hereditaments where I now live in the Township of Hempstead, shall be sold by my executors, by public vendue or by private sale. Also the remainder of my moveable estate, excepting my wearing apparel, which I give my three sons equally to be divided. Out of the proceeds of such sale my executors shall pay all my just debts and funeral charges, and out of the overplus I give my son William the sum of £300; and the like to my son John; and £300 to my son Timothy. To my daughters, Susannah, Ann, and Elizabeth, I give the sum of £200 each, to be paid to them respectively as soon as the money can conveniently be collected, incoming by the sale of my estate (my sons being first paid their respective legacies), and as to the surplus money, if any be, after paying my debts, and all and every, the legacies, I give and bequeath the same to my three sons above named in an equal proportion. As to my son Timothy, being in his nonage, I order that his share shall be put and kept at interest, and the proceeds applied towards his maintenance and education during his nonage, and the residue of his legacies, gifts or bequests, paid him at his majority or marriage, which shall happen first. I make my sons, William and John, my daughter Susannah, and well-beloved friend, Henry Van Flack, of the City of New York, merchant (or such and so many of them as shall think fit to " qualifie " themselves), executors.

Dated June 14, 1756. Witnesses, Elias Doughty, John Cromwell, Sarah Doughty, Quakeress. Proved, April 5, 1781.

Page 159.—Know all men by these presents that I, ISAAC RUSHMORE, of the Township of Oyster Bay, in Queens County, on Nassau Island, yeoman, being this seventeenth day of the seventh month called July, 1779, will and order that all my just debts be paid out of my moveable estate. I leave to my two sons, Stephen and Edmund, one fourth part of a fifteen shilling patent right in the undivided Brushy plain, and in the undivided marshes in the South Bay, all in the Township of Hempstead, being a right that fell to my wife, Sarah Rushmore, by her father, Edmund Titus, by his father, Silas Titus, and also the third part of a five shilling patent right in the undivided plain land, in the Township of Hempstead. To my two sons all my lands and buildings when of age. My executors are to let my lands and buildings for the use of my family until my son Stephen comes to the age of twenty-one years, and then he to have all my lands and buildings unto his possession, and to be at all necessary expenses in bringing up my son Edmund until he shall arrive at the age of " twenty " years, and then my will is that all my lands and buildings be equally divided between them. If there be any overplus arise from the use of my lands and buildings, more than is necessary to be expended for the use of my family, then such overplus to be equally divided between my three daughters, Phebe Downing, Mary Rushmore, and Jane Rushmore. My son Stephen shall have my watch when he comes to age. To my two sons aforesaid I leave my wearing apparel (except my new " bever hatt ") to be divided between them; that my three youngest children should be brought up and educated in a becoming manner both as to learning and otherwise according to the discretion of my executors. I leave to my daughter, Mary Rushmore, £70, to my daughter, Jane Rushmore, £70 to be paid " on her day of marriage, or when she arrive to the age of eighteen years," both which foregoing legacies to be paid out of my moveable estate; the other part of my moveable estate together with my lot of salt meadow at Matinacock be equally divided between all my daughters, viz.: Phebe, Mary, and Jane. I leave to my son-in-law, Silas Downing, my new beaver hat. I make my brother-in-law, Willets Kerby, my brother-in-law, Henry Post, and my friends, Jacob Underhill and Gedion Seaman, executors.

Dated July 17, 1779. ·Witnesses, Samuel Willets, Jacob Underhill, Thomas Prior, of Oyster Bay, quaker. Proved, April 23, 1781.

Page 162.—Know all men by these presents that I, JAMES ELLISON, of the Township of Hempstead, in Queens County, this nineteenth day of February, 1780. All my ·just debts be fully paid together with my funeral charges after my decease, out of my moveable estate. I leave to my loving and well-beloved wife, Elizabeth Ellison, one feather bed, bedding furniture and appurtenances, and one cow, and my bay mair, and my cubbord and round table, and all my grain both cut and on the ground, and my three swine, all to be at her own disposal. To my son, William Ellison, all my wearing apparel, and also my black colt, to his own disposal. I direct that my sorrall mair and the remainder of my neat kind be sold, and the proceeds, when collected, to be equally divided amongst my surviving daughters; and that my said wife shall have the use of all the remainder of my moveable estate, both within doors and without, together with the use of five acres of woodland (it being the east part of my woodland), for and during widowhood, but no longer, and after that time my daughters, Elizabeth and Hannah, shall have each of them one feather bed and appurtenances to their own disposal; the remainder of my household goods shall be equally divided amongst my daughters, Freelove, Elizabeth, Mary, and Hannah, or the survivors of them. I leave to my sons, James and William, all the remainder of my moveable estate without doors. To my two sons, James and William, my homestead, my dwelling house and land, whereon I now dwell, situate on the north side of Hempstead Plains, equally to be divided between them. I make my trusty friend, Peter Titus, Jr., and my son, James Ellison, executors.

Witnesses, David Losee, Benjamin V. D. Water, Richard Ellison, quaker, of Hempstead. Proved, March 24, 1781.

Page 164.—In the name of God, Amen. I, WIL-HELMUS WYCKOFF, of New Town, in Queens County, on Nassau Island, the colony of New York, yeoman. All such debts and dues as I owe in law or conscience to any person or persons be justly and truly paid within some convenient time after my decease by my executors out of my moveable estate, and also my funeral charges. I leave to my dearly-beloved wife Phebe the use and income of my farm during her widowhood, and all my real and personal estate, excepting paying the sum of £10 a year to my mother, Adrajana Wickoff, during her life, but if my wife should remarry she is to have one negro wench named Sara, and £50 to be

paid out of my moveable estate in lieu and " stide " of
her dower out of my said estate. To my loving son
John the farm where I now live upon, or the land and
meadow that formerly did belong to William Leverich
with all improvements, house, orchard and barn, with
rights thereunto belonging, excepting a free passage
for his brother, Peter Wickoff, down to a Landing
place; to my dearly beloved son Peter the farm that
did belong to John Wickoff, all that to the western of
a division line as it has been divided before. To my
loving daughter, Cornelia Wickoff, £500, two hundred
and fifty to be paid by her eldest brother, John Wickoff,
and £250 by her brother Peter. I make my loving wife,
Phebe Wickoff, Cornelius Rapelje, John Vander Veer,
Sr., and Nicholas Schanck, of Kings County, executors.

Witnesses, John Lawrence, Samuel Lawrence, yeoman, Daniel Lawrence. Proved March 21, 1781.

[Note.—Phebe Wyckoff (now Phebe Cornell), Nicholas Schanck and Cornelius Rapelje renounced and refused to take upon them or either of them the execu-
torship; letters of administration were granted to
John Wyckoff, of New Town, yeoman, eldest son of
Wilhelmus, on April 25, 1781.]

Page 166.—These presents witnesseth that I, Permenas Jackson, of the Township of Hempstead, in
Queens County, January 14, 1781. I leave to my wife,
Elizabeth Jackson, the whole of her portion that she
brought me, likewise the sum of £100; to each of my
two daughters, Elizabeth and Rosannah, £500; to each
of my two sons, Permenas and John, £100. I leave to
my wife and four children all the residue of my moveable estate, after all my just debts and funeral charges
are first paid, and my children brought up, all which
several bequests to my wife are in lieu of her dower in
my estate. To my two sons and two daughters equally,
the use of all my real estate, until my son Permenas is
eighteen years old, to be hired out by my executors for
the benefit of my children. To my two sons, Permenas

and John, my real or " fast " estate, after my son Permenas is eighteen years old. It is my will that the whole of my real estate be possessed and enjoyed by my son Permenas from the time he is eighteen years old until my son John shall marry, or is eighteen years old. The whole of my moveable estate, except what I had with my wife, be put to sale and sold, and the proceeds to go to my wife and children as above given. I make my brothers, Obadiah Jackson, Thomas Seaman, and John Jackson, executors.

Witnesses, Jacob Seaman, yeoman, Elijah Smith, of Hempstead, yeoman, Nathaniel Whitson. Proved, March 19, 1781.

Page 168.—To all people to whom these presents shall come know ye that I, JOHN WEEKS, SR., of Oyster Bay, being this thirteenth day of March, 1780, very weak in body. I leave to my beloved wife Rebeccah the use of all the houses and lands, during her widowhood, and all my household furniture, three cows and £50, to be paid her out of my estate, all which I give to her in lieu of her right of dowry; to my beloved daughter Jane I give my house and lot of land where I now live, which she is to have after her mother's decease or day of marriage, bounded as followeth: beginning. at the southwest corner, joining to the street at the northwest corner of the homestead that is possessed by the widow of my son John, deceased, and running easterly to the northeast corner of the aforesaid homestead to the road that leads by my son Augustine's barn on the east, and by said road till it comes to John Parish' land, and on the north by said Parish land, and on the east partly by said Parish land until it comes to the southeast corner of Henry Powel's land, thence by said Powels until it comes to the southwest corner, and from thence on straight line to the northwest corner of my garden by my house, thence by the highway to the front " Bounder " containing within said Bounds 20 acres more or less. Also one piece of woodland lying near Norwich, bounded on the north by the highway that leads from Norwich to John Nostrant's, on the east by the said Nostrant's land, and on the south and west by Henry Cocks and John Wright's land, containing ten acres each, to her after her mother's decease or day of her marriage. To my son Augustine that piece of meadow ground and swamp lying northward of my garden, bounded on the west by the highway, on the north by the watering place, and on the east by Henry Powel's land, and on the south by the land I gave to my daughter Jane. To each of my granddaughters, Anne, Elizabeth, Judah, Ruth, and Charlotta Weeks, £20, to be paid out of my estate. To my grandsons, William, John, and Rafine Weeks, £10 each, to be paid out of my estate at the discretion of my executors. To my daughter-in-law, Elizabeth Weeks, the third part of the use of the homestead she now lives in, with the use of the third part of the house and barn, and the use of the third of all the out land that I give among my son John's children. I give among my grandchildren, viz., William, John, Anne, Elizabeth, Judah, Ruth, and Charlotta Weeks, all that house, barn and land that they now live in, bounded on the west by the highway, on the south by George Weeks' and land of William Butters, on the east by a highway, and on the north by land that I have given to my daughter Jane, and also half of all my out-lands and meadow that is not disposed of. I give to my son, Augustine Weeks, all the remaining part of my lands and meadow that I have not disposed of. I make my son, Augustine Weeks, of Oysterbay, executor.

Witnesses, Samuel Townsend, Esquire, Micheal Butler, Thomas Wright. Proved, April 7, 1781.

Page 170.—In the name of God, Amen. The 28th Day of May, 1777. I, BENJAMIN RAINER, of the Township of Hempstead, in Queens County. I leave to my beloved wife my best bed and furniture, one horse and saddle, one round table, half a dozen chairs, two iron pots, one dozen pewter plates, one iron trammel, two pewter platters, two basons, one wash tub, one pair hand irons, two cows and calves, all the meal and provisions I have, and my grain in the ground and elsewhere of every kind, and all my " Cloath "; all which articles I give in lieu of her dower and not otherwise. To my loving wife Anna one sixth part of all my moveable estate and also my negro boy named " Stephneg," and also the use of all my lands and tenements during widowhood, nevertheless my two sons, Joel and Isaac, shall have the privilege of living in the house with my said wife as long as she remains my widow; at her marriage or decease I give and bequeath unto my three sons, Amos, Joel, and Isaac, all the proceeds of the sale of my lands and tenements. My executors are to sell my lands and divide the proceeds equally among my three sons. My son Isaac shall have the privilege of disposing of his part of the money as he thinks proper, notwithstanding what is said above. I leave to my son Isaac one cow and calf; to my two sons, Joel and Isaac, my plow and all my farming utensils; to my daughter Anna one bed and furniture, one cow and calf, one chest, eight sheets, two flannel blankets, ten pillow cases, four towels, and two table-cloths. All the remainder of my moveable estate not already bequeathed I leave to my five daughters, viz.: Bithia Hall, Anne Smith, Mille Bedel, Abigail Mott, and Anna Rainer, excepting £10 which I give over and above to daughter Anne. I make my son Amos, and my son-in-law, John Hall, executors.

Witnesses, James Searing, " practitioner of physick," Benjamin Bedell, David Batty, yeoman. Proved, August 9, 1777.

Page 172.—I, MARY ROWLAND, of the Township of Hempstead, in Queens County, November 12, 1776. I leave to my daughter, Zorada Rowland, two of my best feather beds, six pair of sheets, four " coverleds," two bedsteads and the furniture, two of my best pewter platters, six pewter plates, three table cloths, six towels, all which she may choose, and my cupboard and chest. All the residue and remainder of my estate after my just debts and funeral expenses are all paid and discharged (excepting the legacy ordered for me in my father, Robert Marvin's last will and testament) I leave to my three daughters, Abigail Thorne, Phebe Hagner, and Zorada Rowland, equally divided amongst them. My will and my mind is that the legacy above mentioned shall be equally divided amongst all my children, Marvin Rowland, and my daughters above mentioned, provided my said son is a loyal subject to his majesty, King George the Third, and a true friend to Government; if my son is otherwise, the legacy shall be equally divided amongst my daughters. I make my two friends, Samuel Denton and James Cornwell, both of Herricks, in the Township and County aforesaid, executors.

Witnesses, John Searing, William Hewlett, yeoman, Emry Hewlett. Proved, November 27, 1776.

Page 173.—I, RICHARD MOTT, of Herricks, in the Township of Hempstead, in Queens County, being this 12th day of the eighth month, 1779, in a weak state of health. I order my executors to collect all my moneys due to me, and with the same to pay all my just debts, funeral charges and incidental expenses that may happen in executing my will and testament. I leave all my wearing apparel to my brother, Samuel Seaman Mott; my bed and furniture to my sister, Sarah Manlove; to my executors the sum of £4 to be paid into the hands of the Treasurer of the monthly meeting of Friends at Westbury for the use of said meeting; all the remainder of my estate not heretofore willed I leave to the children of my brother, Seaman Mott, to the children of my sister, Sarah Manlove, and to the children of my sister, Elizabeth Seaman, to be equally divided among them, and to be possessed thereof when

they arrive respectively to the age of twenty-one years,
or their respective days of marriage. I desire my executors to put each " Legates " part out at interest for
their advantage. I make my kinsman, Jiles Seaman,
and Richard Seaman, sons of my uncle, Jiles Seaman,
of Oysterbay and County aforesaid, executors, and
that my executors be reasonably paid for their time,
trouble, and expense in its execution.

Witnesses, Thomas Pearsall, John Searing, yeoman,
Sarah Lake, spinster. Proved, July 28, 1780.

Page 175.—I, JACOB VAN NOSTRANT, of the East
Woods, in Oysterbay, in Queens County, yeoman, being
this 30 day of March, 1779, weak and low in body. All
just debts and funeral charges to be paid before any
division be made in my estate. I leave to my wife Cornelia my best bed and furniture and cupboard to her
own disposal, and the use of my house during her
widowhood, all which I give her in lieu of her dower
and not otherwise. I leave to my children, viz.: Albert, Leanah, Esberite, Maria, Garrit, and Aaron, all
the remainder of my estate whatsoever, both in lands
and moveable, that lyeth in Oysterbay or elsewhere
(except my son Garrit that at present is indisposed)
to be equally divided between them and him the said
Garrit with the rest if he should get better of his in-
disposition, which matter is hereby left discretionally
to my executors as they shall think fit, at such time
as they shall think fit to make a division in my estate,
and I further leave at their discretion to sell and
dispose of my whole real and personal estate when
they shall think best for my family's support, and the
payment of my just debts. I make my friend, Samuel
Van Wyck, and my son, Albert Van Nostrant, executors.

Witnesses, Anne Wortman, John Van Nostrant,
yeoman, Nathaniel Whitson. Proved, April 20, 1779.

Page 177.—In the name of God, Amen. I, HANNAH
BEDELL, of Hempstead, in Queens County. I leave to

Catharine Bedell, daughter of Silvester Bedell, my bed and all the furniture thereunto belonging. To Mary Bedell, daughter of my brother Jeremiah Bedell, all my wearing apparel, be the same of what nature or kind soever. All the rest of my estate, both real and personal, after all my just debts and funeral charges are paid I leave to " Cozen " Silvester Bedell. I make Silvester Bedell to be my only and sole executor.

Dated October 6, 1776. Witnesses, Samuel Pettet, yeoman, Peter Pettet, Aletty Dorlan. Proved, November 20, 1776.

Page 178.—I, BENJAMIN SMITH, of the Township of Hempstead in Queens County doth this tenth day of January, 1779, make and publish this will. All my just debts and funeral expenses to be paid. My executors to sell such part of my lands as they shall think proper and convenient, sufficient to pay my daughters their portion hereafter mentioned, should my personal estate be insufficient for the same. I leave to my loving wife Hannah the use of two-thirds of the remainder of my real estate until my son Benjamin arrives to the age of eighteen years. This towards bringing up my children, and then my wife and two sons, Niah and Benjamin, to have the use of the same equally amongst them during her natural life. Also to my wife one-fifth of my household goods within doors, my riding chair, my negro man Siah, eight head of cattle, twenty sheep, two horses, and utensils to carry on farming, and £50 cash in lieu of her dower. To my four daughters £1200, equally divided among them when or as they arrive to the age of eighteen years, and their equal fifth part of my household goods within doors. To my son Niah my black mare & black gelding, my negro boy Bill, and ten sheep; to my son Benjamin my bay colt. My daughters, as long as they remain single shall have one room, pasture for a horse, and two cows, and firewood sufficient for one fire; she or they to bear expense of getting the same.

All other personal estate to be sold as my executors
deem advisable, in order to pay off my daughters' legacies, viz.: to Meriam, Phebe, Sarah, and Hannah
Smith. To my sons, Niah and Benjamin, all other
lands and tenements or real estate, with my right in
the undivided lands in the Township. Benjamin to
have my homestead in his division. Should he die under age or before twenty-one years of age, then his
portion to be equally divided amongst my surviving
children. My executors shall improve or put to interest their portion during non-age for the bringing
up and maintaining my children. I make my two loving brothers, Richard Smith and James Smith, and
my loving son Niah, executors.

Witnesses, Benjamin Treadwell, jr., John Marvin
(yeoman), and James Cornwall (yeoman). Proved,
May 6, 1779.

Page 180.—In the name of God, Amen. I, JACOB
PETERSON, of Hempstead in Queens County, yeoman,
make this my will. My just debts and funeral charges
to be duly paid. I leave to Mary, my dearly beloved
wife, all the household goods, and furniture which I
received with her at our marriage; also the sum of
£30, to be paid within one year after my decease. To
my son Zebulon £20, to be levied out of my estate;
to be paid him when twenty-one years of age. All
other estate to be divided into three parts; one part
for my son Zebulon; one equal third to my daughter
Hannah; a like part to my daughter Mary; to be paid
them as they arrive at lawful age. I make my trusty
friends and neighbors, Martin Van Nostrand and Robert Doughty, executors.

Dated November 10, 1776. Witnesses, David Ludlow (yeoman), Rulif Vorhis, Nathaniel Box (yeoman).
Proved, January 25, 1779.

Page 182.—In the name of God, Amen. I, GEORGE
HEWLETT, of the north side of Hempstead Plains in the
Township of Hempstead in Queens County, yeoman,

make this will. All my just debts and funeral expenses to be paid as hereinafter directed. I leave to my son William all that my farm at Hericks in the Township aforesaid, which he now occupies, with all its appurtenances. Also, one full and equal undivided third part of all my shares and rights of undivided marshes at the south side of Hempstead, and of my undivided rights of land at Hempstead Plains not in fence. Also, eight sheep to be chosen for him out of my flock by my executors; two heifers and one yearling horned beast, to be chosen out of my stock by the said William. To my daughter Hannah eight cows and eight sheep, chosen by my executors; also, my negro boy, Jim, and my black mare and riding chair and tackle, and also my household furniture and plate (except my silver tankard, and one bed, pillows, and covering, hereafter disposed of) and the sum of £160 in cash to be paid to her as directed. To my son William my negro named Jacob; to my son Richard my silver tankard; to my son Emry all the rest of my sheep. To my sons, Richard and Emry, one bed with the pillows, sheets and covering. All other estate, real and personal, to my sons, Richard and Emry, to be equally divided between them as tenants in common, subject nevertheless to the payments of all my debts and funeral expenses, and £160 to my daughter Hannah; the one-half thereof to be paid within six months, and the other half within one year next after my decease. I expressly charge the payment of the said debts, etc., and the legacy as a Lien on the real estate devised to my sons, Richard and Emry, to be bound and paid by them equally. I make my brother, Benjamin Hewlett, of Great Neck, Valentine Hewlett Peters, Esq., of Hempstead, and Benjamin Hewlett the younger, of the same place, executors.

Dated February 12, 1778. Witnesses, Joseph Kissam, Esq. (attorney at law), Benjamin Kissam, and Martha Carman (spinster). Proved, November 10, 1778.

Page 184.—The twenty-seventh day of April, 1778. I, Daniel Huelett, senior, of Hempstead on Long Island, will that all my just debts be well and truly paid. I leave to my beloved wife Elizabeth all my personal estate and all my possessions of what kind soever during her natural life. Likewise one feather bed and furniture. My son John shall live on the said personal estate and possessions with my wife Elizabeth. To my son John one negro wench named Rose; to be put in his possession or disposal as he and my executors shall agree upon. Also, to him, all my personal estate after the decease of my wife Elizabeth. To my three sons, Daniel, William, and John, all my plain lands, and marsh, to be equally divided between them. My executors, with the consent of my wife and son John, to sell all or any part of my personal estate for the benefit of my wife and son. I make George Huelett and Daniel Huelett, executors.

Witnesses, George Hewlett, Jemime Hewlett (spinster), and Matthias Cooke (yeoman). Proved, May 20, 1778.

" The will of Stephen Martino recorded in Liber B of Wills, Page 119, &c."

The above entry is made on the margin of page 185, Liber 34. Search has been made in the Hall of Records and in the New York County Clerk's office; inquiry has also been made in Richmond County, where the will was probated, August 4, 1779. Cornelius Martino, Benjamin Martino, and Stephen Martino, were named as executors, and subsequently qualified.

Page 186.—In the name of God, Amen. I, Peter Van De Water, of Flushing, in Queens County, cordwainer, do make this will. I leave to Elizabeth, my dearly beloved wife, one feather bed and furniture, including two pairs of sheets and pillowcases, one case of drawers, six sitting chairs, six pewter plates, two pewter platters, six knives and forks, two iron pots, one trammel, one tea kettle, one copper kettle, my burnt china bowl, and my negro woman named Silvia. Unto my daughter Elizabeth the feather-bed which belonged to her aunt, Winche Van De Water, with its furniture, three silver table-spoons, three silver tea-spoons, one small case of drawers, one pair of gold buttons, and one gold ring. Unto my daughter Winche one feather bed and furniture including two pairs of sheets, three silver table-spoons, three silver tea-spoons, one pair gold buttons, one gold ring, and one " Bilsted " chest. Unto my son, William Sherlock, all my wearing apparel, silver tankard, my negro boy named Harry, and one feather bed and furniture, including two pairs of sheets. Unto my daughter, Mary Sherlock, as much of my estate as I have above given to my above named daughters. All my estate, real and personal (except what is above given) to be sold as soon as deemed advantageous for my children; the proceeds of such sale to be divided equally amongst my wife and children. I make my trusty and loving friends, John Rodman and John Field, executors.

Dated May 27, 1777. Witnesses, Daniel Hitchcock (house carpenter) Pepperrell Bloodgood, and Robert Hinchman (Deputy Clerk of Queens County). Proved, April 13th, 1780.

Page 188.—In the name of God, Amen. I, JOHN BEATTY, of the South Division of Richmond County, yeoman, make this will. I leave my beloved wife, Ann Beatty, during her natural life, one bed with all the bed furniture belonging to it, six chairs and a table, one pot, one kettle, six tea-cups and saucers and tea-spoons, one tea and sugar pot; at her decease whatever is left shall go to the children. Unto my wife and son John the use and possession of the farm I now live upon; together with two horses, two cows, one waggon, one plough and harrow, and other farming utensils, for the term of three years after my decease; they paying yearly for the same, £10, if they choose to accept the conditions of this article. My three daughters, Elizabeth, Ann, and Charity, shall live with their mother and brother, and work for their mother, who shall provide them with every necessary during the three years as she now provides for them. At the expiration of said term the remaining part of my whole estate to be sold and turned into money. If my wife and son John shall agree to live on the place as above mentioned, then all the rest of my personal Estate that is not allotted for their use to be sold and turned into money; my just debts and funeral expenses to be forthwith paid. When said term expires and the residue of my estate is turned into money, the proceeds shall be divided into seven equal parts; of which my wife and five children, Edward, John, Elizabeth, Ann and Charity shall each have one part, and the remaining seventh part to be equally divided among the four children of my daughter, Isabel Vanderbilt, deceased, viz.: John, Aris, Catharine, and Isabel Vanderbilt. Should any of my children die under age his or her part shall be equally divided among the surviving grandchildren. I make my loving wife Ann, and my two sons, Edward and John Beatty, and my trusty friend, Daniel Leake, jr., now living at the mill on the Great Kills, executors. Dated August 27, 1778. Witnesses, Peter Cortelyou, Joseph Guyon, and John Guyon (yeoman). Proved, May 7, 1781.

Page 190.—In the name of God, Amen. I, JOSEPH HOWARD, of the Township of Flatbush in King's County, yeoman, make this will. All my just and lawful debts and funeral charges be duly paid out of my moveable estate. I leave to my grandson, Christoffel Howard, son of my son William, late deceased, all my lands which lie on the westerly side of the highway or road that leads from my dwelling house to Brooklyn Ferry; being the most part thereof in the bounds of Flatbush and part in the Bounds of Brookland; together with the orchard, woods, and other appurtenances thereunto belonging. Also, my two lots of wood-land, containing ten acres, which I bought of the sons-in-law of Johannes Rapalje, deceased; also, the equal third part of my meadow. Unto my grandson William (also a son of my son William), so much of my land in number of acres as I conveyed to my said son William in his lifetime (as by a certain instrument in writing thereof may appear), adjoining thereto on the southwesterly side thereof. Unto my two grandsons, Joseph and William Howard, sons of my son William, my dwelling house, barn and all and singular the rest of my lands, wood-lands and real estate. Unto my daughter Mary, the now wife of Cornelius Sebring, the sum of £1,200. Unto each of my granddaughters, Hilletye, Grietye, and Femmetye (daughters of my son William) £200; £100 whereof to be paid to each of them one year after my decease; that is to say, to them that shall be of lawful age; and the other £100 one year thereafter; and to each of them which shall then not be of lawful age, £100 when they shall arrive at lawful age, and the other £100 one year thereafter. Unto my three said grandsons, equally, my horses, wagons, farmer's tools and utensils. Unto my said daughter Mary, and my said granddaughters, all my household goods and furniture to be equally divided amongst them. To my said grandsons and granddaughters all the residue of my estate to be equally divided. My grandchildren to be brought up and maintained out of the use, incomes, and profits of my estate until they arrive to lawful age, or marry, which shall happen first. My daughter-in-law Femmetye to continue to dwell in my house for so long a time as she shall remain the widow of my son William, but shall in the meantime be liable to assist in the bringing up and maintaining my grandchildren. I make my grandson, Joseph Howard, my cousin, William Howard, of New Town, my cousin, Cornelius Wyckoff, and my neighbor, Johannes Lott, executors. Dated November 25, 1777. Witnesses, Jacob Snedeker, Jurrien Lott (yeoman, of New Lotts), and Johannes Snediker. Proved, May 24, 1781.

Page 192.—I, JOHANNES ELDERT, of the New Lotts in the Town of Flatbush in Kings County, yeoman, will that all my just and lawful debts and funeral charges be paid out of my estate. I leave unto Femmetje, my beloved wife, all and singular my real and personal estate, so long as she remains my widow. At her death or remarriage I give to my two sons, namely, Hendrick and Isaac, all my certain piece or parcel of land whereon I now dwelleth so as it now lyes in fence; being seven lots or thereabouts, to each of them the equal half thereof; to Hendrick the easterly side with the dwelling house, barns, orchards, and gardens (except my dwelling house, barn, orchard, and garden and five acres of land from the east side of my dwelling house and barn, wherein my son Isaac now dwelleth) to the westerly half of my land along the road. Unto my son Isaac the westerly equal half with the dwelling house (wherein he now dwelleth) barn, orchard, garden, and five acres of land. Also, unto my said two sons, all the residue of my lands and meadows and real estate, equally; they and their respective heirs to pay unto my daughter, Grietye, the now wife of John Van Deveer, jr., the sum of £200; each of them £50 two years after my decease, and yearly thereafter the sum of £50 each, until the whole sum be paid. Unto my sons, Hendrick and Isaac, and my daughter Grietye (after my wife shall cease to be my widow, and my lawful debts and funeral expenses be paid) all the rest of my moveable estate, to be equally divided amongst them. I make my sons, Hendrick and Isaac Eldert, executors.
Dated February 15, 1777. Witnesses, Johannes Lott, Jacob Snedeker, and Johannes Lott, jr. (yeoman). Proved, June 8, 1781.

Page 194.—I, CORNELIUS WILLETT, of the Borough of West Chester, in the county of West Chester, gentleman, will that all my just debts and funeral charges be duly paid and satisfied in some convenient time after my decease. I leave unto my well-beloved wife Elizabeth, during the time she remains my widow, and no longer, the use and improvement of my two farms and salt meadows, together with all my houses, barns, and stock of creatures of every kind, and all the tools and utensils of husbandry upon or belonging in any wise to my said farms; as also my plate, linen, beds, and household furniture, and all my negroes not herein particularly mentioned to be disposed of otherwise. Unto my wife, for life, my negro men Robert, Israel, and Andrew, and boy Henry. My executors to permit my said slaves Robert, Israel, and Andrew to choose their own masters at what time they are disposed of. Unto my wife, as her own property, at her disposal, my negro woman Caroline, my clock, worked chairs, large looking glass, a feather bed and curtains with a bed-stead and a bedding for the same, six large silver table-spoons, a silver milk pot and pepper box, and all the pictures hanging in my parlor. Unto my daughter, Rachel Haviland, my negro girl named Nanny; unto my daughter, Mary Graham, my negro man named Phillip; unto my daughter Martha my negro girl named Nelly; unto my daughter Sarah my negro boy named Joseph. Unto my grandson, Willett Leaycroft, all my right, title, and interest in a certain tract of land commonly called the Flat Lands in Kings County on the Island of Nassau. In case he should die before he attains to the age of twenty-one years, not having lawful issue, I revoke and annul my said devise; then my executors to sell said tract, and the proceeds to be divided as the rest of my estate. Unto my grandson, Cornelius Willett Vanranst, the sum of £100, and my negro boy named Robert. Unto my grandson, James Graham, my negro boy named Harry; but he is not to have him until the death of my wife. Unto my granddaughter, Amelia Ogilvie, my negro girl named Hannah. Whereas my daughters,

Martha and Sarah, are unmarried, my executors to
pay unto each that shall remain unmarried at the time
of my decease the sum of £50 to be as an outset. On
the death or remarriage of my wife, my executors are
to sell and dispose of either at public or private sale,
as they shall think best, all my estate, real and personal, not hereinbefore given and devised. In case
my executors shall think it will be more for the advantage of my wife and children to sell my upper farm
during my wife's widowhood they have full power and
authority to sell it at any time after my decease. After the payment of all my just debts and legacies hereinbefore given, all the proceeds of the sale of my lands
and meadows, together with all the residue of my estate, real and personal, are to be divided into six
equal shares for my children and grandchildren in the
following manner: viz.: one sixth part unto my daughter, Rachel Haviland, and to her son, Willett Leycraft,
to be equally divided between them; a sixth part unto
my daughter, Mary Graham (except £50 of her division, which sum I give to her eldest son, Cornelius
Willett Vanranst); a sixth unto my grandson, Edward
Stevenson; a sixth part unto my daughter Martha; a
sixth to my daughter Sarah; a sixth unto my two
granddaughters, Elizabeth and Amelia Ogilvie, to be
equally divided between them. In case either of my
said granddaughters, Elizabeth or Amelia, should die
before they attain to the age of twenty years or marry,
·her share shall be given to her surviving sister; should
both die before the age of twenty years, or marry, then
their share I give to my surviving children and grandson, Edward Stevenson, to be divided between them
as the last division of my estate is to be made. Should
my said grandson, Edward Stevenson, die before he
is twenty-one years old, not having lawful issue, what
I have given him shall be considered part of my estate
and be divided as before. Should any of my children
or grandchildren die before the last division of my
estate, having lawful issue, such issue shall have por-

tion of my estate as his or her parent would have had if then living. My Executors to put out at interest all such sums of money as shall belong to any of my children and grandchildren before-named, that may be under age at the time of my decease; such portions, with the interest due, to be given at the time of marriage, or when twenty-one years of age.

Whereas there are divers sums of money which I have paid on account of Augustin Graham, husband of my daughter Mary, whatsoever money that shall appear to be due to me from him shall be deducted out of the share of my daughter Mary when the last division of my estate is made; excepting the interest of £100, which I give to my son-in-law. My executors shall, at their discretion put out my grandson, Cornelius Vanranst, to such trade or calling as they shall think most suitable to his circumstances.

What I have given my beloved wife Elizabeth is in lieu of her dower or thirds; also, that she is at the pains and cost of bringing up and maintaining my two granddaughters, Elizabeth and Amelia Ogilvie, during the time of her widowhood. But in case their father, George Ogilvie, or their guardians, shall refuse and not permit them to live with my wife, then she shall be free from any obligation to maintain them.

I make my dearly beloved wife, Elizabeth Willett, my daughter, Martha Willett, my nephew, Isaac Willett, and my trusty friends, Doctor Daniel White and Theopilus Bartow, executors.

Dated January 19, 1781. Witnesses, Robert Hunt and Cornelius Leggett (yeoman) and Ebenezer Leggett. Proved, June 11, 1781.

Page 198.—I, WILLIAM PHILLIPS, of the Royal Regiment of Artillery, and Major General in his Majesty's service, being of sound mind and in present Health of Body, Do make this my last Will and Testament in my own handwriting at New York this fifth day of January, 1781. I recommend myself to God the Father of all in a belief of His infinite Goodness and Mercy. I leave to Mrs. Elizabeth Brown, now or late of High Street, Mary la Bonne, London, lately the wife of John Brathwaite, but now divorced in due course of Law, all I shall stand possessed of at my death in Estates, real or personal. In case the said Elizabeth Browne shall die before me, I leave William Collier, Lieutenant in the Royal Regiment of Artillery, to Thomas Forsyth, Esq., William Faqahar (Surgeon of Marlborough Street, London), and to Major Drummond of the Royal Regiment of Artillery, all my estates, real and personal, In Trust to be by them given in equal shares to my natural children, William Edward Browne, Charles Browne, Charlotte Browne, and Emeily Browne, at the time the children shall arrive at the age of twenty-one years.

In case of all their deaths, to Lt. Collier of the Royal Regiment of Artillery. To be first paid out of my real and personal estate at my death unto Miss Caroline Williams, now in the care of Mrs. Levina Brundenell, the sum of £500 sterling, and to be placed in the Funds for her use until her age of twenty-one years. Should the said Caroline Williams die before that age, the interest of the legacy to go to Mrs. Levina Brudenell for her life; after which the principal and interest to go to my heirs as before described. Out of the receipts of my real and personal estate £30 per annum be paid to Mrs. Lucy Phillips, otherwise Thomson, during her life. I acquit Lieut. Collier of any Debts he may owe me at my Death. Unto Miss Catharine Van Horn, of Flatbush, Long Island, 100 guineas, to be paid her at my death.

Witness my hand this fifth day of January, 1781. Witnesses, John Yorke, Mungo Noble (Captain in his Majesty's 60th Regiment of Foot), Edward Fage, and Edward Thecher (gunner in Royal Regiment of Artillery). Proved, June 8, 1781.

Page 200.—In the name of God, Amen. I, HANNAH SMITH, of the Township of Hempstead in Queens County, do this fourteenth day of January, 1780, make this will. I leave to my four daughters, Meriam, Phebe, Sarah, and Hannah, all my whole estate (after my just debts and funeral expenses are paid) within doors and out, equally divided among them. I make my two brothers-in-law, Richard Smith and James Smith, executors.

Witnesses, Nier Smith (yeoman), William Wright, and James Conwell (yeoman). Proved, March 16, 1781.

Page 201.—I, JOHN DORLON, of Hempstead, in Queens County, do make my will as followeth: First, I leave to my son John all the farm, or the lands whereon my said son now lives, lying on the west side of the highway that leads from my now dwelling house to the house where the widow Burlugh, deceased, formerly lived; and fifteen acres of land to be taken off the south end of the farm whereon I now live, beginning at Samuel Williams' field (so called) and running southerly to Noah Comb's land, and extending as far west as to make fifteen acres. Also, all the remaining part of my meadow which I have not heretofore given my late son Elias a deed for. Likewise one half of all my plain land that is already laid out to me, and also one half of all my timber or swamp land that lies at Hungry Harbour Neck adjoining the Boggs, and one half of all the undivided right in the Township of Hempstead which now belongs to me, which was my father's, also one half of all my land at Hick's Neck. Unto my daughter-in-law Hannah, the widow of my late son Elias, the entire use and benefit of a good room in the dwelling house where my son lately lived, and also to get firewood for her own use (on the lands I have hereafter given to my grandsons, Joseph and Linninton) the firewood to be cut and brought home to her by my aforesaid grandsons. Also give unto her pasture for a cow on the farm where I now live. My grandsons shall find sufficient hay for wintering the cow; all which for the use of my daughter so long as she remains my son's widow, and no longer. Unto my grandsons, Joseph and Linninton, children of my late son Elias, all the remainder of my lands, rights and shares of land, with the buildings thereon, to be equally divided between them. Also unto them, all that part of the house or lands which I have heretofore given the use of unto Son Elias' widow. Unto my son Samuel, and unto my son Joseph's children, and unto my daughters, Mirriam and Anne, and unto my daughter Mary's children, all my moveables, be the same of what nature or kind soever, to be equally divided between them. But my son Joseph's children and my daughter Mary's children are to have a share equal to one of my other children. I make my son, John Dorlon, and my friend, John Williams, executors.

Dated June 16, 1778. Witnesses, James Burtis, Elias Burtis (yeoman) and James Burtis. Proved, June 5, 1781.

Page 203.—These presents witnesseth JOHN DERYEE, in Queens and province of New York, this nineteenth day of October, 1779, do make my will. My estate, real and personal, to be put to sale at the discretion of my executors (except my desk and silver watch and one of my beds with its furniture). I leave my son Rulof £100 and my desk and silver watch; unto my son Pratt £100; unto my well-beloved wife Nancy one bed and its furniture. The remaining part to my wife Nancy and to my two sons and three daughters, viz.: Catherine, Mary, and Nancy; to be equally divided. I make Nancy, my well-beloved wife, my brother-in-law, John Pratt, and Samuel Seamen, of Jerusalem, executors.

Witnesses, Obadiah Seaman, James Birdsall, and Thomas Seaman, of Hempstead (schoolmaster). Proved, May 30, 1781.

Page 204.—In the name of God, Amen. On the tenth day of March, 1780, I, ADAM CARMAN, of Hempstead in Queens County on Nassau Island, being in a poor state of health. I leave to my daughter Hannah the bed that I now lay on, together with the bedstead and cord with all the covering belonging; also the looking glass; and £5 to be levied out of my estate and paid soon after my death. Unto my daughter Nancy £5 raised and paid as above. All my out-door moveable estate to be sold soon after my death; the proceeds to pay my just debts, funeral charges, and the legacies. Also to them, the use of all my fast estate for the expiration of four months after my death; but all my in-door moveables over and above not already disposed of, to be sold, and all lands and tenements, together with all the Rights of Lands that I shall happen to have, to be sold four months after my death; of the proceeds of all sales one fifth part to my loving daughter Phebe, wife of James Antony; a like part to each of my daughters; Elizabeth, wife of Daniel Thurston; to Hannah Carman; to Nancy Cadman; and the remaining one-fifth part to my grandchildren (children of my daughter, Mary Rainer), Mary and Almy Rainer, equally to be divided, and to be paid as they arrive at the age of eighteen years. I make my trusty friends, Samuel Cadman and Uriah Bedle (both of Hempstead), executors.

Witnesses, Abraham Mall (yeoman), Caleb Southard, and Isaac Denton (yeoman). Proved, February 20, 1781.

Page 207.—In the name of God, Amen. October the seventh, 1776. I, DAVID PINE, of Hempstead in Queens County on Nassau Island, yeoman, being sick and weak, leave (my just debts and funeral charges being first satisfied) to my well-beloved mother, Sarah Pine, a decent maintenance, such as house-room, clothing, utensils, washing & lodging and every necessary of life; at her death, a decent funeral; all to be raised out of my estate. I make my well-beloved sister, Sarah Pine, and my loving cousin, John Linninton, and my loving cousin, Elias Dorlin, the 3d, and my loving friend, James Wood, executors; and empower them to sell and convey such lands and meadow or both, as they shall think proper before paying my just debts and funeral charges. Unto my loving sister, Sarah Pine, my house, barn, orchard, fences, land and meadow, and all my moveable estate, such as cattle, sheep, horses, farming utensils; together with all my moveable estate, also all my undivided Rights in the Township of Hempstead. If any person or persons shall raise a dispute about any of my rights, lands or meadow I give my executors full power to answer in law as though I were present myself.

Witnesses, John Smith, Amos Smith, and William Pettit (yeoman). Proved, November 20, 1776.

Page 209.—In the name of God, Amen. I, DANIEL COLLIER, late of Connecticut, at present of New York, mariner, leave (after my just debts be paid) the remainder of all my personal or real estate to my brother, William Collier, of Hartford in Connecticut. I make David Gregg, of the City of New York, innkeeper, executor.

Dated June 29, 1780. Witnesses, William Cumming and John Welsh. Proved, June 25, 1781.

[NOTE.—Coleman Fisher, of the City of New York, merchant, being of the people called Quakers, affirmed and declared that he saw the testator and the above two witnesses sign, etc. The executor named, Daniel Gregg, died before the probate, and made Jane Fegan his sole executrix, who was made administrator of Daniel Collier's estate.]

Page 210.—Be it known unto all men to whom these Presents shall come, or in any ways concern; that I, ROBERT ALLEN, of Mill Neck in the Township of Oysterbay in Queens County, being this sixteenth day of December, 1778, weak in body. My executors are to dispose of such a part of my estate, as they shall think most proper, to discharge all my just debts. The estate otherwise to be left for the use of my wife and children until my youngest child becomes of age; then the residue to be sold for the benefit of my children, except what I leave to my wife. Unto my wife Hannah one cow, one bed, such as she shall choose, with the furniture; one cupboard, one table, one pewter platter, one large bason, and one half dozen pewter plates, and one trammel. Unto my second son, Baruch, £15 for his own use and purpose. All the rest of my estate to my children as follows: a double portion to my sons, viz.: Darias, Baruch, Robert, and Abraham; unto the daughters, viz.: Freelove, Lorete, Phebe, Sarah, and Hannah. I make my friend, Thomas Cock, and my friend, Thomas Smith, jr., and my wife, Hannah Allen, executors.

Witnesses, Henry Ludlam, Daniel Allen, of Oysterbay (yeoman), and Sarah Ludlam. Proved, June 4, 1781.

Page 211.—Know all men by these presents that I, JOHN MOTT, of Cowneck in the Township of Hempstead in Queens County, being this 28th day of the second month, 1773, well in health of body. All my real and personal estate, both lands and moveables, to be sold as soon as convenient after my decease. The proceeds, all moneys due to me upon Bonds and otherways to be collected; with the same my just debts, funeral charges and incidental expenses in executing this will, or that may otherwise happen, to be paid. The residue of my estate to be for uses and purposes after mentioned.

Whereas, my brother Edmond Mott has been and is at this time in a " Delarious " unsettled condition of mind, not of a capacity fit to have the Disposal of any Temporal Enjoyments, therefore my executors are to assist and support him out of my estate as long as he continues in this unsettled state of mind. Should he recover his understanding and come to right state of mind, and my executors should judge him of a fit Capacity to have the Disposal of what I have committed to their Trust, he is to have all my estate then in trust (except, as I am at this time possessed of a negro man named Hance, who has been for some time at his Liberty respecting Slavery, notwithstanding what is above written, the negro man to be continued his Liberty, and brought under no restraint as to Slavery; my executors to have the care and oversight of him, and also keep and retain such a part of my estate in their hands as they shall think proper for his support should he become necessitous). After the death of my brother, and the death of the negro Hance, and all charges paid respecting them, then all remaining in the hands of my executors to go as follows: Unto each of my executors £50; and £100 to the use of the poor belonging to the Society of Friends within the Province of New York, or otherways to be disposed of as the Yearly Meeting of Friends within said Province shall think proper. The residue of my estate to go to my niece, Margaret Smith, wife of Melancton Smith, and Richard Sands and Adam Mott, both of Cowneck in said Town and County, my executors.

Witnesses, John Willis and Stephen Mott (Quakers and yeomen), and Elizabeth Mott. Proved, March 16, 1781.

Page 213.—I, Sarah Seaman, widow of Richard Seaman, near Herricks in the Township of Hempstead in Queens County, being this seventeenth day of the eighth month, 1780, far advanced in age, but of a tolerable state of health. All moneys due to me on bonds and otherwise to be collected; the same to pay all my just debts, funeral charges, etc. I leave to my daughter, Sarah Lake, wife of Joseph Lake, my best bed and its furniture, all my wearing apparel and old riding "Shaise." To the intent my daughter Sarah should have some place of residence after my decease, she is to have the use and profits of all my lands during her natural life; at her decease they to be for all her children then living equally to be divided. The residue of my estate, not above willed, to be divided into equal parts; one of which to be for my daughter Sarah; the other half to be for six of my grandchildren, equally to be divided, to wit: my son Richard's three children, viz.: Elizabeth, Richard and Benjamin, and my three grandsons, Richard, Daniel, and Joseph Lake, children of my daughter Sarah. My executors to take care of that part given to my grandson, Benjamin Seaman, until he attains the age of twenty-one years. 'I make my friends, Adam Mott, John Searing, and Gedeon Seaman, of Hempstead, and Jiles Seaman, jr., of Oysterbay executors.

Witnesses, Daniel Toffey (yeoman), Mary Searing, jr. (spinster), and Susannah Searing.

Proved, March 16, 1781.

Page 215.—In the name of God, Amen. The third day of October, 1776. I, ADRIAEN HEGEMAN, jr., of the Township of Oysterbay in Queens County on the Island of Nassau, yeoman, being at present weak in body. After all my lawful debts are paid and my funeral charges defrayed, I leave my daughter, Doortie Hegeman, my Dutch Psalm Book for her birthright, before any division is made of my Estate. All such, real and personal estate (except such as in hereafter named) to be sold for the discharging of my lawful debts. Any money remaining I give to my loving wife Egbertie one sixth part; to my five dear children, namely, Doortie, Jannetie, Maria, Hendrickie, and Geurtruy (except the one-sixth for my wife), share and share alike. Unto my loving wife my cupboard, together with all the things in the same; one of my best beds with curtains thereto belonging, one horse and saddle, one brown dining table, one looking glass, six common chairs, two cows, one churn, four keelers, two pails, one tray, three pewter dishes, one pewter bason,

twelve pewter plates, two iron pots, one tea kettle, one
pair hand irons, shovel and tongs, one large brass kettle, one spring wheel, one wool wheel, one dresser, one
gridiron, one large iron ladle, all the tea pots, cups,
saucers and bowls, one Dutch Psalm Book and another small Dutch Book, one large wash tub, one pair
wool cards, one frying pan, and three knives and forks.
Unto my dear children, Doortie, Jannetie, and Maria,
one large brown chest for their joint use. To my other
dear children, Hendrickie and Geurtruy, one common
chest for their joint use. To my child Jannetie my silver shoe buckles. To my five children all my wearing
apparel, my executors to do with the same most advantageously for my children; and they shall take
charge of the children that they may obtain knowledge
or learn trades; the money in the hands of the executors to be applied for this use if it is wanted. I make
my loving wife, Egbertie Hegeman, my executrix; my
loving father, Adriaen Hegemen, my loving father-in-
law, Jan Van Noorstrandt, and my worthy friend,
Anthony Van Noorstrandt, executors.

Witnesses, Folkert Rappalje, Tunis Rappelje (yeoman), Engerbert Lott, jr. Proved, March 14, 1781.

Page 217.—Know all men by the Presents, that I,
JANE HEAVILAND, widow, of the Township of Hemp-
stead in Queens County, being this sixteenth day of
October, 1780, sick and weak in body. All my just
debts being fully paid out of the money I have by me,
I leave to my granddaughter, Sarah Smith, my black
Cloak. Unto my granddaughter, Jean Smith, my silver shoe-buckles. Unto my granddaughters, Sarah
and Jane Smith, and the daughters of my son, Joseph
Heviland, my wearing apparel to be equally divided;
only my silver sleeve buttons which I give to the said
Jane Smith. Unto my son, Joseph Heaviland, my
gold sleeve buttons and all my Jack coats and Briches
silver buttons. Unto my son John the bond I have
against him and also my silver beaded Chain, and sil-

ver spoon. Unto my son Joseph as much of my household goods as will make him equal with the bond I have against my son John; he to have such of the goods as he likes best. Unto my sons, John and Joseph, the bond of £58 against them. Unto my granddaughter, Hannah Heaviland, my green cloak and best bed. Unto my granddaughters, Sarah and Jane Smith, and to Jane, Jerusha, Jemima, Phebe, Hannah, and Jane Heaviland, the daughters of my son Joseph, all the remainder of my household goods, to be equally divided; which shall be left in the hands of my son Joseph until they arrive to the age of eighteen years, or day of marriage. Unto my sons, John and Joseph, all my moveable estate without doors, and the remainder of my money equally to be divided between them. I make my sons, John and Joseph Heaviland, and my son-in-law, Silvanus Smith, executors.

Witnesses, Micajah Combs, Cornel Smith (yeoman), and Richard Ellison. Proved, January 21, 1781.

Page 219.—Know all men by these Presents, that I, JONATHAN SMITH, of the Township of Hempstead in Queens County, yeoman, being this twenty-second day of June, 1777, not well in body. I leave to Mary Smith, my wife, two feather beds, bedding, furniture, and appurtenances. My executors to sell all my homestead where I now live, and land adjoining; situate in the South woods within the Township; and my land with fences on the plains; together with all my rights of lands and meadows, of what kind soever, within the patent of Hempstead; also, all my moveable estate not above disposed of, after my decease. The proceeds to be disposed of as follows: Unto Mary, my wife, £10; to my daughter-in-law, Conericke Smith, £10. All my just debts and funeral charges to be paid; but of proceeds of sale of real and personal estate I give to my three granddaughters, Jane, Sarah, and Mary Smith, each £20 in money to be put to interest for them, and paid to each arriving to age of eighteen years. Unto

Thomas Smith Rock, son of Thomas Smith, deceased, £6. Unto my grandson, Jonathan Smith, £10; to be put to interest and paid to him when he is twenty-one years old. Unto my two grandsons, viz.: Silvanus and Jonathan Smith, all the residue of my real and personal estate, equally to be divided (excepting my great Bible, which I do give to Jonathan). The executors shall put the money to interest for the use of my two grandsons, for their education and bringing up, and to put them to such trades as they shall most incline to, and pay to each his equal part on coming at the age of twenty-one years. I make my trusty and loving friends, Richard Hewlett, Esquire, of Rockaway, and my brother, Cornell Smith, and Benjamin Hewlett, jr., executors.

Witnesses, John Van Nostrand (yeoman), Zabulon Smith, and Richard Ellison (yeoman). Proved, January 20, 1778.

Page 221.—In the name of God, Amen. I, JACOBA GOUVENEUR, of the City of New York, being in perfect health. I leave to my sister, Marie Farmer, £600; to be paid her immediately after my decease. Also, all my plate (except one silver tankard), she paying therefor to my estate at the rate of 9 shillings per oz. Likewise, all my china, whole and broken, she paying £8 for the same. All or any part of my household goods, furniture, and linen which she shall elect, she paying such price as the same or any part shall be valued at by my executors. I give to her all my wearing apparel, leaving it to her discretion to give the whole or any part thereof to my niece, Hester Governeur. And as I received the whole estate that was left by my sister Elizabeth, of which estate my sister Maria was entitled to one-half part thereof, my said sister Maria must also have and receive out of my estate the half of the clear amount of which I received of my sister Elizabeth's estate. Secondly, unto Nicholas Governeur my silver tankard on which is engraved my father's Coat of Arms. Unto Isaac Low, of the City of New York, merchant, an Arabian gold pocket-piece; also, a small picture burnt on glass. The residue of my real and personal estate, with the gold and silver belonging to and worn about my body shall be sold, and disposed of, and the proceeds thereof put out at interest upon good and sufficient security; the interest to be paid annually to my niece, Hester Gouveneur, during her life. If at her decease she have any lawful issue, the produce of the remainder of my Estate, with the interest to the child or children of the said Hester; if more than one, to be divided. Should she die without issue, then unto my nephew, Abraham Gouveneur, during his life. After his decease, if he should die without lawful issue, then one-fourth part of the said principal to Samuel Gouveneur; a like part to Magdalen Hall, sister to Nicholas Gouveneur; one eighth part to Frances Sharpe, wife of Jacob Sharpe; one eighth to Rineir Skates; a like part to Peter Farmer; the remaining eighth part to Jasper Farmer. I make Nicholas Gouveneur and Isaac Low, executors.

Witnesses, Gerard Walton, of the City of New York (gentleman), Richard Ray and Samuel Ray. Proved, June 25, 1781.

Page 223.—These Presents Witnesseth that I, Cornelius Hoogland, of the Township of Oysterbay in Queens County, being this sixteenth day of May, 1777, much indisposed in body. I leave to my beloved wife Sarah one bedstead, bedding, and other furniture. Unto my three sons, viz.: Tunis, William and Cornelius, in equal shares, all my carpenter's tools, shoemaker's tools and weaver's tools. Unto my son Tunis my Great Bible; to my daughter Mary, a bed, bedstead, bedding and other furniture. The remainder of my estate is to be sold, both lands and moveables, and turned into money at some convenient time after my decease. Of such proceeds (after my debts are first paid), unto my daughter Mary £30, to be paid her be-

fore a general division be made; and to my three sons
£100 each to and for the purpose of supporting their
mother, my wife, with all things necessary and convenient for her natural life. The remainder to be
equally divided amongst all my children, namely: Tunis, William, Cornelius, Margaret Vanderbelt, Catharine Simonson, Mary Hoogland, Anne Bennett, and
Phebe Duryee. I make my son Tunis and my son
William, executors; giving them discretionary power
to adjust all differences and contests. Whereas, I
have given to my daughter, Catharine Simonson, a
legacy there expressed, but upon further reflection, I
bequeath to all her children that legacy which I gave
to her, in equal shares.

Dated May 16, 1770. Witnesses, Daniel Birdsall,
Peter Luister (or Luyster), yeoman; and William
Seaman. Proved, June 12, 1781.

Page 224.—I, JAMES SEAMAN, of Jerusalem in the
Township of Hempstead in Queens County, being
weak in body. I leave to Martha Seaman, my well-
beloved wife, half of all my lands, meadows, and buildings during her natural life, or as long as she remains
my widow. After her death or marriage the said
lands, meadows, and buildings unto my son Benjamin,
together with the other or remaining half of my lands,
after my just debts and funeral charges are paid out
of it. To my wife, my negro woman named Mime, and
one bed and bedding, all my linen, one " bilstale " table
and chest, one great chair and two small chairs,
and my riding chair. After the death of my wife my
negro woman Mime to have her freedom. Unto my son
Benjamin my negro boy named Tim and my negro
girl named Lender; my farming utensils and my grain
of all sorts, threshed and unthreshed, lying, standing,
or growing; as also my flax, dressed and undressed;
and all my hay or fodder. Unto my daughter Phebe
£40, 11 shillings; to my daughter Martha £28, 8 shillings; to my three daughters, Phoebe, Martha, and

Mary, all the remainder of my moveable estate in equal shares. I make my son Benjamin and my kinsman, Thomas Seaman, executors.

Dated, June 22, 1777. Witnesses, Jonathan Pratt, Obadiah Seaman, and Jacob Seaman (yeoman). Proved, June 19, 1781.

Page 226.—Know all men by these Presents, that I, Samuel Seaman, of Oysterbay Township in Queens County, on Nassau Island, this sixteenth day of ye Second month, 1780, do make this present writing to contain my last will. My just debts to be fully paid and all necessary charges that may happen. I leave to my daughters, Rachel Hicks, Martha Titus, Abigail Willets, Phe Hicks, Meriam Robens, and Ester Sands, each £100 and all my household goods, in equal shares. Unto my grandchildren, viz.: Samuel Seaman, Samuel Robens, and Samuel Hicks, my grandsons; and Martha Hicks, Martha Willets, Martha Seaman, Martha Titus, and Elizabeth Seaman, all my granddaughters, £10 each, to be preserved in my executors' hands for their use, and paid as each shall come of age. Having taken into consideration that I am now in possession of divers black-people, do hereby by virtue of these presents give them all, both male and female, their freedom and fully discharge all them from me and my heirs forever at my decease, feeling an entire freedom so to do in my mind. The residue of my estate, real and personal, unto my three sons, Willet, Obediah, and Samuel Seaman. But having deliberately considered the legacy given to my son Obediah, I have thought it proper for his benefit and advantage to impower my executors to take his equal portion of lands and goods into their care and possession, and carefully to let my son have the privilege and benefit of all his portion during his life. In case they have any of my Estate in their hands at my son's decease, then his wife, Phebe Seaman, should have the use of one-third of the Estate left by him, and the

other two-thirds to go to his children in the following
manner: Unto his sons, two-thirds; and to his daughters, one-third, as they respectively come of age. Further observe, the legacy given to my son Obediah Seaman's wife is to be understood given to her during her
widowhood, and no longer. Her portion to go to Obediah's children as their portions be directed. I make
my brother-in-law, John Williams, Samuel Way, and
my kinsman, Henry Post, executors.

Witnesses, Jonathan Wright, Joshua Titus (yeoman), and Henry Post. Proved, June 12, 1781.

Page 228.—I, COLES CARPENTER, of Moscheto Cove
in the Township of Oysterbay in Queens County, being
under infirmity of body. All my just debts be paid by
my money or moveables at the discretion of my executors. I leave to my wife Sarah during the time she
remains my widow, the use of one-third part of my
real estate; and also a bed and furniture and other
necessaries for keeping house. My wife at her discretion to distribute the residue of my in-door moveables amongst my three daughters; Elizabeth, Deborah, and Freelove Carpenter. Should my wife marry
again then she is to have £50 in money, together with
all her wearing apparel, in lieu of her dower, to quit
the place. Should my executors see best to sell the
place or any part, then my wife to have the use of one-
third part of the money arising from such sale. Noth-
ing herein contained to be construed to eclipse my wife
of her thirds and the articles above mentioned during
her widowhood. Should she marry again, to quit her
thirds and to take the above-mentioned £50, together
with said wearing apparel. Unto my oldest son Maurice, £15 in money. Unto my four sons, Maurice, Benjamin, Latting, and James, all my lands, meadows,
and real estate, in equal shares, to come into their
hands when the youngest son that lives comes of age,
on conditions that they shall pay to my three daughters the sum of £100 apiece; the same £300 to be paid

as soon as my youngest living son comes of age. My
sons are to have all the overplus money, if any there
be (after legacies be paid and just debts discharged),
together with all my stock and farming utensils, equally amongst them. If either of my sons or daughters
die without lawful issue, the survivors of the sons to
have the deceased brother's part equally amongst
them; and also the surviving daughter or daughters
to have in like manner the deceased sister's part. I
make my kinsmen and neighbours Charles Valentine,
David Valentine, and William Mudge, executors.

Dated the sixth day, fourth month, 1779. Witnesses, Thomas Kirkley, Jacob Downing, and Mary
Crooker. Proved, June 23, 1781.

Page 229.—In the name of God, Amen. I, THOMAS
THORNE, of Cowneck in the Township of Hempstead,
yeoman, being at present indisposed in body. My just
debts and funeral expenses to be paid. I leave to my
daughter Sarah such parts of my household furniture
as are particularly mentioned in a list or schedule
bearing even date, signed by me in the presence of the
witnesses to my will. Which several articles are to be
chosen and delivered to Sarah by her mother. Likewise to Sarah £80 in cash to make her equal to what
I have heretofore given to each of her sisters. Unto
my son Thomas, junior, the sum of £200; to be paid
as hereinafter directed. All the rest of my household
furniture and plate, all my hogs, my riding chair, and
my negro wench Teen to my dearly beloved wife Mary,
to her own use and disposal. Also, for and during her
widowhood, all my dwelling house, and farm, together
with four milch cows and two horses, to be chosen by
herself, and all my farming utensils; to be used by her
during the said term. Also unto my wife, my negro
man Jack so long as she shall continue in the actual
occupation of my said farm; but whenever the same
shall be sold or be rented, then, the said Jack to belong
to my sons, Amos, Richard, and Thomas, equally. All

bequests made to my wife are in Barr and in lieu of all claim or right of dower in my estate. The rest of my stock of every kind, not before disposed of, I order to be sold, and the proceeds, together with the cash that may be left, after paying Sarah's legacy, be applied to the payment of the above legacy of £200, as far as the same will extend. Should there be any surplus, the use and interest thereof to my wife during her widowhood. I authorize my wife, together with both or any one of my executors at any time during her widowhood to sell the said farm and real estate. In case of such sale in her widowhood, my wife to have the interest of the moneys during such term. Should the farm be unsold during my wife's widowhood, then, at her death or remarriage it is to be sold. Should the provision above made for the legacy of £200 be insufficient, then, at the death or remarriage of my wife, the deficiency be made up and paid out of the proceeds of sale of the farm. The remainder of the proceeds, and whatever else is herein given to my wife during her widowhood (except the said negro man) is to go, at her death or remarriage, to all my children, to wit: Philip, Mary, Joseph, Susannah, Amos, Richard, Thomas, Catharine, and Sarah, in equal shares. Should either of my children die during my lifetime, leaving a child or children, then his, her or their share or shares of my Estate respectively unto their respective child or children in equal shares. Should any of my children so dying in my lifetime leave no child or children, then the share or shares of each of them so dying unto my surviving children in equal shares. I make my wife Mary and my two sons, Joseph Thorne and Thomas Thorne, junior, executors.

Dated February 20, 1778. Witnesses, Benjamin Kissam, John Burtis, and James Burr. Proved, October 17, 1778.

Page 231.—In the name of God, Amen. I, Amos Thorne, of Cow Neck in the Township of Hempstead in Queens County, farmer, do order all my just debts and funeral expenses to be fully paid and satisfied. I leave all and singular my farm, messuages, and tracts of land situate on Cow Neck (which I lately purchased of my father's estate, and whereon I now live), unto my brother, Richard Thorne, subject to the right and interest of my mother in the same, and to be possessed by him after her death or remarriage, and not before. Also to the several clauses, articles, etc., in and by a certain writing of agreement made and indented between me and my mother, bearing date the sixteenth day of December, 1778; on my part and behalf to be performed, reference being had, he paying for the same at the death or remarriage of my mother, and when the same shall come into his possession, the respective sums following, to wit: to each of my brothers and sisters, Philip, Thomas, Mary, Susannah, Catharine, and Sarah, the sum of £80; and to each of my brother Joseph's children, viz.: to his sons, William and Thomas, £30 each, and to his daughters, Hannah and Margaret, £10 each. Unto my brother Richard's son Amos my small piece of salt meadow lying near Rockaway at a place called Hungry Harbour (which I purchased of my father). My brother Richard must pay to his son Amos the sum of £20 when he arrives to the age of fifteen years; my brother Richard having the use of the money and said meadow till his son Amos comes to said age, he giving a bond to my executors for the payment of the money and the delivery of the meadow. The residue of my personal and moveable estate unto my brother Richard for his own full use and disposal forever, provided always in case my brother Richard shall refuse or neglect to pay the said several legacies above ordered to be paid by him, then my executors are to sell and dispose of my farm and lands to the best advantage. After the death or remarriage of my mother the surplus, if any, of the proceeds of sale shall go to my brother Richard. I make my loving brothers,

Philip and Thomas Thorne, and my respected friend, Joseph Pearsall, executors.

Dated January 16, 1780. Witnesses, Adrian Onderdonck (yeoman), David Brooks, and George Onderdonck (yeoman). Proved, May 27, 1780.

Page 234.—I, SAMUEL CORNELL, of the Town of Newbern & Province of New Carolina, merchant, but at present residing in the City of New York, leave all my estate, both real and personal, after my just debts are paid, as follows: Unto my sister, Hannah Brown, £400, New York currency; to each of my granddaughters, vizt.: Susannah and Rebecca Edwards, £500, like money, payable to each at the age of eighteen years. I give for the sole use of the Church at Flushing, Long Island, £200 payable to the parson and church wardens for the time being. Unto my five daughters, Mary, Susannah, Sarah, Hannah, and Elizabeth, all the residue of my estate, both real and personal, in equal shares; observing at the same time that my daughter, Mary Edwards, has already received from me in part of her proportion of my Estate, £5000 proclamation money of North Carolina, which sum must first be deducted out of her fifth share in order that all my children may be put upon an equal footing. Should any of my children die without leaving issue lawfully begotten, then such child's or children's share of my estate shall devolve to the surviving sisters; should one or more of my daughters die, leaving issue lawfully begotten, then such child or children shall be equally and fully intitled to their mother's share of my estate; provided, nevertheless, that should such child or children also die without issue lawfully begotten, then such child's or children's share shall revert to my own children, or such of them as may at that time be living. All my outstanding debts to be collected as soon as possible in order to make a general settlement of my estate, and that each child, vizt.: Mary, Susannah, Sarah, Hannah & Elizabeth, may receive their dividend or share agreeable to the intent of this will. I make Thomas Haslen, Jacob Blount, and William Low, Esq., of the Province of North Carolina, & the Honourable Henry White, Esq., of the City of New York, executors.

Dated February 24, 1781. Witnesses, Archibald Hamilton, James Barclay (merchant) and Samuel Camfield (merchant). Proved, July 2, 1781.

Page 236.—I, JESSE CARLL, of Dicks Hills in the Township of Huntington in Suffolk County, this tenth day of February, 1781, being sick and weak in body. All my just debts and funeral charges to be paid. I leave to my loving wife Temperance Carll, all the things that she brought to me, also the sum of £50, and two cows, also the use of my negro girl named Tamer so long as she remains my widow, and no longer. All which shall be in lieu of her dower. Unto my son Israel all that tract of land and house standing on the same (which I bought of Solomon Platt and Ephenetus Platt), being about 300 acres, more or less; also, 20 acres that I bought of Daniel Wickes, all joining to the road leading from Town to Selah Carll's, and two rights in the squa pits purchase, and one right and a half in the old purchase, and a right and a half in the Beach and Islands; all which is to my son Israel. Unto my son Eliphalet all the tract of land near my homestead on which my house stands, being about 137 acres, more or less, and also about two and a half acres called Homestead, on which my orchard and house now stands; also, one piece of land, about six acres, lying between the land of Platt Carll and the land of Ananias Carll, near the house of Simon Totten; and also about four acres southward of said Totten's, both joining to the highway; and also one lot of meadow lying on the west side of the little Neck, at south joining to the creek, which I bought of Joseph Whitman; also two rights in the Squa Pits Purchase. Also, to my son Eliphalet, that tract of land in which

my barn stands, being about seven acres, with all the
appurtenances thereto belonging. Unto my son Eliphalet my great Bible; to my son Israel my silver
tumbler. My daughter Batsheba shall have £100,
and all my household goods not disposed of, except
one bed and furniture. Unto my two sons Israel and
Eliphalet, one bed and furniture and all my stock of
all kinds, and all farming utensils in equal shares (except the two cows which I give to my wife). My son
Israel shall have my negro boy named Seneker; to my
son Eliphalet my negro boy named Frank; my executors to sell all the rest of my negroes, & to give titles
for the same. The proceeds and the residue of my
money and moveables unto my two sons in equal
shares. I make my cousins, Ananias Carll, Platt
Carll, and Gilbert Carll, executors.

Witnesses, John Kelcey (yeoman), Jonathan Kelcey and Solomon Ketcham. Proved April 3, 1781.

Page 238.—Know all men by these presents, that I,
TIMOTHY CARLL, senior, of the Township of Huntington in Suffolk County on Nassau Island, yeoman, being at present in a pretty good state of health, but far
advanced in years, will and direct that all such debts
as I shall justly owe at the time of decease, and funeral
charges and expenses be in the first place paid out of
my personal estate as soon as conveniently may be
after my Decease. I leave to my eldest son Selah all
that farm or tract of land where his dwelling house
now stands adjoining the land of Sylvanus Balden.
Unto my son Selah all that certain piece or tract of
land which I purchased of Ebenezer Blatchly, lying
northward of Samuel Townsend's land and containing
eighty-one acres, more or less. Unto my son Selah a
Two Hundred Right in the Squaw Pitt Purchase. Unto
my son Gilbert all my lands called Whitman's Hollow,
and the little Hollow, and all my meadow on Saxter's
Neck, & all my right in the said neck, and all the remainder of my rights in the said Squaw Pitt Purchase

not disposed of as above, and all my buildings not before granted, and all the remaining undisposed real estate wherever situate, the whole with their appurtenances to my son Gilbert. Also one bed, two pair of sheets, two pair of pillow cases, two coverlits, my silver tankard, loom and farming utensils. Unto my grandchildren, Jonathan or Scudder Valentine, Gilbert Valentine, Abigail Valentine and Ruth Valentine, each £20 apiece, to be put out at interest on good real and personal security, and to be paid to them principal and interest as they respectively arrive to full age or marry. Unto my grandchildren Scudder and Oliver Ketchem, Phebe, Sarah, Jerushe, and Mary Ketchem, each £20 apiece and paid in like manner as before directed with respect to my other grandchildren. All the residue of my personal estate unto my daughters, Abigail Youngs and Sarah Valentine in equal shares. I make my good friends, George Youngs, late of Oysterbay in Queens County; Joshua Wood and Jesse Ketchem of the Township of Huntington in Suffolk County, executors.

Dated May 15, 1776. Witnesses, Lindley Murray, Silas Carll (yeoman), and Elles Carll.

Codicil. I, the said Timothy Carll, do give to my daughter, Abigail Youngs, £20 more than I have herein before disposed of to her. Unto my grandchildren, George Youngs and Timothy Youngs, £20 apiece out of my personal estate, to be paid at full age, or the time of their marriage. And I desire that this may be taken as a part of my will hereto annexed.

Dated May 15, 1776. Witnesses, Lindley Murray, Silas Carll (yeoman), Elles Carll. Proved, June 15, 1781.

Page 241.—In the name of God, Amen. October the seventeenth, 1776. I, SARAH PINE, of Hempstead, in Queens County, on Nassau Island, being sick and weak. My just debts being first satisfied, I leave to my well beloved mother, Sarah Pine, a decent maintenance, such as house room, clothing, victuals, washing, lodging, and every necessary of life, during her natural life; at her death, a decent funeral. Whereas my brother, Daniel Pine, in his will has ordered his executors to sell land and meadow to pay off bonds that I have against him, and other of his debts, my executors are to act agreeable to his will. Unto my two cousins, Salvenas and Philop Pine, sons of John Pine, all my houses, lands, and meadows, but not to be enjoyed by them till after the death of my mother. Unto Hannah Dorlin, wife of Elias Dorlin, and to Sarah Smith, wife of Joshua Smith, all my household goods such as beds, pewter, pots, chest of drawers, and the like. Unto Hannah Linninton, daughter of John Linninton, one full suit of cloath, and the rest of my wearing apparel, unto Hannah Dorlin and Sarah Smith. The household goods and clothing are not to be enjoyed by the persons they are given to, till after the death of my mother; she to have the use of them as long as she lives. Unto Hannah Dorlin, wife of Elias Dorlin, and to Sarah Smith, wife of Joshua Smith, and to John Carl, junior, all my cattle, horses, sheep, swine, & farming utensils, together with all my moveable estate, and that my mother have her maintenance out of it; my just debts and funeral charges paid out of it; but it is not to be enjoyed by them till after the decease of my mother. I make my well-beloved cousin, Elias Dorlin, and my loving friends, James Wood and Thomas Dorlin, executors.

Witnesses, Benjamin Barker (yeoman), Thomas Tredwell (yeoman), and Millicent Van Nostrand. Proved, November 20, 1776.

Page 243.—In the name of God, Amen. I, JACOB VANDERBILT, of the half Hollow Hills in the Township of Huntington in Suffolk County, being this twenty-fifth day of May, 1779, weak in body. My just debts and funeral charges of every kind be paid. My executors are to sell so much of my moveable estate and lands as will raise money sufficient to pay all my debts. I leave to my well-beloved wife, Lucretia Vanderbilt, one bed and cloathes thereto belonging; likewise, one table, one chest and trammel to her free disposal (if taken by her for her Right of Dower and not other-ways). Unto my beloved wife all the profits of the residue of my estate for her support and my children's during her widowhood, and no longer; or until such time as the children come of age. I make my trusty friend, Jacobus Nostran, of the half Hollow Hills, and Wilmot Oakley, executors.

Witnesses, Jesse Ketcham (yeoman), Richard Wiggins, and Charity Ketcham. Proved, June 15, 1781.

Page 245.—In the name of God, Amen. I, JAMES BRADLEY, Soldier in his Majesty's Seventh Regiment of Foot, native of Broomsgrove, Worcestershire, Great Britain, being of sound mind and memory. After all my just debts be paid I leave to Mr. James Bennett, of the City of New York, jeweller, all my real and personal estate, whatsoever, in Great Britain or elsewhere; desiring the said James Bennett to pay to Mr. Samuel Harrison £20 sterling for favors received. Likewise I make the said James Bennett, my executor.

Dated April 17, 1779. Witnesses, Thomas Dixon, William Milbourne, and Ann Smith (spinster). Proved, July 16, 1781.

Page 246.—In the name of God, Amen. I, TIMOTHY KELLEY, a seafaring man out of the City of New York, being of sound mind and memory. All my just debts to be paid and discharged. I leave to Mr. James Dillitt, of the City of New York, my real property both by sea and land. I make the above said James Dillitt, executor.

Dated October 26, 1778. Witness, Nicholas Connery. Proved, July 16, 1781.

Page 247.—In the name of God, Amen. I, JAMES DESBROSSES, of the City of New York, distiller, being in good health of body. My just debts and funeral expenses to be paid. I leave to. my son, James Desbrosses £100. Unto my daughter, Mary Ann Desbrosses, all my linen, silver plate, household and kitchen furniture. To my son James one half of my real estate and the other half to my daughter, Mary Ann Desbrosses. I make my son James, my daughter, Mary Ann, and my brother Elias, executors.

Dated October 27, 1774. Witnesses, Pelatiah Haws, Jr., Theopilus Anthony (blacksmith), and Michal Garret. Proved, July 16, 1781.

Page 249.—In the name of God, Amen. On the seventh day of February, 1778, I, WILLIAM SMITH, JR., of Hempstead in Queens County, being sick and weak in body. All my just debts and funeral charges to be paid out of my estate, and after such payment I leave to my well-beloved wife, Martha Smith, my best feather bed and furniture to the same; one good cow, she to take choice, one table and chest, one iron pot and kettle, frying pan, one wash tub and pail, one great wheel and one half of all my pewter. All the residue of my estate, real and personal, to be sold to the best advantage; the proceeds to go to my loving son Samuel; £8 to be paid when he arrives to the age of twenty-one years. Unto my well-beloved son, Johanas Smith, £8, when twenty-one years old. All the overplus is to be equally divided between my wife and four children, namely: my wife Martha, and my sons, Samuel and Johanas, and my daughters, Sarah and Jean Smith. All the money left to my children to be put at interest, and paid to my wife toward the bringing up of my family till my children are of age; but in case that is not sufficient, my executors are to let her have as much of the principal as they shall think proper. What I have already given to my beloved wife Martha to be in lieu of her thirds and dowry, and not otherways. My executors are to put my children to apprenticeship to such trades as they shall choose. I make my trusty friends, William Jonson and Isaac Denton, both of Hempstead, executors.

Witnesses, Micael Demott, of Hempstead (yeoman), Joshua Pettit and James Pettit. Proved, July 10, 1781.

Page 251.—In the name of God, Amen. This nineteenth day of May, 1781, I, WILLIAM SMITH, of the Township of Hempstead, Queens County, being in a weak and low state of health. My just debts and funeral expenses to be paid. I leave to my daughter Elizabeth, the wife of Jacob Downing, £200; to be paid to her within six months after my decease. Unto my sons, John, William, Tredwell, and Joseph, all my real estate, and the residue of my personal estate, equally to be divided among them as tenants in common. In case my sons Tredwell and Joseph, or either of them shall die under the age of twenty-one, and without lawful issue, the share is to go to my surviving sons. In case my daughter Elizabeth shall die before the time of payment of her bequest, then the £200 to go to such child or children as she shall have at the time of her death. Should she die without any children before the time of payment, and such child or children die before they attain the age of twenty-one years, then I give the same equally among my above-said four sons. I do expressly declare my sons, John and William (altho' hereby appointed my executors), shall be accountable to my other children for their shares of money now due, or that shall be due to me from them (my sons, John and William, or either of them), at my death, as part of my personal estate above bequeathed; it not being my intention by the appointment of my two eldest sons as my executors, to release or discharge them from such debts. I authorize my executors at any time during the nonage of my youngest surviving son (if they think it best and most advantageous) to sell all or any part of my lands and real estate. I make my loving sons, John and William, and my loving brother-in-law, Samuel Birdsall, executors.

Witnesses, George Rapelje, of Hempstead, Jno. Kissam, and Thomas Appleby, Jr., of Hempstead. Proved, July 9, 1781.

Page 253.—In the name of God, Amen. On the twenty-eighth day of June, 1779, I, THOMAS TREDWELL, of Hempstead in Queens County, being in a reasonable state of health. I leave to my well-beloved wife Phebe, two of my best feather beds and furniture to the same, six sitting chairs, cupboard and two tables, and all the linen that I shall have in the house at my death, together with all my silver plate (except my silver tankard), also my best horse and riding chair, two cows and calves; she to take choice out of my stock. Also, £20 to be raised and levied out of my moveable estate and paid to her soon after my death. All the above I have given to my well-beloved wife Phebe to her own disposal over and above what I have already given to her. Also, the use of my dwelling house and of the equal fourth part of all my land and meadow, with the use of the equal fourth part of my barn, and my negro man Sias and my silver tankard during her natural life or widowhood. All above I give in lieu of her thirds and dowry, and not otherways. The same tankard I leave to my grandson, John Tredwell, son of my son Benjamin. All the remaining part of my moveable estate to be sold. Of the proceeds, the £200 in money already given to my wife Phebe is to be paid, and unto my grandsons, Tredwell Jackson and Samuel Jackson, the sum of £25 each. All the money remaining over and above, after paying the above legacies to be for paying my just debts and funeral charges; should the money fall short of paying the legacies, then so much of my lands to be sold to make up the deficiency. And also 10 shillings to my granddaughter, Charity Tredwell, daughter of my son

John, to be paid when she is eighteen years of age. All legacies, debts, and funeral charges being paid and the remaining and undisposed of part of my estate to go to my son Benjamin, together with all my Pattent Right in the Pattent of Hempstead, over and above what I have already given to him. Also, unto him, after my wife Phebe's death or marriage, all that I gave her the use of (except my silver tankard). I make my loving son, Benjamin Tredwell, and my trusty brother-in-law, Benjamin Smith, and my friend, Isaac Denton, all of Hempstead, executors.

Dated June 28, 1779. Witnesses, Benjamin Carman, Michael Demott, of Hempstead (yeoman), and Isaac Denton, Jr. Proved, July 10, 1781.

Page 255.—Know all men by these presents that I, JACOB DEREA, of Jericho within the Township of Oysterbay in Queens County, yeoman, being this twenty-seventh day of August, 1779, weak of body. My just debts and funeral charges and other expenses be paid out of my moveable estate before any division be made. I leave to my well-beloved wife Sarah the just and full sum of £50 and all the household goods and furniture she brought to me, at her free disposal, and the use of my "mair" and chair to ride in as long as she remains my widow, and no longer. All the residue of my estate, real and personal, to be sold at the discretion of my executors, and turned into money and to be put at interest until my children shall arrive at lawful age; then to be equally divided between my three sons, George, Joshua, and Garred. Should my wife be with child then it should have its equal share with the rest, and my estate equally divided among my surviving children, who are to be brought up to learning suitable to their circumstances, and all to have trades or mechanical branch as they shall choose. Unto my well-beloved wife Sarah all the cattle, or as many as she brought to me. I make my brother-in-law, Nethanial Smith, of Hempstead, and my neighbour, Willets Kirby, and John Wortimon, both of Oysterbay, all of Queens County, executors.

Witnesses, Joshua Smith, of Hempstead (yeoman), Abraham Probaseo, and John Wright. Proved, July 30, 1781.

Page 257.—Know all men by these presents, that I, CORNEL SMITH, of the Township of Hempstead in Queens County, yeoman, being this twenty-eighth day of May, 1781, weak in body. I leave to my loving and well-beloved wife Mercy my best feather bed and furniture, two cows and calves, two horses and my farming utensils, ten sheep and £30 in money; all at her own disposal and in lieu of her right of dower. My wife shall have the use of all my household goods and four cows; and the use and profits of my dwelling house and land, viz: all the land belonging to my homestead that derived to me from my deceased father, and also the lot of salt meadow and upland that I bought of Abijah Bedel, so long as she shall remain my widow, towards the education and bringing up of my children until my younger sons shall be twenty-one years of age. Unto my daughter Susannah, one feather bed, bedding and appurtenances; unto my son Amos, my gun and "cutlash"; and the sword that was my son Elijah's, unto my son John. The remainder of my moveable estate, not above disposed, to be sold; the proceeds to pay the above sum of £30 to my wife, to my daughter Susannah £60. All my just debts and funeral charges to be fully paid. It is to be understood that my negro slaves are to be sold as my moveable estate. Unto my son Jacob all the residue of my farm or land that I bought of Nehemiah Sammis, only excepting the south part that I have already conveyed to my son, Cornell Smith, Jr. Unto my son Amos all the land that I purchased of my brother Jonathan, deceased, it being about ten acres, and also all the land that I purchased of Jonathan Smith, Jr., deceased, adjoining to the said ten acres; and also a

piece of plain land and hollow ground that I purchased
of Silvanus Smith. Unto my two youngest sons,
namely, John and David, my homestead, where I now
live, and appurtenances, viz., my dwelling house and
land near and adjoining that derived unto me from
my deceased father, Jonathan Smith, together with
my lot of salt meadow and upland situate on Cove's
Neck, that I bought of Abijah Bedel; and a small hay
house on said Neck to be removed thereon; and also
five acres of woodland, part of the land that I purchased of Samuel Clowes and James Wood adjoining
to the west side of the path that leads to Samuel Mott's
mill, all which is to be shared equally by my sons, John
and David. Should they die in nonage without issue,
then all the land and meadow that is herein given to
them is to be equally divided amongst my surviving
sons. Unto my sons, Cornell, Jacob, and Amos, my
lot of salt meadow and upland lying on Coes Neck,
that I purchased of Elisha Bedel, excepting a small
house thereon. Should either die in nonage and without issue, then his part shall be equally divided between the surviving brothers. Unto my said sons,
Cornell and Amos, all the remainder of the woodland
that I bought of Samuel Clowes and James Wood.
Should my said daughter Susannah die before she
come to be eighteen years of age, or day of marriage,
the said £60 given to her shall be divided between
said wife and daughter, Mary Rainer, to their own
disposal. My wife is to have £30 out of my moveable
estate in addition to the above £30. The residue of
my moveable estate, not above disposed of shall be
equally divided amongst my wife and two daughters,
Mary Rainer and Susannah Smith. I make my loving
wife, Mercy Smith, and my trusty friends, Uriah
Bedel and Richard Mathews, both of the Township of
Hempstead, executors.

Witnesses, Hannah Whaley, Moses Cornelius, and
Richard Ellison, of Hempstead (yeoman). Proved,
July 28, 1781.

Page 259.—In the name of God, Amen. I, Isaac Willet, of the Borough Town of West Chester, in the County of West Chester, gentleman, being at present weak in body. All just debts to be paid. I leave to my dearly beloved wife Margaret, for life, all that my neck of land called Cornwell's Neck, where I now live, and after her death to be divided into two equal parts, by one or more lines beginning at a large white oak tree which I have marked with two notches on four sides; from thence to run as will most equitably divide said neck, having regard to wood and timber. The eastermost half part according to such division, with the buildings and improvements thereon and the remainder and reversion thereof, I give to my nephew, Isaac Willet, subject nevertheless to the finding and providing thereout a good and sufficient maintenance of my brother, William Willet, during his life if he survives me and my wife; and subject also to a devise hereinafter made of the use of the salt meadows at Black Rock to my brother, Cornelius Willet, for his life, if the same or any part thereof shall fall within the eastermost half so devised to my nephew Isaac. The other westermost half part of the Neck unto my nephew, Lewis Graham, subject to a devise, hereinafter made, of the use of the salt meadow aforesaid at Black Rock, to my brother, Cornelius Willet, for his life, if the same or any part thereof shall happen to fall within the westerly half part so devised to Lewis Graham; and subject also, with the rest of my estate devised to him, to the payment of £600, hereinafter charged upon the same. I think proper here to declare that this last mentioned moiety given to Lewis Graham was intended for my nephew, Gilbert Colden Willet, but his grandfather, Governor Colden (who I suppose is well able to make handsome provision for him), has treated me and my wife very unkindly in removing my nephew, Lewis Graham, from the office of Sheriff of this County, which I resigned in his favor expecting it would have been some provision for him;

and my wife, in consideration of the devise to Lewis
Graham, has consented that the lands in the Mohawk's
Country (which I had expressly engaged to devise to
her by will) should by my last will be otherwise disposed of as I should think fit. I give all my personal
estate to my wife, to her own use and disposal, for
this Reason, That all my present slaves, except three,
came by her, and her industry and prudence has procured the greatest part of my personal estate, and she
will, by this devise to her, have in her own Power to
reward those who treat her with respect and civility.
As I have no children of my own to provide for I think
this bequest highly just and reasonable. But I nevertheless request of my wife that as long as my nephew,
Isaac Willet, behave dutifully and kindly to her, that
she will assist him in his maintenance; and also request that she will take the care and charge of bringing up Anna McElworth, and allow her a maintenance
out of my estate until she come of age or marry, if
she shall behave in such manner as to deserve it; of
which, however, my wife is to be the sole judge. In
case my brother William survives me, that my wife
allow him out of my estate a good and sufficient maintenance during his life. Unto my nephew, Lewis
Graham, the part of Cow Neck in the Borough of West
Chester which is in the possession of Ichabod Lewis,
and on which he now lives; he paying within three
months after my decease to my brother, Cornelius
Willet, if then living, the sum of £200, which in such
case I give to said Cornelius. Should my brother be
not then living the £200 is to go to such of his children as shall then be living, in equal shares. Unto
my brother, Cornelius Willet, the use of my salt
meadow at Black Rock for and during the term of his
natural life. Likewise unto him all my lands, tenements, hereditaments and real estate at Barren Island
or Flat Lands in Kings County, and elsewhere upon
Nassau Island. As I heretofore conveyed to Lewis
Graham a small farm which I had in the Manor of

Cortlandt, and on my informing him that I provided for him in my will he has requested I would charge him with the payment of £600 as I should direct, as a consideration for said farm, I do therefore expressly charge upon the lands and estate herein before devised to him the further sum of £600, to be paid within one year after my decease for the use and purposes hereinafter declared. I order my lands in the Mohawk's Country (which were given to my wife by her father, and by her conveyed to me before marriage), to be sold. Out of the proceeds and the above £600 I direct £500 put at interest; the income to be applied toward the maintenance and education of Thomas McElworth; the said principal sum of £500 I give to him at his majority. Also £500 to be kept at interest, both principal and interest I give to Anna McElworth when she is twenty-one years of age, or marry. In case of death of Thomas under twenty-one years, then what is devised to him is to go to Anna at her majority or marriage. In case of her death before coming to majority or marriage, then the said £500 and interest thereof to go to Thomas at his majority. Should both die under twenty-one, and Anna being unmarried, then the whole sum of £1,000 and interest due on Anna's part, to go to my nephew, Isaac Willet. Out of the residue of the proceeds of sale of land in the Mohawk's Country, and the said £600 charged on my estate devised to Lewis Graham, all my just debts shall be paid; and the surplus, my executors are to apply towards assisting my nephew, Gilbert Willet, if he shall then be living, and in such a situation that a small sum of money can be of service to him, but not to pay his debts. I particularly recommend to my nephews, Isaac Willet and Lewis Graham, who have both been brought up in my family and on equal shares of my fortune, to live together in brotherly love and friendship, and to endeavor to promote each other's interests and happiness upon all occasions. I make my wife Margaret, my brother, Cornelius Willet,

Lewis Graham, and my nephew, Richard Morris, Esq., executors.

Dated January 30, 1770. Witnesses, Israel Honeywell, Gillead Honeywell, and Samuel Downing.

Codicil. Whereas, I, the before-named Isaac Willet, in and by my aforegoing will have directed, that if there be any surplus after the payment of the two legacies amounting to £1,000, and my debts out of my estate appropriated for such purposes, that my executors apply the whole or such part at their discretion towards assisting my nephew Gilbert, I have since thought it most prudent to limit this exercise of discretion, and for that purpose do declare that the sum shall not exceed the aggregate of £150. In case that after the payment of particular legacies, and debts directed to be paid from proceeds of sale of lands in the Mohawk's Country and the £600 charged on Lewis Graham, and the further bequest to Gilbert Willet, there shall still remain any surplus, I do give such surplus to my wife Margaret, the better to enable her to perform the particular matters requested of her.

Dated January 30, 1770 (same witnesses). New York Secretary's Office, August 12, 1774, certifies that the original will and codicil of Isaac Willet is on file, and that a true copy has been made.

The preceding is a true copy of our official copy of the original will and codicil of Isaac Willet issued by me as appears by the preceding certificate signed by my own hand on the date therein mentioned. Examined with the said official copy this seventh day of August, 1781.   SAM. BAYARD,
                                        Junior Secretary.

Page 264.—In the name of God, Amen. I, GRIFFIN CORY, of Hempstead in Queens County, being weak of body. My just debts to be paid. I leave to my well-beloved wife Sarah £120; to be raised out of my estate lying or being on Cortlandt Mannor in West Chester

County. All my moveable estate and every other individual I now have in the Township of Hempstead unto my wife Sarah. Unto my two daughters, Hannah and Elizebeth, £20 apiece; and unto my eldest son, Thomas, £20; to be raised and levied out of my estate. All the residue to be equally divided between my eight sons, namely: Thomas, John, Gilbert, Amos, Silvenus, Griffin, Lewis, and Morris, at the discretion of my executors; and the last-mentioned equal division not to be made until this present war between Briton and the Americans be settled; after such settlement my executors to make the best of my estate and pay out to the legatees when they come to the full age of twenty-one years. Should one or more happen to die in nonage then the survivors to have such portion or portions in equal shares. I make my well-beloved wife Sarah, and my two eldest sons, Thomas and John Cory, executors.

Dated August 19, 1780. Witnesses, Joseph Place (yeoman), John Place, and Robert Dingee (yeoman). Proved, December 1, 1780.

Page 266.—In the name of God, Amen. I, John Hitchcock, of the Borough Town of West Chester, being sick. I leave my loving wife all my estate, real and personal, after my just debts and funeral charges are paid. At her death or remarriage, to go to my son, Jeremiah Hitchcock, all my lands and tenements whatsoever, he paying such legacies hereafter mentioned. Unto my eldest son, John, the sum of £12; unto my sons, Samuel and Miles, £10 each; unto my two daughters, Mercy and Mary, £10 each. Should my son Jeremiah neglect to pay the legacies in some convenient time after the death of my wife, the lands to be sold to pay the legacies. My moveables to be divided amongst all my children. I make my wife and my sons, John Hitchcock, and Jeremiah Hitchcock, executors.

Dated in the year of Our Lord, 1780. Witnesses,

David Oakley, yeoman, Joseph Reynolds, and Mary Buckee. Proved, August 14, 1781.

Page 267.—In the name of God, Amen. I, Isaac Rodrigues, now of the City of New York, mariner, being of sound mind and memory. After all my just debts be paid and discharged, I leave to John Roberts of the City of New York, tavernkeeper, all my estate, real and personal, of whatsoever kind it be, and I make him executor.

Dated June 18, 1779, and in the 19th year of his Majesty's reign. Witnesses, Richard Hall, grocer, and John Graham. Proved, August 14, 1781.

Page 269.—In the name of God, Amen. I, John Schau, formerly of Norfolk, Virginia, merchant, but at present of the City of New York, being of sound mind and memory. After all my just debts be paid I leave to Ann Fraiser, at present of the City of New York, spinster, tho' born in Roshier in Scotland, all my estate, real and personal, and mixed. I make Niel Jamison, of the City of New York, merchant, executor.

Dated July 23, 1781. Witnesses, John Falthausen, William Ketcham, Esq., and John L. C. Roome, Esq., public notary. Proved, August 14, 1781.

Page 270.—In the name of God, Amen. The first day of March, 1758, I, Joshua Pell, of the Manor of Pelham in the County of West Chester, yeoman, being sick and weak in body. All my just debts and funeral charges to be fully paid as soon as conveniently can be done after my decease. I leave to my well-beloved son, Joshua Pell, Jr., £5, to be paid within one year after my decease. Unto my well-beloved wife, Phebe Pell, the use and command of the best room in my house, a bed, bedding, and other household goods for her comfortable subsistence; also, a sufficiency of provision and clothing for her and my younger children during her natural life or widowhood; to be provided and allowed her by my two sons,

Joshua Pell and Edward Pell. Also £7 yearly under same conditions. In case she marries after my decease, £100 is to be paid her immediately, and the other above specified privileges to cease. Unto my son, Gilbert Pell, one negro boy slave named Michael to be delivered to him at the expiration of his apprenticeship, which he is now serving with Joseph Latham at New York, also £100, to be paid to him as follows: £20 at said expiration, and £80 as hereinafter specified. To my son Philip £100, to be paid as hereinafter specified; £100 to my son Benjamin under like conditions. To my daughter, Mary Latham, £20, likewise. To my daughter, Phebe Pell, £100 and one negro girl slave named Arabella, to be paid and delivered to her at the day of her marriage. To my daughter, Sarah Pell, £100, and £100 to my daughter, Jerusha Pell, and one negro slave named Hagar. None of the above-mentioned legacies, nor any part thereof (except such as are expressly limited to a time of payment) be liable to be paid until my youngest child arrives to full age, and then all to be fully paid and discharged. In case any of my six youngest children, viz.: Gilbert, Philip, Benjamin, Phebe, Sarah, and Jerusha, should die before they come to lawful age, or without lawful issue, their share to be divided among the survivors of them. All such parts of my moveable estate as my executors shall think necessary to pay all my just debts and funeral charges to be sold for that purpose; the use or profits of the remainder to be employed in the maintenance of my wife and the educating of my younger children. The remainder, if any, to be divided among my six younger children. Unto my two sons, Joshua Pell, Jr., and Edward Pell, all my lands, meadows, and tenements, in equal shares, in the following manner. To begin at a water-fence where a small creek puts up on the southermost side of a ditch commonly called Ben's Ditch, and to run an easterly line so as to divide the whole into two equal parts. The northermost half

to my son, Joshua Pell, Jr., the southermost half part
to my son, Edward Pell. Unto my son Edward the
whole of a Hammock lying in the west meadows, commonly called the West Hammock. The lands to be
freely possessed and enjoyed by my two sons immediately after my decease. In case either of them should
die without lawful issue, his land shall go to my next
oldest son upon the same conditions as is hereinafter
mentioned. My son Joshua, in consideration of the
above devise of one half part of my land, shall pay
£500 as his part towards discharging the legacies
bequeathed to my wife and other children; payable
when due. My son Edward, under the same consideration, shall pay £220 as his part, for the same purposes. To Joshua, my cane and my large Bible. I
make my said son, Joshua Pell, and my trusty and
loving son-in-law, Joseph Latham, of the City of New
York, ship-wright, my executors in trust.

Dated March 1, 1758. Witnesses, Charles Vincent,
Sr., of West Chester (yeoman), Philip Pell, Robert
Rolfe. Proved, August 14, 1781.

Page 273.—In the name of God, Amen. I, MARGARET
CISK, late of the City of Philadelphia, in the Province
of Pennsylvania, but now of the City of New York,
widow, being sickly but of sound and disposing mind
and memory. After my interment, all my just debts
to be paid, and after which I leave to my loving
friends, Joseph Thomas and Hannah Thomas, his
wife, and their two children, Mary and Elizabeth
Thomas, all my wearing apparel for their own use,
but none to be made sale of; and all my plate and
household furniture, except what I shall mention hereafter, and all sums of money, lands, tenements, etc.,
to go to my loving friend, Joseph Thomas, aforesaid,
and I make him my sole executor.

Dated August 8, 1781. Witnesses, John Hicks, surgeon mate in his Majesty's Hospital, Juliana White,
married woman.

Page 275.—I, Samuel Latham, of Cowneck in the
Township of Hempstead in Queens County, physician,
being this twenty-fourth day of the fourth month,
1780, in a tolerable state of health and of a sound mind
and memory. I order my executors to collect all monies due to me on Book and otherwise; with the same
to pay all my just debts, and funeral charges. I leave
to my adopted son, Singleton Latham, son of my
brother-in-law, Robert Mitchell (on conditions hereinafter mentioned) all my mills, houses and buildings
with all the lands whereon they stand; and all the
lands to the North of my dwelling house and to extend so far southward along the mill-pond and brook
that a west line across to the bay will contain 100 acres
of land. All which is devised to him on condition he
pays (immediately after my decease) to my executors
£2,000; which sum I bequeath to my respected brother,
Thomas Singleton Latham. Should he refuse or neglect to pay the £2,000, as above directed, then I order
my executors to sell such part of the lands, buildings,
and mills willed to him as will pay the above legacy.
All my lands not above willed, unto my nephew,
Charles Mitchell, on condition he pay to my brother-
in-law, Robert Mitchell, Adam Mott, or Austin Mitchell, my executors, £1,200 within one year after my
decease. Should he refuse or neglect to pay the sum,
my executors are to sell all the lands willed to him, the
proceeds to be for such uses and purposes as hereinafter directed. Unto my said nephew, Charles Mitchell, £1,000, to be paid him immediately after my decease. Unto my cousin, Samuel Mitchell Latham,
son of Robert Mitchell, £2,000, to be paid to him
when he is twenty-one years of age. Unto my sister, Mary Mitchell, wife of Robert Mitchell, the use
and profits of £400 during her natural life; at her
decease, the said sum unto two of her sons, namely:
Joseph and George Mitchell, in equal shares. Unto
my cousin, Jane Mitchell, daughter of Robert Mitchell,
£300; unto Priscilla Mitchell, daughter of Robert,

£200; unto Ann White, a young woman that for several years has been in my service, £100. I desire my executors to take care of each legatee's part of what I have willed to them, during their nonage, for their advantage; and that they be well educated, schooled, and brought up out of the issues and profits arising from what is devised to them; and that they fully enjoy and possess the same when they come of age, viz.: the boys at twenty-one and the girls at eighteen. If it should happen that Samuel Mitchell Latham or Singleton Latham should decease before they attain the age of twenty-one years, not leaving lawful issue, the survivor of them is to have and enjoy such deceased legatee's part. If Jane or Priscilla Mitchell should decease before they attain to the age of eighteen years, not leaving lawful issue, the deceased child's part I will to the survivor of them. Further, if Joseph or George Mitchell should die before they receive what is willed to them, then the £400 that my sister Mary has the use of (willed to her), I will to the survivor of them. I direct my executors to dispose of my stock of creatures, farming utensils, and household furniture at their discretion; the proceeds for the discharge of legacies above given. I make my brother-in-law, Robert Mitchell, my friend, Adam Mott, my cousin, Charles Mitchell, and my friend, Austin Mitchell, executors.

Witnesses, John Morrell, Stephen Mott, Sarah Mott. Proved, August 7, 1781.

Page 277.—To all Christian People to whom these Presents Shall come or in any way concern: Know ye, that I, Joost Dereay, of the Township of Oysterbay in Queens County, yeoman, being this first day of April, 1781, in but a weakly state of health, but mind and understanding quick and good and well. I order my executors to fully pay all my just debts and funeral charges. I leave to my well-beloved wife, Willimpey Dereay, two of my best beds and full furniture, my best horse and riding chais, my cubboard, two tables, looking glass and household furniture of all sorts and all kinds that is in my house (sufficient to furnish her for housekeeping), with sufficient meat and bread corn to last her one whole year after my decease; with two of my best swine, and the use and profits of all my lands which my son, George Dereay, leased to me and my wife. Unto my wife £200; to be paid her by my executors within three months after my decease. All which is to her free disposal. Unto my daughter Willimpey the next choice of my beds and full furniture; and £30; to be paid her within four months after my decease. Unto my grandson George, son of Jacob Dereay, £10; to my grandson Rulof, son of John Dereay, £10; all current money to be put on interest until they arrive at lawful age. Unto Nealey Noostrand, £20. Unto my son George one shilling Right of Land in the Common in the Township of Hempstead, which I bought of James Pearsall of Huntington. Likewise unto my son George twenty-one acres of plain land, which I bought of Jonathan Pratt, situated in Oysterbay Plain, with all my " Wites " of land whatsoever that is not already given away. Unto my son Charles 5 shillings; which makes, with what I have before given him, his full share of my estate. My executors are to sell all my estate not already disposed of, and divide the proceeds in the following manner. Unto my son George four eleventh parts; to my grandchildren (children of my son John, deceased), two eleventh parts, to be put on interest until they come to age, to my three grandsons (sons of Jacob, deceased), two eleventh parts, to be put on interest until they come of age; unto my daughter, Mary Bennet, one eleventh part; unto my daughter Willimpey one eleventh; unto my son-in-law, Garret Noostrand, the interest of one eleventh part, as long as he liveth, and, provided my daughter Cornelia should have lawful children, then the principal shall be divided between such children. In case my daughter should live to be a widow, I give the one eleventh part to her free disposal. I also give to Nelas a Lawfull Bond I have against her husband, Garret Noostrand, dated ye twenty-first of March, 1781. Condition of one hundred pound, fourteen shillings, three pence, to be paid them when they arrive to lawful age, and the interest yearly paid to their mother, Nealey Noostrand. In case that Nealey should not have lawful issue and should decease before her husband, Garret Noostrand, then I direct that her eleventh part and the money due on Noostrand's bond be equally divided into six parts, George Dereay to have two parts; John Dereay's children to have one part; Jacob Dereay's children to have one part; Willimpey Dereay to have one part; and Mary Bennett one part. I make my friends and neighbor, John Wortimon, Willits Kirby, Gabrial Dereay, and Abraham Monfoort, executors.

Witnesses, Isaac Wright, George Montfort, John Wright (yeoman). Proved July 30, 1781.

Page 280.—In the name of God, Amen. I, JAMES FORBES, late of Aberdeenshire in North Britain, now residing in New York, merchant, being very sick and weak in body. After payment of all my just debts and funeral charges, I leave to my well-beloved wife Dorothy all my household and kitchen furniture, bonds, bedding, plate, jewels, and whatsoever I use appertaining to housekeeping. All the residue of my estate to be sold, which, with my ready money is to be divided as follows: one half to my wife; two third parts of the other half part to my honored mother, Anne Forbes, and my beloved brother Alexander (now commonly called and known by the name of Alexander Gall) to be equally divided; the remaining one third of the half part to my other brothers and sisters, in equal shares. I make my worthy friend, Richard Sause, of the City of New York, merchant, and John Thompson of said city, stone-cutter, executors.

Dated August 11, 1781. Witnesses, David Masterton, Thomas Bartow (merchant), Bartholomew Crannell, Esq., Notary Publick. Proved, August 27, 1781.

Page 282.—In the name of God, Amen. I, PETER DU BOIS, of the Wall Kill in the County of Ulster, being of sound mind, memory and understanding. All my just debts to be fully paid and satisfied, for which purpose I do hereby authorize my executors to sell so much of my real estate as shall be necessary. I give the remainder of all my real and personal estate to my dear, most excellent and amiable wife, Catharine Du Bois. I make my very good and worthy friends, the Honourable Henry White, Esq., James Duane, Esq., Jacob Walton, Esq., and Samuel Ver Planck, Esq., executors; hereby recommending my said wife to their friendly care and protection.

Dated March 14, 1772. Witnesses, John Bowles, Wm. Banyar, Crean Brush. Proved, September 15, 1781; by John Kelly, Esq., and Philip A. Schuyler, merchant, both of the City of New York, who identified the handwriting of John Bowles, William Banyar and Crean Brush, and also of Peter DuBois. On September 14, Henry White and Jacob Walton refused to be executors, and James Duane and Samuel Ver Planck " being not at present resident within the protection of his Majesty's government of the Province," the said Peter Du Bois became intestate; letters of administration were granted to his widow, Catharine Du Bois, at Fort George in the City of New York on September 20, 1781.

Page 284.—I, AMOS WOOD, of Huntington in Suffolk County on Nassau Island, being this ninth day of January, 1776, in weak and low circumstance of body, but understanding sound and memory quick and good. I order my executors to dispose of all my houses, lands, and tenements in the bounds of Huntington, also my equal part of the moveable estate that was my father's and all that was my own (except my oldest horse). All my lawful debts to be paid. I leave to my sister, Mercy Wood, my bay horse before mentioned; and £200 arising from my estate. Unto my sister's son, Daniel Oakly, £100. All the residue of my estate I leave to my three sisters, Sarah, Hannah, and Deborah, in equal shares. I make my friends, Nathaniel Oakly and Jacob Willits, Jr., of Islip in Suffolk County, executors.

Witnesses, Richard Willits, Arthur Dingee, Stephen Abbet (weaver). Proved, September 1, 1781.

Page 286.—In the name of God, Amen. I, ALIDA CUYLER, of the City of New York, spinster, being weak and low in body. I order all my debts and funeral charges to be paid. I leave to my niece, Catherine Cuyler, daughter of my deceased brother, Henry Cuyler, my silver coffee pot. I hereby discharge and emancipate my negro wench Nan from slavery, and desire my executors to release her from servitude. Unto my sister, Hester Cuyler, all the residue of my personal estate, and one half of all my real estate. The remaining half of my real estate to my nephew, Henry Cuyler, son of my deceased brother Henry, and to my nieces, Catherine Cuyler and Alida Ogden, daughter of my sister, Hannah Ogden; to each one third part. In case Alida should die without issue before she attains the age of twenty-one years, her part to go to her mother, Hannah Ogden. I make Stephen Skinner, Esq., and my sister, Hester Cuyler, executors.

(This will is not signed nor witnessed.)

NOTE.—On October 1, 1781, Christian Marschalk, widow; Hannah Farmer, spinster; and Samuel Farmer, merchant; all of the City of New York, made declarations before the Surrogate. The first named declared that on the third day of September last, the testatrix desired the deponent to put down her will in writing, saying, "You know how I always told you it should be done." That agreeable to her desire the deponent did put in writing what the testatrix had be-

fore dictated to her; and desired the above-named
Samuel Farmer to copy it over in some better form.
This was done without any substantial difference from
the original. The deponent read the copy over twice
to the testatrix, who approved of it and desired that
it might be given to an attorney to be put in form that
she might execute it. Before the same could be done
and executed the said Alida Cuyler died. Also, that
at the time, the copy of the notes, from which the preceding will was drawn, and contains the same in sub-
stance, was read to the testatrix. She was of sound
disposing mind and memory, etc. That the said notes
first taken and those copied by Samuel Farmer have
been lost or mislaid and cannot now be found; but the
preceding instrument in writing contains the sub-
stance, etc. Hannah Farmer and Samuel Farmer cor-
roborated the declaration of the first witness.

Page 288.—The last Will and Testament of SAMUEL
WOGAN, Captain of the American Legion. Viz.: First
paying all just debts and Demands that shall appear
Due of me. I leave to Rachel Davis, late of Rhode
Island, 100 guineas; together with what Effects of
mine now in her possession. Unto my mother, Mrs.
Amy Wogan, widow, the remainder of my property,
which I have left in Alexander I. Hamilton, late Lieut.
of the 45th Regiment's Power to Receive from the
undermentioned Persons, Viz.: Alexander & Miller's
acknowledgment to me for £407, 2 shillings and 11
pence, sterling, out of which I have received 60
guineas. To the amount of my account with Cox, Mair
& Cox, Lieut. Col. Bayard, Dr., 25 guineas. Lieut.
Simson, 17th Regt., Dr., 8 guineas.
    Dated December 18, 1780.
    Richard Ness, and Robert Rolls, both Captains in
the American Legion identified the handwriting of the
testator. Proved, October 1, 1781.

Page 289.—In the name of God, Amen. I, ELIZA-
BETH SLEIGHT, widow, and relict of Mathew Sleight,

late of the City of New York, merchant, being in good
health of body. I leave to my beloved son, Mathew
Sleight, my whole estate, both real and personal. My
executors are to sell the whole of my real and personal
estate (except such part of my furniture as they shall
think proper to keep for the use of my said son), the
proceeds to be put at interest for the use of my son.
My son Matthew to live with my father and mother,
Samuel Pell and Mary Pell, and my sister, Hester
Pell, during his minority, and they to be his guardians.
My executors to pay to my said guardians, the interest
on the money left to my son by his father, Mathew
Sleight, for his support, maintenance, and education,
so long as he shall live with them. If he dies without
lawful issue then my whole estate to go to my father
and mother, Samuel and Mary Pell, and one-third part
thereof to my sister, Hester Pell. I make my sister,
Hester Pell, my friends, Evert Banker, and Henry
Van Vleck, executors.

Dated June 24, 1765. Witnesses, Cary Ludlow,
Surrogate, Barnard De Forest, Abraham Ferdon.
Proved, October 8, 1781.

Page 291.—In the name of God, Amen. I, Sebastian Lucas, of the City of New York, white-smith, being of sound mind and memory. After all my just
debts be paid, I leave to Mrs. Judith Lester, of the
Parish of St. Giles, widow, £20 sterling. In case of
her death the legacy to go to her youngest son. All
the residue of my estate, real or personal, to my son,
Sebastian Lucas, when of age. Should he die without
lawful issue, then the remainder as follows: To Mrs.
Judith Lester, £100 sterling. To my niece, Nancy
Lucas, daughter of my sister, Nancy Lucas, £100 sterling. To my nephew and godson, Sebastian Lucas,
son of my brother, John Lucas, of Birmingham, £100
sterling. The remainder of my estate to my nearest
relation that shall be living at the time of my said
son's decease. I make my friends, Miles Sherbrook,

Esq., of the City of New York, merchant, to be guardian to my son, for whose support I set apart the interest arising from my estate. I also make the said Miles Sherbrook, Esq., to be sole executor.

Dated September 12, 1781. Witnesses, Luke Bird, blacksmith, Thomas Goudge, wheelwright, Samuel Deall. Proved, October 15, 1781.

Page 293.—I, THOMAS WHITE, of the City of New York, being weak in body. All my just debts and funeral charges be first satisfied out of my estate, the whole of which I make liable to the payment thereof. I give the use of my dwelling house with the furniture to my beloved wife Ann, during her widowhood. My executors are to place at interest £1,000 for the uses, trusts and purposes hereinafter named. In trust to permit and suffer my wife to receive the interest thereof during her natural life. After her decease, in trust, to pay the principal to such child or children of mine as she by her last will and testament shall direct, and to and for no other uses and purposes. Unto my wife Ann £200, annually, said annuity being in lieu of her dower. In case of her again intermarrying, I give her £500, and she is to relinquish one-half of the annuity of £200. I give to my son, Thomas White, £500 and my dwelling house with the lot of land and buildings, situate in Elizabeth Town in the Province of New Jersey (in which house Broughton Reynolds heretofore lived) in right of primogeniture. I order that my children shall be clothed and educated out of the rest of the interest until they attain the age of twenty-one years, or day of marriage; and are to live with their mother until such time shall arrive, if it should be their respective choice, they severally paying her for such living or maintenance a reasonable compensation. It is my desire that such education shall be as good as can be procured for them in the opinion of my executrix and executors, in whose candor and integrity I repose the utmost confidence, and it is also my request and desire that my sons be brought up to some profession or business, in the choice of which I would have their natural inclinations consulted; and if my youngest son should be inclined for a military life, I would have him indulge therein. The residue of my estate, my five children, Thomas, Matthew, Daniel, Charlotte, and Amelia, equally. It is my express desire that if either of my said daughters should marry before twenty-one years of age with the approbation of my executors, then I order that £1,500 shall be paid to each of them so intermarrying; the same to be deducted out of the shares of my estate. I make my wife Ann, executrix, and my son, Thomas White, and my friends, Alexander Wallace, Robert Ross Waddell, John Thurman, and John Kelley, all of the City of New York, executors.

Not dated. Witnesses, the Honourable Hugh Wallace, Esq., John Marston, merchant, John Miller, merchant, all of the City of New York. Proved, August 15, 1781.

Page 296.—In the name of God, Amen. I, REBECCA SIPKINS, of the City of New York, widow, this nineteenth day of March, 1747, do make and declare my will. After payment of just debts and funeral expenses by my executors, I leave to my grandchild, Christina Breested, daughter of my late son Gerrit Breested, deceased, £100. Unto my grandchild, Cornelia Waldron, daughter of my late daughter, Elizabeth Griffith, deceased, £150; unto my three grandchildren, John, Rem, and Rebecca Remsen, children of my said daughter Elizabeth, deceased, each £50; unto my grandchild, Maria Van Der Heul, daughter of my late daughter, Johanna Van Der Heul, deceased, £150; unto my grandchild, John Taylor, son of my daughter, Rebecca Griffith, £150. My executors are to put out at interest the several legacies given to my grandchildren, and the interest shall be applied towards educating and maintaining them until they come to age.

All the residue of my estate, real and personal, unto my well-beloved daughter, Rebecca Griffith. I make my daughter Rebecca and her husband Will ml   , executors, and guardians of my grandchildren.

Witnesses, Wm. Bogert, Cornelius Boghart, Simon Johnson, Esq. Proved, December 5, 1755.

NOTE.—The several blanks in this Record being defacements in the said probate and copy of the Will when put into my hands.   SAM. BAYARD,
                                                        Junr. Sec'y.
New York, Secretary's Office, October 29, 1781.

Page 300.—In the name of God, Amen. I, ARTHUR HELME, of the City of New York, mariner, this twenty-sixth day of January, 1747, do make this Will and Testament. All my just debts and funeral expenses to be paid. I leave to my dear and loving wife Jane the rents, issues, and profits of all my real estate during her widowhood, in order for her better maintenance and support, and the better to enable her to educate, bring up and maintain my children. After the remarriage or death of my wife, all my real estate to go to my well-beloved children, William, Francis, Benjamin, Jane, and George Helme, and unto the child or children wherewith my wife now goeth and is pregnant, to each an equal part. The interest of all my personal estate to be used toward educating, maintaining, and bringing up my children, until they arrive at majority or marriage, then my personal estate to go to my wife. I make my dear and loving wife Jane, and my loving and good friends John Coe and William Helme, executors.

Witnesses, Thomas Heysham, William Heysham, Catherine Heysham. Proved, October 29, 1781.

NOTE.—Letters of administration were granted on October 29, 1781, to Francis Panton, of the City of New York, shopkeeper, son-in-law of Arthur Helme, deceased, who became intestate by the death of Jane Helme, John Coe, and William Helme.

Page 302.—In the name of God, Amen. I, JOHN AMAR, master carpenter to the Board of Ordnance, and late of Pensacola, but at present of the City of New York, being of good mind, etc. After all my just debts are paid I leave to my brother, Daniel Amar, and to my sister, Deborah Amar, both of the Parish of Bromham, near the Devises Wilsts in the Island of Great Britain, the sum of £50 sterling each. The remainder of my estate I give to my beloved wife Sarah, and I make her and my friend, Thomas Austin, Overseer of Works to the Board of Ordnance, executors.

Dated September 19, 1781. Witnesses, Wm. Hingston (Kingston), grocer, Wm. Cook, John L. C. Roome. Proved, October 29, 1781.

Page 304.—In the name of God, Amen. I, DANIEL PROVOOST, of the City of New York, merchant, now residing at my country seat on New York Island, being weak in body, but in perfect state of mind, memory, and understanding. My executors to pay all my just debts and funeral expenses. I leave to my daughter-in-law, Mary Provoost, widow of my late deceased son John, £200; also the use, income, and profits of my farm at Dover, in New Jersey, during her widowhood. After her decease or remarriage I give the said farm to the children of my deceased sons, John and William. Unto Mrs. Sarah Bolton Loftus, who has for a long time past, and at present does reside with me in the capacity of a housekeeper, £350, to be paid to her brother twelve months after my decease, £50 whereof she may lay out in a suit of mourning. Whereas she by her faithful services and great attention to my interest during the time she has resided in my family has been a great means of preserving and increasing my estate, I do therefore hereby further give her the use, increase, and profits of my house and lot of ground at the Old Slip, now rented to James Wier, also the use, increase and profits of my lot of ground fronting Smith Street and King Street and which I leased to the late Mr. Nathaniel Marston, since deceased; also of my lot of ground fronting Wall Street, which I leased to the late Simon Johnson, Esquire, since deceased; also of my farm with the buildings thereon, situate at Hallets Cove on Nassau Island, during her natural life. I ratify and confirm the deed of gift which I have heretofore executed to the said Sarah Bolton Loftus for the farm, buildings, and improvements thereon on which I now reside, situate on the East River and commonly called the Lowvee, and also will such other deeds and instruments in writing as I have heretofore executed to the said Sarah Bolton Loftus. After her decease I give one half part of that part of my estate hereby given to her during her natural life, to and among the children of my said deceased son, John Provoost. I give to my executor £300. Whereas the management of my estate will require great pains and attention I do further give to my executor £2 ten shillings on every hundred pounds he shall receive and pay out of my estate. All the remainder of my estate, both real and personal, I give in manner and form following: One half part thereof to the children of my deceased son, John Provoost, and the other half to the children of my deceased son, William Provoost. I make David Matthews of the City of New York, Esquire, to be sole executor.

Dated September 1, 1781. Witnesses, Robert Ross Waddell, merchant, Robert Waddell, John Hardenbrook, gentleman, David Richardson. Proved, October 29, 1781.

Page 308.—In the name of God, Amen. I, ELIAS ELLIS, of the City of New York, being weak in body, yet of a sound and perfect understanding and memory. All my just debts and funeral expenses be discharged, and the rest and residue of my worldly estate I dispose of as follows: I leave to my son, Henry Ellis, £5 in consideration of his birthright, also to him together with my daughter, Yaneka Day's children (whom I will and order shall have and share their mother's part equally among them), also my daughter, Elizabeth Steenbarge, and my daughter, Mary Kip, my son, William Ellis, and my granddaughter, Margaret Devue, who shall also share her mother, Margaret Quackenbusses full part: unto the aforesaid children and grandchildren all my real and personal estate; being one half lot binding on my son William's, next to George Duncan's; also one house in Crown Street, next to my son William's; and one other house in Derick Dye Street, lately occupied by Benjamin Quackenbuss, deceased; likewise one house and two lots of ground in the Bowery Lane on the west side of the road formerly belonging to Hendrick Hellisa, deceased, joining the land of Nicholas Bayard, together with all my goods and chattels, to be divided into six equal parts. My son Henry to have one part; my daughter Yanake's children to have one part, my daughters, Elizabeth, Mary, my son William, and my granddaughter, Margaret Devue, each one part. I make my sons Henry and William, and my son-in-law, Abram Day, executors.

Dated August 7, 1775. Witnesses, Roelef Westerveldt, Michael Smith, John Aldrington, captain of a company of guides and pioneers in his Majesty's service. Proved, October 29, 1781.

Page 310.—In the name of God, Amen. I, ELIAS DUBLON, of Hempstead, in Queens County, being now weak in body. I leave to my loving wife Hannah one cupboard which now stands in my dwelling house with all such linen as may happen to be in the same at the time of my decease, and also such beds and bedding which I have lately had from the family of Daniel Pines; also one cow such as my wife shall choose, and all the pewter, all of which I give her in lieu of her right of dower. Unto my daughter Hannah one negro girl named Tish, and as much household goods or other things as will make her equal with what my daughter Mary has already had. All the remainder of my estate, both real and personal, I give to my sons, Joseph and Linninton, upon the condition that they pay all my just debts and funeral charges, also that they shall at all times hereafter support and maintain my wife in a decent manner with meat, drink, washing, lodging and apparel, or pay to her £15 yearly during her life, which my wife shall choose. In case my sons shall refuse to pay all the legacies, my executors are to sell as much of my estate as will pay and satisfy my debts and legacies. Whenever any of the debts which are owing to me from persons in Dutchess County are received, I order that all such debts shall be divided amongst all my children. I make my son Joseph, and my friends, Sylvanus Bedell and Timothy Clowes, executors.

Dated April 6, 1778. Witnesses, David Bedell, George Weeks, Jacamiah Bedell, of Hempstead. Proved, October 24, 1781.

Page 312.—I, DANIEL BLACHLY, of the Township of Huntington, in Suffolk County, the twenty-first day of February, 1781, being in health of body and of sound disposing mind and memory. Executors to pay all my just debts and funeral charges. I leave to my loving wife Prudence all the moveables and money that fell to me or to her by the decease of her uncle, John Scudder, except two cows which I have kept for the use of my family, but my executors are to let her have two cows instead of them; also, to my wife, one bed and furniture; also, the use and improvement of half of all the lands and buildings that I shall hereafter give to my son Moses, during her widowhood and no longer, with the proviso that she cut no more timber than is necessary for firewood and to repair fences. I leave to my son Benjamin all that piece of land whereon his house stands; also all that piece of land that I bought of the "Sammises," lying on the second tier of lots joining to the land of Eliphelet

Sammis; also ten acres of land on which his barn stands, joining to the land of Ezekiel Wickes, with the house and barn where he now liveth. I leave to my son Ebenezer all that tract of land that lyeth to the southward of my house joining to the south side of the homestead of Nathaniel Buffett, jr., which did formerly belong to Jeremiah Platt, deceased. I leave to my son Moses four " Dieces " of land all joining to the Country Road, the " eastermost " piece joining to the Clay Pits road, the next piece lying east of Buffets Barn, the two westermost " Dieces " on which my house and barn now stands, except the ten acres above given to my son Benjamin. My executors are to sell the remainder of my estate. I leave unto my four daughters that are not married, viz.: Jemima, Rhoda, Jane, and Experience, each £50, which makes them equal with my daughters that are already married. I leave to my two sons, Ebenezer and Moses, £20. If either of my two sons, Ebenezer or Moses should die under age, his part shall be divided between my two surviving sons; if either of my four daughters that are single should die under age her part shall be divided between all my daughters without exception. I make my good friends, Joseph Lewis, Ananias Carle, and Zebulon Buffet, executors.

Witnesses, Jonas Williams, Isaac Rogers, Solomon Ketcham. Proved, October 19, 1781.

Page 315.—On the 10th day of June, 1772. I, THOMAS HICKS, of Hempstead, in Queens County, on Nassau Island. All my just debts to be paid out of my moveable estate. I leave to my loving wife my " Riding Cheer and ye best Hors or Mare that I may have at ye time of my Deth "; to my son Thomas the best cow and calf that I shall have; to my sons, Jacob and Silas, my two negro men called Luke and Ceser, also the two best working horses that I shall have, that is not already given, together with all my utensils for farming. I leave to my wife and to my daughter

Elizabeth as much out of my moveable estate as to make each of them equal with what I have given to my daughter Hannah. All the rest of my moveable estate to my wife and my daughter Elizabeth and to my grandson, Charles Cornell. I give to my wife and daughter Elizabeth the use of the best room that I have in my house, the use of the bedroom adjoining my chamber, and my cellar, and the liberty to " appels or frute " out of my orchard for their own use till they marry. I leave to my two sons, Jacob and Silas, all my lands and meadows with all my buildings and improvements thereon, but Jacob and Silas shall pasture three cows and one horse for my wife and Elizabeth, and to bring them firewood to the door and to cut it fit for the " Fier," and to find hay for three cows and one horse for them as long as they shall remain unmarried; and Jacob and Silas shall find my wife her " Bred " Corn and meat as long as she remains my widow, and to pay her £3 yearly during her widowhood. My said sons shall let my son Thomas cut six load of grass in my meadow a year. They shall pay to my son Austin £300, in six equal payments, and board him till they pay him the last payment. If either shall refuse to pay the legacies, I order my executors to sell as much of my land and meadow that I have given to the said Jacob and Silas as will pay the £300 to my son Austin, with all the other legacies. I make my brother, John Hicks, my cousin, Silas Hicks, and my two sons, Jacob and Silas Hicks, executors.

Note.—All the lands and meadows that I have above given to Jacob and Silos is given equally between them.

Witnesses, Charles Hicks, yeoman, Stephen Hicks, John Mott, yeoman. Proved, March 25, 1776.

Page 317.—In the name of God, Amen. I, Hezekiah Rogers, of Huntington, in the Province of New York, yeoman. All just debts to be paid out of my estate. I leave to my loving wife Ruth all the cash

I have now by me, and also the use of one cow as she shall choose. My son Alexander shall provide sufficient meat and bread, firewood, etc., that my wife shall have need of in lieu of her dowry or power of thirds. I leave to my sons, Isaac, Muha, Hezekiah, Ezekiel, and Topars half of the money that shall arise from the sale of a certain piece of meadow which I shall hereafter order to be sold. I leave to the five children of my son Obadiah, viz.: Ruth, Zobulon, Isaac, Platt, and Abel, the other half of said proceeds. I order my executors to sell a certain piece of meadow land lying near Fleets on the north side of the east neck so called, and to dispose of the money as above mentioned. I leave to my two daughters, Phebe Rogers and Ruth Sammis, £10 each. I give to Isaac Rogers, son of my son Obadiah, all that certain tract of land lying on the north side of the road leading from Huntington to Coldspros, fifty-two acres, more or less, with all the fencing and all thereunto belonging. I give to my two grandsons, Platt Rogers and Abel Rogers, the house and barn, as also about twenty acres, called the Homestead, my son died in possession thereof, and built thereon, as also a field on the other side of the road, containing about fifteen acres, more or less, as also a piece of meadow land that I bought of Nathaniel Wickes both salt and fresh, excepting two roods on the west side, which I give to my son Alexander as far up as a certain Ditch, also a lot of upland and meadow called the North lot, all being on a neck called the Great Neck. My daughter-in-law, Mary Rogers, shall have a privilege in the buildings and lands that I have given to her children until they come of age, or so long as she shall remain a widow. I leave to my son Alexander my dwelling house, barn and all my lands and meadows, and all my real and personal estate that I have not heretofore disposed of. I make my son, Alexander Rogers, and my friend, John Brush Miller, executors.

Dated September 22. 1778. Witnesses, Samuel

Conklin, Matthew Hopper, John Shannon. Proved, October 19, 1781.

Page 319.—In the name of God, Amen. The 20th day of June, 1777. I, JOSIAH RAYNER, of the Township of Hempstead, in Queens County. I leave to my well-beloved wife Elizabeth my best bed and furniture, two cows, two iron pots, one tramble, one frying pan, one pair of tongs, one iron shovel, one warming pan, all my pewter, one square table, one wash tub, one cupboard, all the linen and yarn I have in the house, all my Tea tackling, all the provisions and wool, all the grain on the ground and elsewhere of every kind, and flax on little Dutch wheel and great Wheel in lieu of her dower; also the use and benefit of all my lands and tenements, and the interest of £25 during her widowhood, that my son Henry is to be charged with. I give to my loving wife, old white mare at her disposal, also the interest of all the remainder of my moveable estate, not already bequeathed. After her marriage or decease to divide the principal among my daughters and granddaughters as follows: To Elizabeth Roads £5; to my daughter, Sarah Tuttel, £5; to my daughters, Jemima Natorn, Sarah Tuttel, Catharine Covert, and to my granddaughter, Martha Doxee, the remainder of my moveable estate. I leave to my son Samuel six shillings; to my son Henry all my lands and tenements in the Township of Hempstead, and all my Rights of Land upon condition he pays the money that I owe in the Loan Office in Queens County and £25 at the decease of my wife Elizabeth to the uses above mentioned; in case he should refuse to pay the £25, my executors are to sell two pieces of land situate southard of Benjamin Rainer's one piece, bounded north and south by my brother, Joseph Rainer's land, and one piece bounded south by my brother Joseph Rainer's land and north by my cousin, Benjamin Rainer's land, containing in both pieces about fourteen acres, more or less. My just debts be paid, and proving my will, and funeral expenses out of my moveable estate. I make my respected friends, Timothy Clowes, and Joseph Hall, both of Hempstead, and my wife Elizabeth Rainer, executors.

Dated June 20, 1777. Witnesses, Elijah Rainer, Ezekiel Rainer, David Batty, of Hempstead, yeoman. Proved, October 24, 1781.

Page 321.—In the name of God, Amen. August 27, 1781. I, JOHN HAGERMAN, of Hempstead, in Queens County, on Nassau Island. I leave to my well-beloved wife Ann one good cow, she to take her choice out of my stock; also my best feather bed and bedstead and cord and furniture belonging to the same. I leave to my daughter Mary one feather bed and furniture to the same, and one cow. My real and personal estate that remains to be sold at the discretion of my executors; the proceeds to pay all my just debts and funeral charges, and of the remainder I give £100 to my well-beloved wife Ann, to my daughter Mary £20; to my daughter Hannah £15 to be paid out of my estate when my youngest son Aureyon is twenty-one years old. The remainder I give equally among my three sons, John, Joseph, and Aureyon. My executors are to put my sons to apprenticeship. I make my loving wife Ann, and my trusty cousin, Benjamin Hagerman, in Queens County, my executors.

Witnesses, Charles Dorlin, Benjamin Jackson, Isaac Denton. Proved, October 13, 1781.

Page 323.—In the name of God, Amen. I, JOSEPH LEWIS, of Huntington, in Suffolk County, this 10th day of September, 1781. My executors within one year after my decease to sell such of my moveables as they shall think will be the most benefit for the children, and pay all my just and lawful debts out of my moveable estate. I leave to my oldest son Azel, and my third son Concklin, all my part of the mills, dams, houses, and lands, etc., at Cow Harbor, and my house and lands at Cuby, which I bought of Alexander Lewis. Likewise I give to my sons, Azel and Joseph, one pair of oxen, which I bought of William Hubbert in lieu of one span of horses they now claim. I give to my second son, Joseph, and my fourth son, Richard, all my houses, out houses, lands, rights, and privileges to the same belonging in the "Townd spot" of Huntington, and likewise my tract of land that lays adjoining the south part of Zebulon Platt's homestead, containing about forty-five acres, more or less. I give to Richard Lewis the yearling colt. I give to my four daughters, namely: Abigail, Elizabeth, Amelia, and Naomi Lewis, all my moveable estate, except what I already disposed of. If any of them should die under age, my will is that it should be equally divided among the survivors, and if any of my four sons should die under age their part shall be equally divided among the surviving sons, except £200 of the deceased part, and that shall be equally divided among the surviving daughters; if any of my sons so die then his partner shall have the refusal of his part, and that my executors shall make the valuation. I give to my son Concklin my silver watch. I make my friend, John Squire, and my brother, Scudder Lewis, executors.

Witnesses, Nathaniel Harrisen, Epenetus Conklin, yeoman, Phebe Bayles. Proved, October 19, 1781.

Page 325.—In the name of God, Amen. July 15, 1781. I, PEARSON LANGDON, of Hempstead, in Queens County, on Nassau Island. I order my executors to sell so much of my moveable estate as shall pay all my just debts and funeral charges, and after so doing the remaining part of my estate, both real and personal, I give my wife Nancy the use of, during her natural life or widowhood, provided she brings up my children till they are able to get their own living. After my wife's death or marriage the whole to be sold by my executors and the proceeds I give to my well-beloved daughters, namely: Nancy, Phebe, Almy, and

Hannah to be equally divided among them. In case my wife Nancy should bare a child within nine months from the date hereof, if it be a female I order my whole estate equally among the five; if it be a male child, give to him all my estate, provided he pays to each of my daughters £30; in case he neglects or refuses paying to my daughters the above mentioned £30, the whole money that shall arise by the sale of my estate to be equally divided among my children. All that I have given to my well-beloved wife Nancy I give to her in lieu of her thirds and dower. I make my loving brother, Joseph Langdon, and my loving cousin, Adam Pearsall, executors.

(Signed PEARSALL LANGDON.)

Witnesses, Thomas Combs, John Langdon, Isaac Denton. Proved, October 13, 1781.

Page 327.—In the name of God, Amen. I, ALEXANDER EAGLES, of the City of New York, sadler. After my just debts be paid and discharged I give to my loving wife Elizabeth all my estate, both real and personal, and I make her executrix.

Dated January 11, 1775. Witnesses, Jas. Giles, schoolmaster, Jacob Bogart, Jno. Burger. Proved, November 12, 1781.

Page 328.—In the name of God, Amen. I, DANIEL WIER, Esq., Commissary Genl. to His Majesty's Army in North America, now residing in the County and Province of New York. After paying all my just debts and funeral expenses I give to my beloved brothers, William Wier and Thomas Wier, £2,000 sterling, each; to my dear sisters, Frances Wier and Grace Wier, £2,000 sterling, each; to my friends, Captain Colebrook Nesbitt, of the 82d Regt., Thomas Wilkinson, son of my friend, Jacob Wilkinson, Esq., of London, and Thomas Aston Coffin, my Secretary, £5,000, sterling, each. Also, I give to my friends, Mrs. Susannah Nesbitt, widow of Arnold Nesbitt, Esq., late of

Grafton Street, London, Colonel George Garth, of the
1st Regt. of Guards, and Thomas Lee, son of Richard
and Jane Lee, of Leeds, £2,000 sterling, each. To my
friends, Jacob Wilkinson, Esq., of London, John Lodington, son to my Aunt Lodington, and John Wier,
surgeon to the Hospital of the Northern Army, £1,000
sterling, each. To my friends, John Burke, Esq., of
London, and Captain Mungo Noble, of the 60th Regt.,
£500 sterling, each. To my friends, Henry White,
Esq., of New York, Joshua Loring, Esq., Commissary
General of the Provinces, and Gregory Townsend,
Esq., Assistant Commissary to the Army, £200 sterling, each. To my godson, Daniel Wier James, 100
guineas. Also as a testimony of my regard I give to
my friends, Sir William Home, Major General Charles
Grey, Major General Edward Mathew, Major General
James Pattison, Lieut. Colonel James Marsh, Lieut.
Colonel Edmund Stevens, and Dr. Robert Roberts,
£100 sterling, each. Also I give to my friend, Lord
Cornwallis, as a testimony of my regard, my antique
ring which I now wear. Also as a testimony of my
regard I give to my friend, Major Henry Bruin, my
watch which I now wear with the chain and seals.
Also as a testimony of my regard I give to my friend,
Major General James Pattison, my spectacles set in
gold. I give to my godson, Isaac Wallace, my silver
Turrenne. I give to my butler, William Marshall,
£100 sterling, with all the linen, wearing apparel,
horses, carriages, and household furniture I may be
possessed of at the time of my death. To all the servants at the day of my death I give £20 sterling, each.
To my aforesaid brother, William Wier, I also give
and bequeath all my plate. To the aforesaid Thomas
Aston Coffin I give all my books and shaving case.
To the aforesaid Joshua Loring, Esq., I give my emer-
ald ring. To the aforesaid Dr. Robert Roberts, I also
give my gold snuff box and gold-headed cane. Lastly,
it is my desire that the remainder of my estate be
secured at interest by my executors, the interest there-

of to be equally divided between my aforesaid brothers and sisters, William, Thomas, Frances, and Grace Wier, and the survivors or survivor of them, and each of them, during their natural lives and after their deaths I give the said residue and remainder of my estate to the aforesaid Thomas Wilkinson and Thomas Aston Coffin to be equally divided between them. I make Jacob Wilkinson, Henry White, Gregory Townsend, and Thomas Aston Coffin, executors.

Dated August 31, 1781. Witnesses, Edward Goldstone Lutwyche, gentleman, Robert Ross, gentleman, William P. Parsons, gentleman. Proved, November 19, 1781.

NOTE.—On the same day, Thomas Aston Coffin, one of the executors named in the will, was duly sworn to the true execution and performance before the Hon. Cary Ludlow, Surrogate for the City and Province of New York.

Page 330.—Know all men by these Presents that I, MOSES FOWLER, of the Township of Flushing, in Queens County, carpenter. I order my just debts and funeral charges all be fully paid and satisfied. I give to Anna, my beloved wife, all my estate both real and personal, and I make her and my brother, Thomas Fowler, and Captain Samuel Cornwell, executrix and executors, all of the Township of Flushing.

Dated August 16, 1781. Witnesses, Stephen Carman, yeoman, Thomas Fowler, Luke Cumming, yeoman. Proved, October 11, 1781.

Page 331.—I, THOMAS KELLAM, of the Township of Huntington, in Suffolk County, the 23d day of July, 1781. My executors to pay and discharge all my debts and funeral charges. I leave to my loving wife Levinah two cows and one sorrel mare and two swine; also the use of one third part of my farm and buildings, and firewood as it stands, so long as she remains my widow; also the use of all my household goods and

furniture (except what I shall hereafter dispose of);
also I give to my wife what new cloth there is in the
house for the use of the family, all which is in lieu of
her dower. To my daughter Jemima one bed and furniture without curtains, and one cupboard, to be taken
as soon as she shall see fit, and so much money, with
what household goods she shall have, as to make her
equal with her sisters, with liberty to live in the house
so long as she remains single. All my grain and provisions and swine not disposed of shall be applied for
the use of all my family. I leave to my three sons,
Ebenezer, Jesse, and Joshua all my lands, meadows,
and buildings, both on Santepogue at South, and all
at or near the long swamp, to be equally divided between them. My son Ebenezer shall have his third
part of all my lands at or near the Long Swamp, taken
off the north part of that piece of land lying west or
southwest from my house, from Daniel Smith's land.
Also to my son Ebenezer £50 including what he hath
already had to make it up to £50. My two daughters
that are married shall have all the moveable estate
that they have already got. Unto my wife that piece
cloth that was carried to the fulling mill, to be used
in the family. My three sons shall find hay for their
mother's cows and horse, during her widowhood. To
my son Ebenezer one red pied heifer and one steer;
to my son Jesse my loom and tackling, and my bay
mare and colt and one steer; to my son Joshua my
other mare; to my three sons all my farming utensils,
to carry on farming. There shall be one creature fat-
ted for the use of the family. All my wearing apparel
shall be equally divided between my three sons. My
wife shall have what money there is now in the house.
My executors shall sell of the remainder of my creatures and moveable estate (except all the flax which
is to be applied for the use of the family), as soon as
they shall think proper; but the oxen not to be sold
until they have done getting of hay. After the debts
and legacies are paid by my executors they shall divide

all the remainder of the money between my three daughters. I make my good friends, Jonah Wood, and Ananias Carl, executors, and my wife, executrix.

Witnesses, David Smith, yeoman, Josiah Smith, Solomon Ketcham. Proved, October 19, 1781.

Page 334.—I, MARY SAMMIS, spinster, of Huntington, in Suffolk County, this twenty-fourth day of October, 1781, being in perfect mind and memory, etc. My executors to pay and discharge all my just debts and funeral charges as soon as convenient after my decease, out of my estate. I leave to my loving sister, Margaret Plumb, all my household goods and wearing apparel (except one bed, which I give to her daughter, Mary Plumb). Unto my sister, Margaret Plumb's children, all the residue of my estate; and appoint my good friends, Silvanus Chichester and Peleg Wood, executors.

Witnesses, Jeremiah Wood, junior, yeoman, Alexander Denton, yeoman, John Ketcham, yeoman. Proved, October 27, 1781.

Page 335.—In the name of God, Amen. May 20, 1768. I, JAMES REEVE, of Southold, in the County of Suffolk, yeoman, being in perfect health and of sound mind. I leave to Mary, my beloved wife, her full power of dower according to law, in all my lands, buildings, and meadow, with all my personal estate whatsoever, to enable her to pay all my just debts and for her comfortable support, and to dispose of at her discretion among my six children, excluding my son James. Unto my son Isaac all my land and meadow which I purchased of David Brown's executors, and of Barnibas Ferrell, with my three rights in the manor called Ferrell Manor, and my two rights in the manor called Mapes Manor; also the privilege of cutting the same hay off of my meadow as my said son usually hath done in time past, to do still for twenty-five years after my decease. Unto my son Selah my farm, purchased of James Hoell, and my land called Coleman lot, with the remainder of my land in the manor aforesaid, being seven rights; also his privilege of cutting the same meadow twenty-five years next after my decease which his brother James usually cut when he lived on the farm, and also privilege of cutting wood of the same piece of woodland, said son James used to cut on, for the same term of years. Unto my son Ebenezer all my land in the Manor of St. George, with all my right at a town called Andover or Other Creek, and my half right at Susquahannah. I make Mary, my beloved wife, my sole executrix.

Witnesses, John Case, joiner, David Arnold, John Case, junior. Proved, May 10, 1781.

Page 337.—I, SOLOMON KETCHAM, of Huntington, in Suffolk County, this 20th day of September, 1781, being in perfect mind and memory. My executors to pay and discharge all my just debts and funeral charges. I leave to my loving wife Hannah one riding chair and one horse, my negro girl named Leah, and six cows, and so many swine as my executors shall think proper, and all my household goods (except what I shall hereafter dispose of). I give her the use of half of the buildings where I now live, and the use of one fourth of my farm, so long as she remains my widow. All which I give to my wife in lieu of her dower. Unto my daughter, Mary Sands, my negro girl named Merea; to my daughter, Mary Sands' four children, Elizabeth, Sarah, Daniel, and Hannah Sands, £100, to be equally divided between them; to be paid when they are of lawful age or at the day of marriage. Unto my daughter, Sarah Ketcham, one bed and furniture and £100. Unto my daughter, Hannah Ketcham like articles, and like sum, all to be paid to my daughters as they arrive to the age of eighteen years or day of marriage. Unto my son Philip £100; to my son Solomon £30. My four sons, Philip, Solomon, Conkling, and Platt should improve and carry on,

jointly together, all my lands and meadow till such
time as all my just debts and legacies above given are
paid.   After all my debts and legacies are paid I give
unto my four sons all the remaining part of my estate.
If either of my sons should die under age, his part to
be divided between the surviving brothers.   My executors shall give a pass to my negro James and his
wife to look a master for themselves. I make my good
friend, John Ketcham, and my two sons, Philip and
Solomon, executors.

Witnesses, Israel Wood, of Huntington, farmer,
Jeremiah Wood, Jr., Alexander Denton, of Huntington, beaver.   Proved, October 22, 1781.

Page 339.—In the name of God, Amen.   This 2d
day of July, 1767.   I, PARROT FLEET, of Huntington, in
the County of Suffolk, Island of Nassau, yeoman, being sick and weak in body.   My executors to pay all
my just debts.   I leave to my loving wife Abigail all
my whole household goods of every kind that I shall
not dispose of in this Will; likewise four cows, fifteen
sheep, a horse, the creature as she shall choose, also
my riding chair, a full year's provision of every kind.
I give to my wife forty bushels of wheat as also thirty
bushels of indian corn, also a fat beast, fifty pounds
of flax, every year my wife shall continue my widow.
I also give to my loving wife four good swine as she
shall choose.   I also order my wife full liberty of this
my dwelling house during her remaining my widow.
Unto my three sons, my whole estate in lands, upon
the north side of this Island to be equally divided.
Unto my youngest son, Jesse, one half of all my lands
and meadow on the south side lying on the neck called
Little East Neck.   Unto my two sons, Simon and Jeremiah, the remainder of my lands and meadow to be
equally divided.   My son Jesse shall have a free right
in the south house.   My three sons to pay every article
to their mother as above mentioned in good order year
after year.   My three sons to pay to my three daugh-

ters, Deborah, Sarah, and Anna, £50 each. Unto each of my daughters, one bed and furniture as also a home, as long as they shall continue single in this my house I now dwell in. I make my loving brother-in-law, Jeremiah Wood, and my sister's son, John Bryan, my sole executors.

Witnesses, John Johnson, Peter Scudder, Gilbert Potter, all of Huntington, yeomen. Proved, October 20, 1781.

Page 340.—In the name of God, Amen. The 21st day of July, 1781. I, SAMUEL MILLS, of Jamaica, in Queens County, cordwainer, being at the time very sick and weak in body. All my just debts and funeral charges to be paid. I leave to my well-beloved daughter, Martha Mills, £100, to be raised out of my estate; also my best bed and bedding complete, all the linen in the cupboard, one looking glass, one Bilsted Chest, some chairs, six pewter plates, four platters, one stand. All the remainder of my estate, both real and personal, I order to be sold and the proceeds of the sale I give to my three well-beloved sons, Henry, Samuel, and Stephen, to be equally divided, and paid to them as they arrive at the age of twenty-one years. I make my brother, Amos Mills, and my brother-in-law, Nicholas Ludlam, executors.

Witnesses, James Everit, yeoman, Barnardus Hendrickson, Hendrick Hendrickson, yeoman. Proved, September 14, 1781.

Page 342.—In the name of God, Amen. I, ANN ANTILL, at present of the City of New York, in North America, being of sound mind but old and infirm, etc. I leave to my son Edward my lands in the County of Bergen, in the Province of New Jersey, left to me by the last Will of John Corbett, Esq. I desire that my money in the hands of Charles Lowndes, Esq., given to me by the Will of my deceased sister, Euphamia Norris, be divided into five equal parts and disposed of as follows, viz.: to my grandson, John Collins Antill, son of John Antill, Esq.; to my granddaughter, Isabella Graham Antill, daughter of my son, Edward Antill, Esq.; to my granddaughter, Ann Cochran, daughter of Richard Cochran, Esq.; to my granddaughter, Sarah Morris, daughter of Lieut. Colonel John Morris; and to my granddaughter, Elizabeth Colden Antill, daughter of my son, Lewis Antill, deceased. As to the money given to me by my late beloved husband, Edward Antill, Esq., and any other money I may die possessed of, I desire it may be equally divided among my children. I make my son, John Antill, Esquire, my sole executor.

Dated March 27, 1778. Witnesses, Thomas Davies, Ann Morris, Thos. Skinner, baker. Proved, November 20, 1781.

NOTE.—On December 3, 1781, John Antill, Esq., appeared before the Surrogate for the City and Province of New York, and was duly sworn to the true execution and performance of said Will.

CARY LUDLOW,
Surrogate.

Page 344.—In the name of God, Amen. I, STEPHEN LAWRENCE, of Flushing, in Queens County, yeoman, this 30th day of December, 1779, being well in body and of perfect mind and memory. All my just debts and funeral charges be well and truly paid. I leave to my loving son, Somerset Lawrence, £1,000; to my loving son, Leonard Lawrence, £400; to my loving son, Robert Lawrence, all my real estate which I have in Flushing. I give all the remainder of my moveable estate to be equally divided between my three loving sons. I make my son Leonard and my trusty friend, John Field, executors.

Witnesses, Thos. Cornell, John Cornell, Oliver Cornell, yeoman. Proved, September 22; 1781.

Page 345.—In the name of God, Amen. The 5th day of May, 1779. I, JOHN GEORGE WEDDERHANE, of the

Out Ward of the City of New York, butcher, being in
health of body and of perfect mind and memory.
First I will that all those debts and duties as I do owe
in right or conscience to any manner of person or persons whatsoever shall be well and truly contented and
paid in convenient time after my decease by my executors.   I leave to Mary Magdalene, my dear and well-
beloved wife (whom I likewise make my only and sole
executrix), all and singular, my lands, messuages,
tenements, buildings, household furniture, moveables,
money, and sums of money, due or becoming due to
me by books, or bond, or otherwise, from any person
or persons whatsoever, by her fully to be possessed
and enjoyed.

Witnesses, Nicholas Lackman, sugar baker, George
Kline, bread baker, Peter Sparling. Proved, November 19, 1781.

Page 347.—In the name of God, Amen. I, CATHA-
RINE KIBBLE, of the City of New York, widow and relict
of Stephen Kibble, late of the same City, Assistant
Deputy Commissary General, deceased, being sick and
weak in body. My just debts and funeral charges to
be paid. Immediately after my funeral is over I order
all my furniture and plate of every kind to be sold and
disposed of at public auction or vendue. I leave to my
sister, Jane Wallace, who now lives with me, my house
I now reside in, the same being in Wall Street, the
corner of New Street, opposite the old Presbyterian
meeting. Unto my much-esteemed friend, Mrs. Mary
Butler, wife of William Butler, Esq., ten guineas, in
order to purchase her a mourning ring. Unto my
loving niece, Dorothy Wallace, a bed and window curtains, and six pair of good Rusia Sheets, and six pair
of pillow cases; I further give her twenty guineas to
purchase her mourning. Unto Thomas Cumpston,
my executor, hereinafter named, a large case now
in my cellar containing twelve large case bottles each
of which case contains two and one half gallons.

My executrix and executors are to fully liberate and manumit my negro wench called Phillis, and that she be by no means sold nor otherwise disposed of, as a reward for her faithful services. All the remainder of my estate, real or personal, I give to my beloved daughter, Catharine Kibble, provided that if my daughter Catharine should depart this life before the age of twenty-one and day of marriage, then I give all the estate to Sally, Betsey, and Penelope, sisters of my husband, Stephen Kibble, deceased, and to my sister, Jane Wallace, and Dorothy Wallace, my said niece, to be divided between them in equal portions. I direct that my said daughter Catharine shall be and remain under the tuition and guardianship of my much-valued friend, William Butler, Esq., in order that she may be properly taught, instructed, and educated. I direct that my ear-rings, buckles, gold watch, and other things of the like kind, together with all my wearing apparel be kept and reserved for the use, wear, and clothing of my daughter Catharine. I make my sister, Jane Wallace, executrix, and Thomas Cumpston, and Benjamin James, Esq., Assistant Deputy Commissary General, executors.

Dated April 14, 1781. Witnesses, John Faulkner, cabinet maker, Peter R. Ludlow, merchant, Will Cock, Esquire.

Codicil. Whereas, I did will that all my wearing apparel be kept and reserved for the use, wear, and clothing of my daughter Catharine, now I, the said Catharine Kibble, out of love and affection to my niece, Dorothy Wallace, and considering that it will be a long time before my wearing apparel is fit for the use of my daughter Catharine, I direct that my daughter Catharine shall have five of my richest dresses and no more, and that all the remainder be given to Dorothy Wallace to her use for ever. I do further order that all my Shifts be given to my niece Dorothy, except twelve which I desire may be kept for the use and wear, and given to my daughter Catharine. All that set of china which was sent to me by Mrs. Kibble, mother of my deceased husband, from London, together with the Tea Board on which the said set of china is usually placed, and which was purchased here, be given to my niece Dorothy.   And wherever I have now in the house one piece of purple sattin, I dispose of the same as follows, to wit: half part be given to my loving sister, Jane Wallace; the remaining half part be given to my nurse, Elizabeth Daniel, as a reward for her care and attention to me.

Dated May 18, 1781.   Witnesses, Chas. Shaw, John Scott, Will Cock.   Proved, November 20, 1781.

Page 351.—In the name of God, Amen.   On the 14th day of December, 1778, I, MICHAEL FLOWER, of Hempstead, in Queens County. . All my just debts and funeral charges to be paid out of my moveable estate. I leave to my well-beloved wife Mary the use of all the remainder of my moveable estate, together with the use of all my lands and meadow, during her life or widowhood, provided she brings up my children in a decent manner and gives them Common Learning, till my sons, John and William, are twenty-one years old, and my two daughters, Elizabeth and Ann, are eighteen years old.   At the time my executors deliver my moveable estate to my wife Mary, I order that she shall give security to make good the value of my moveable estate at her death or marriage.   In case my wife refuses or neglects bringing up my two sons, my executors are to sell as much of my " Fast Estate " as shall bring them up to the age of twenty-one, and my two daughters till they are eighteen.   After my wife's death or marriage I give to my well-beloved sons, all my lands that shall then belong to my estate to be equally divided.   All the moveable estate that shall remain I give to my well-beloved daughters to be equally divided.   I order my executors to put my sons to apprenticeship as they think proper, to such trades as my sons shall choose.   I make my loving brother,

John Flower, and my trusty friends, Luke Eldert, and Isaac Denton, all of Hempstead, executors.

Witnesses, Harman Flower, Timothy Flower, Gilbert Flower. Proved, November 19, 1781.

Page 353.—In the name of God, Amen. I, WILLIAM RICE, of his Majesty's ship *Iris,* being of sound and disposing mind and memory. I leave to my friend, George Mitchell, of his Majesty's ship Iris, all sums of money as shall be due, owing and payable to me for wages, prize money, or any other account whatsoever, as also my wearing apparel and personal estate. I make the said George Mitchell, executor.

Dated October 17, 1781. Witnesses, Jam. Callam, Peter Malone, mariner, Joseph Bulkeley. Proved, December 4, 1781.

Page 355.—In the name of God, Amen. I, JACOB PARCELL, of New Town, in Queens County, on Nassau Island, yeoman, being at this time weak in body. All debts with my funeral charges be justly paid. I leave to my beloved grandson, Jacob Parcell, son of my son, Nicholas Parcell, £5, as his full proportion with what his father hath received out of my estate. I omit the heirs of my son, Jacob Parcell, as he hath received more than his proportion out of my estate. Unto my beloved granddaughter, Rebecca Hornbrook, £100 to be paid her in one year after the last legacy, hereinafter named, shall be paid. Unto my beloved daughter, Mary House, my large brass Kittle and Iron Griddle. Unto my grandson, Jacob Parcell, son of Isaac Parcell, my silver watch, at my decease. To my beloved son, and son-in-law, John Parcell and John House, the whole of my estate, they paying all my debts, with the legacies heretofore bequeathed, and those that shall hereafter be named. Unto my beloved children, by name, William, Isaac, Richard, Abram Parcell and Catryntje Melinshaw, £800 to be equally divided and paid in five yearly equal payments. If any of my children should die in nonage or without

lawful issue, that part to be equally divided among
the surviving children. I make my beloved son, John
Parcell, and son-in-law, John House, with my esteemed
friend, Richard Betts, Esq., executors.

Dated September 4, 1781. Witnesses, John Parsall,
yeoman, William Parsell, yeoman, Cornelius Berrien,
yeoman. Proved, November 22, 1781.

Page 357.—New York, August 3, 1781. The last
Will and Testament of Mrs. JANE MALONEY, desires
and requests, if she should die of her present illness,
that her son, James Maloney, should be left in the care
and charge of Mrs. Anna Butler until such time as its
convenient to send said child to Mrs. Anna Councill,
sister to the above Jane Maloney, in Wilmington,
New Castle, unless intercepted by Mr. Peter Maloney,
father to said child. Also I do desire that Mr. Benjamin Gatfield will pay Mrs. Anna Butler whatever
sum of money that shall be adjudged proper by any
two or three honest inhabitants of the City of New
York, as a recompense for her trouble in maintaining my child, and that to be paid to her quarterly. I
desire that Benjamin Gatfield will defray all manner
of charges which may be wanting to me at my burial,
also to advance clothes to my son James when wanting or necessary, all such sums of money advanced
by Benjamin Gatfield to be deducted out of the sum of
£118 which I lodged in Benjamin Gatfield's hands. If
my son James should go to Wilmington the net balance what shall then remain due, must be sent along
with him. If my husband Peter and my son James
should both die, then I desire the balance to be given
to my sister, Ann Councill. The within mentioned
£118 I do acknowledge to have received and promise
to comply with this Will and Testament. In Witness
whereof both Jane Maloney and I do interchangeably
sign our Hands. Jane Maloney, Benjamin Gatfield.

Witnesses, James Hanrahan, trader, William Mc-
Phily. Proved, November 5, 1781.

Page 359.—I, DAVID BISHOP, of the Township of Huntington, in Suffolk County, being this 14th day of August, 1781, being indisposed in body and also pretty far advanced in years. My executors to pay my just debts out of the money arising from the sale of my estate. I leave to the children of my brother, Nathan Bishop, viz.: Nathan, Enos, Sarah, Unas, and Hannah, each £3. Two thirds of the remainder of the proceeds I give to my brother, Parson Bishop and my sister, Hannah Hoit, and my brother's son, Benjamin Bishop, to be equally divided. The remainder of my estate, or the money arising therefrom, I give to my brother James' widow, Sarah Bishop, to my sister Abigail's son, Abraham Chichester, and to Nathaniel Finch's wife Rachel, equally between them. I make James Noorstrant, of the Township of Huntington, and Thomas Pearsall, of Bethpage, in the Township of Oysterbay, executors.

Witnesses, William Stilwell, farmer, Mary Stilwell, Thos. Pearsall. Proved, December 5, 1781.

Page 361.—In the name of God, Amen. I, GEORGE RAPALJE, of the Township of Flatbush, in King's County, yeoman, being sick and weak in body. I leave to Mary, my dearly beloved wife, all the use, incomes and profits of my whole estate, both real and personal, during the time she continues my widow, and which shall be in lieu of her right of dower. After her death or remarriage I give and dispose of my estate in manner following: to my son Daniel £200, and one third part of the remainder of my estate; to my daughter Mary, the wife of Elbert Snedeker, one third; to my daughter Phebe, the wife of Martin Johnson, the other third part. I make my sons-in-law, Elbert Snedeker, and Martin Johnson, and my brother, Cornelius Rapalje, executors.

Dated October 10, 1779. Witnesses, Abram Snedeker, Isaac Snedeker, yeoman, Robt. Hinchman, scrivener. Proved, November 28, 1781.

Page 363.—In the name of God, Amen. I, Basil Bartow, of the Borough Town of West Chester. After my just debts and funeral charges are paid I leave to my wife, Clarina Bartow, all the goods and chattels that are remaining which she brought with her, and was her own property, at or before our marriage, also two good feather beds, bedsteads, bedding, and furniture thereunto belonging, such as she shall choose, the sitting chairs, tables, looking-glasses, and china wear usually kept in the parlour, my riding chair and horse, and the sum of £800 in cash or bonds, to be paid to her within six months after my decease. I give to my wife the use of the room called the parlour, and the chamber over it, in my now dwelling house, the use of the northwest part of the cellar as partitioned off, the use of such part of the kitchen for her wench to live in and do her work in, the use of the east side of the garden and peach orchard on a southerly line from the north gate, as the middle walk now runs to Quinby's orchard fence, her firewood, and apples for eating and cider for her own use, liberty of the wells and liberty to pass and repass to and from the several places of privileges without molestation or hindrance, also pasture for two cows and a horse, during her natural life or as long as she remains my widow and no longer, and is in lieu of her Right of Dower. Unto my daughter Clarina £800, a negro girl called Jude, one feather bed, bedstead, bedding and furniture thereunto belonging; also one third part of my religious books, and household furniture not otherwise disposed of, and the privilege of her living in my now dwelling house with her mother or brother during her natural life or until marriage. My executors to pay the principal and interest of the money to her when she shall be twenty-one years old. Unto my son Punderson, all the lands, buildings and salt meadow which I bought of Sarah Hunt and her son Gilbert; also the lot of salt meadow called the **Parsonage** meadow; also the lot of land, and buildings thereon, called "Haddens Lott," which I bought of my brother, John Bartow; also the lot of land adjoining thereto which I bought of Duncan Reade; also a lot of woodland lying at north part of Cowswamp, adjoining to my brother John's land; also one half of two lots of upland and two water lots at New York, belonging to my brother, John Bartow, and self, and which we hold of the Devisees of Abraham Vanhorne and the Corporation of New York (the water lots were granted to my brother, John Bartow, and the half part of them, by him, released to me) together with one half of the improvements that may be made thereon; also half of my right of the lands on Minefords Island, or the new City so called; also my equal half part of a fourth part of a farm at the nine partners, belonging to my brother and self, which we bought of George Bugbee; also one third part of my religious books and household furniture, not otherwise disposed of, and the sum of £200. Unto my son, Basil John Bartow, all my lands called Homestead, with the buildings and improvements made thereon (excepting a piece of land in the field on the hill adjoining the old orchard of three rods square, two rods in the field westward and one rod eastward into the orchard as it is staked out for a burying ground for myself, my children, and their heirs, brothers, and their families, if they choose to bury there, which I hereby give and grant for the aforesaid use of a burying ground for ever, with the privilege of passing to and from the King's Road through the old orchard to the said burying ground without molestation or hindrance); also my lands and salt meadow called below, and the lot of land known by the name of Scabby Indian, being all the lands and meadows devised to my brothers and self by our deceased father, and which are now vested in me solely by a release of right from my brothers to me, together with a £25 privilege of commonage in the sheep pasture of West Chester; also the lands called and known by the name of "The

Personage Land," and the lands I bought of John Oakley, and the lot of land and salt meadow called the Causeway lot adjoining the Great Creek, and the lot I bought of Hester Nichools, all in the Borough Town of West Chester, and also one half of two lots of upland, two water lots at New York; also an equal half part of one fourth part of the farm at the nine partners, belonging to my brothers and self, which we bought of George Bugbee, also the one half of my right in the lands on Minefords Island; also one third of my religious books and household furniture, not before disposed of. I give to the Minister, Church Wardens and Vestrymen, of the Church of England, known by the name of St. Peter's Church, in the Borough Town of West Chester, £50 towards building a new church in said Borough Town, or repairing and enlarging the present church, to be paid to them when they shall actually engage in such work. My executrix and executors are to sell any part of my personal estate not herein disposed of, together with the shop goods, for the best prices they can get, and the proceeds and the outstanding debts due to me and the other moneys remaining after the aforegoing legacies are paid, be put out at interest for the use of my two sons, Punderson and Basil John, the principal and interest thereof to be paid to them when of age. If my daughter Clarina should die without leaving lawful issue before she attain the age of twenty-one years, the moneys I have given to her I give to my two sons, Punderson and Basil John. My wife Clarina shall have the use of my real estate for herself and my children's support and maintenance. The remainder of my estate whatsoever not herein before disposed of (after my just debts and funeral charges are paid) I give to my said two sons, Punderson and Basil John. My earnest desire and request is that my wife, Clarina Bartow, and my executors do take an especial care that my children be virtuously and religiously educated and kept from associating with vain and idle company, and that they be careful to have them learned to read, write, and cypher, and such branches of the mathematicks and literature as may qualify them for some necessary and useful employment in the world. I make my wife Clarina, executrix, my brother, John Bartow, my nephew, John Bartow, son of Theophilus Bartow, and the Reverend Samuel Seabury, executors.

Dated December 16, 1780. Witnesses, Theophilus Bartow, William Bartow, yeoman, Augustus Bartow. Proved, December 17, 1781.

Page 367.—In the name of God, Amen. I, RICHARD PARSELL, of the City of New York, labourer, considering the uncertainty of this short life, and being of sound and perfect mind and memory, but weak in body, will that all my just debts and funeral charges be paid and discharged. I leave to my loving wife Mary all that sum of money or legacy so called by last Will and Testament of Jacob Parsell, deceased, which was given to me by said Will, and all other estate whatsoever, and all the remainder of my personal estate, goods and chattels of what kind or nature soever. I make my said loving wife, Mary Parsell, sole executrix.

Dated November 19, 1781. Witnesses, Louis Andrew Gauteer, David Mellows, tobacconist, Abigail Fowler. Proved, December 18, 1781.

Page 369.—I, PETER VAN DE WATERS, of Westbury, in the Township of Hempstead, in Queens County, yeoman, being, this 12th day of the fifth month called May, 1781, weak in body, but of sound mind and memory. I leave to my wife Mary my best bed and full furniture, and the use of half of all my other household goods, so long as she remains my widow. My executors are to sell the remainder of my moveable estate and pay all my just debts and funeral expenses. The remainder of the money to be put out at interest,

for the support of my wife during widowhood. If any
part remains after my wife's marriage or death, it is
to be divided in the following manner, viz.: half to
my son John, and the other half equally between my
daughter Mary, the wife of James Lewis, and my
grandson, Benjamin Balding. I also give to my wife
the privilege of living in my bedroom that hath a fire-
place in it. In case that my children shall think best
to sell the farm, then they shall pay her so much money
as my executors may think is as good as the privilege
of living in the said room, and she to quit her right
therein. I give to my son John half of all lands, rights
of land, buildings, and improvements. Unto my grandson, Benjamin Balding, the other half of all my lands,
rights of lands, provided they will each of them and
my son John, give bonds to my executors to return
their proportions for the support of my wife if my
moveable estate shall not be sufficient for her maintenance. Unto my son, daughter, and grandson, all my
bonds, bills, notes, and book debts, to be divided between them in the same proportion as the other part
of my estate, that I have given to them, except a bond
I have against my son, John Van De Waters conditioned for £100. I make my nephew, Benjamin Van
De Waters, and my nephew, Gideon Seaman, executors.

Witnesses, Richard Spragg, of Hempstead, yeoman,
Samuel Titus, of Hempstead, yeoman, Joseph Place.
Proved, December 8, 1781.

Page 371.—Know all men by these Presents That
I, John Smith, of Merrock, in the Township of Hempstead, in Queens County, yeoman, being this 18th day
of August, 1777, well in Health and of sound mind and
memory. I leave to my son Joseph all my houses,
buildings, lands, and meadows at Merrock, and likewise the patent right that lieth in common within the
Township of Hempstead, that derived unto me from
my father, Jonathan Smith, deceased, and my son

Joseph shall pay to my loving wife Rachael, and to my three daughters, Phebe, Anne, and Elizabeth, £30, to be equally divided between them. I likewise give to my said son Joseph my black bald mare and one feather bed and bedding. My family shall have one year's provision out of my moveable estate, after my decease; and my beloved wife Rachael shall have the use of one third part of my Homestead, with the eastermost dwelling room in my house, and the two bedrooms adjoining as long as she shall remain my widow. Unto my three daughters, Phebe, Anne, and Elizabeth, all the patent right to the undivided or common lands in the said Township of Hempstead that I purchased of Samuel Totton, to be equally divided. Unto my loving wife Rachael £43, nine shillings, one horse and riding chair, six sheep, three cows and calves, two feather beds, bedsteads and cords, bolsters and pillows, six coverlids, and eight sheets and pillow cases. Unto my two daughters, Anne and Elizabeth, £86, eighteen shillings, twelve sheep, six cows and calves, four feather beds, bolsters, pillows, bedsteads, and cords, twelve coverlids, sixteen sheets and pillow cases to be equally divided between them. I direct my executors to sell my house and land on the Plains at the East Meadow, and the house and lands I purchased of John Haviland, and also my lands adjoining the lands of Josiah Rainer and Isaac Smith, situate in the south woods in the bounds of Hempstead, together with all my moveable estate, and with the proceeds pay any just debts and funeral charges, and the above legacies. The remaining part of the money to my wife and three daughters. If either of my daughters shall die under the age of eighteen years her part to be divided amongst my surviving daughters. If my said son Joseph shall refuse or neglect to pay the £30 as above directed, my executors shall sell the lot of salt meadow adjoining the south side of the place called the Island, and divide the proceeds amongst my wife and three daughters. All which I

have given to my wife is in lieu of her right of dower.
I make my wife Rachel, my son, Joseph Smith, and
my son-in-law, Benjamin Smith, executors.

Witnesses, Hezekiah Bedell, yeoman, Hannah Bedell, Mary Batty, spinster. Proved, May 20, 1778.

Page 373.—The will of SAMUEL WOGAN, Captain of
the American Legion. (For text see page 288 of this
Liber.)

Codicil. Dr. Hamilton having 35 guineas with me,
I leave a memorandum in my pocket-book for you to
receive it, with which I request your acceptance.
Sam'l Wogan, Staten Island, December 18, 1780.
Witness, Captain Richard Ness. Proved, December
17, 1781.

Page 374.—In the year of our Lord, 1776, August
the fourteenth. In the name of God, Amen. I, LUCES
HEVELAND, of Hempstead in Queens County, being
sick and low, but of perfect mind and memory. All
my wearing apparel I leave to my two brothers, and
to my brother Benjamin's sons, John, Joseph and Benjamin, sons of Benjamin Heveland, deceased, share
and share alike. Unto my niece, Jane Hevaland, one
bed and bedstead with two sheets and two pillows and
blankets, with one " callocow " bed quilt, to be left in
the care of my mother until Jane is married, or arrives
to the age of sixteen. The remainder of my moveables
I order to be sold and my debts to be paid by my
executors, which are as followeth : Cornelius Van Nostrand, and Silvanus R. Smith. The use of my lands I
give to my mother during her life. After her death
I order my lands and meadow to be equally divided
between my two brothers, John Hevaland and Joseph
Hevaland. Unto my niece, Jean Hevaland, my chest
that hath a drawer.

Witnesses, Cornelius VanNostrand, Elijah Spragg,
and Samuel Carman, of Hempstead, merchant.
Proved, December 11, 1781.

Page 376.—In the name of God, Amen. The 14th day of February, 1774, I, HENRY BROWN, of the Town of Southold in the County of Suffolk, yeoman, being weak in body. I leave to my son, Henry Brown, all that land (which I bought of Aaron Howell, which he bought of Jehobod Halliock), bounded on the east by a two-pole way (which I bought of Noah Halliock; and also one lot of meadow lying at the "Brawd Meadows," on the south side of Peconock River, called the short lot, which I bought of Capt. James Fanning. Unto my son Peter all that my land and meadow (which was my Uncle David Brown's, which fell to me at his decease); and also one lot of meadow lying at the Brawd Meadows, on the south side of the Peconock River, called the long lot, adjoining the meadow of Brother John Griffing. Unto my son Richard all that land which I bought of Noah Halliock, whereon I now live; and all that part of the Neck which I bought of said Halliock; and also all my meadow at the creek called "Brush his Creek"; and also two lots of meadow lying at the Brawd Meadows on the south side of the Peconock River called the Long lots. Whereas I stand indebted on account of the land which fell to me at the decease of my uncle, David Brown, that towards canceling said debts my son Peter shall pay £100; my son Richard £45; and my son Henry £15. Unto my son Pain £25; to be paid as follows: £10 to be paid by my son Peter in ten years after my decease; £5 in twelve years; £10 to be paid by my son Richard in ten years. I give my oxen and horses and all my farming utensils to my two sons, Peter and Richard; also their fire arms and swords. To my daughter, Anna Halliock, six sheep. After all my just debts, and funeral charges are paid the remainder to go to my beloved wife Mary. I make my wife Mary executrix, and my son, Peter Brown, executor.

Witnesses, Berick Moore Cleves, yeoman, Phinehas Mapes, Israel Youngs. Proved, April 30, 1781.

Page 377.—In the name of God, Amen. I, MARTHA STRONG, in Brookhaven in the County of Suffolk, widow woman, being in good health and of a sound and disposing mind and memory. I leave to my son Selah £200, to be raised out of my moveable or fast estate. As to my son Benjah (who has already had his portion of estate given to him by his father), I further acquit him of all the bonds or debts that by me are demandable of him. All my household goods and personal estate to be equally divided among my four daughters, Sarah, Charity, Abigal, and Johanna (except Oliver my slave, who I give to my son Selah). My estate of every kind not disposed of to be equally divided between my four daughters and my son Selah. I make my beloved son, Selah Strong, and my faithful son-in-law, Ebenezer Miller, executors.

Dated December 18, 1777. Witnesses, Micah Mills, Jonas Hawkins, yeoman, Eliazer Hawkings. Proved, December 17, 1781.

Page 379.—£500 For Mrs. Muter, wife of Robert Muter; 300 for Mr. Mewburn in Yorkshire; 100 for William Robertson; 100 for Adam Dolmage. The remainder to his nephew, Thomas Parkin in Baltimore, Maryland. The Deceased has remitted a bill for £400 to his kinsman in New York, which he bequeaths to him. His watch to Capt. Robertson. For his servant, William Vincent, whatever is recovered from the Sloop *Patty*, now sunk, by order of the Deputy Quartermaster General. The above bequests were made by the deceased THOMAS PARKINS, ESQR., Dep'y Comm'ry Gen'l at this place to the above persons, this ninth day of October, 1781. In the presence of G. Robertson, Agt. for Transports, Adm. Dolmage, Dep'y Comm'y of Prov's.

Proved, January 9, 1782; by George Robertson, Esq., and Adam Dolmage, who declared that Thomas Parkins, Esq., on the 9th of October, 1781, being the time of his last illness, and some short time before

his decease, gave directions for making his will; which
on the same day at Yorktown in the Colony of Virginia, in the lifetime of the testator was reduced to
writing, read to, and approved by him. That the said
will above mentioned is since lost and cannot at present be found; but that this is a true copy of said
original, made on the same day and within a few hours
after the testator's decease.

On January 16th, 1782, Richard William Parkin,
Esquire, Assistant Commissary of Provisions, then
residing at Jamaica in the Province of New York,
nearest of kin to Thomas Parkin, deceased, having
given sufficient security in the sum of £1,200 was
granted letters of administration.

Page 381.—In the name of God, Amen. The seventh
day of October, 1777, I, RULUF VOORHIS, of Hempstead
in Queens County, on Nassau Island, yeoman, being
at this time very sick and weak in body. All my just
debts and funeral charges to be paid. I leave to Cornelia, my dearly beloved wife, one bed, and bedding
complete for one bed, one spinning wheel and one cupboard. All the residue of my estate, not hereinbefore
given, I order to be sold; the proceeds to be equally
divided between my wife and children; viz.: Cornelia, my wife, my daughter, Catherine Voorhis, my son,
Stephen Voorhis, and my son, Abraham Voorhis. If
any or either of my aforesaid children shall die before they arrive to perfect age that share shall be
equally divided between the survivors. I make Catherine Voorhis, my daughter, my Cousin, Simon Voorhis, and my cousin, John Pratt, executors.

Witnesses, James Everit, David Ludlow, yeoman,
Jacob Peterson, yeoman. Proved, October 27, 1777.

Page 382.—In the name of God, Amen. I, JACOB
SUYDAM, of Flushing in Queens County, yeoman, being
sick and weak in body. I direct that my executors
pay all my just debts and funeral charges out of my

personal estate. I leave to my dearly beloved wife Mary £500; also all the furniture or household goods in my house, and the use and profits of all my real estate during the time that her son, Joseph Totten, shall arrive to the age of twenty-one years; at that time the real estate shall be equally divided between my wife, Mary Suydam, and her son, Joseph Totten. At her death or second marriage, which may first happen, all my real estate to her son, my son-in-law, Joseph Totten, upon conditions of his part of his father's estate which came in my hands by his mother, my wife, Mary Suydam; which considerably overruns his portion that came in my hands by his mother, my wife. All which I have herein given to my wife I give to her in lieu of her dower. To my loving brother, John Suydam, the sum of £1,000. I do order that my negro woman named Lyddea shall, if she choose, work for herself, and if she can support herself without any expense to my estate, and maintain the child she is now pregnant with; if it should live, my will is and do give the said negro child its Freedom. All the remainder of my personal estate to be sold at publick vendue; the proceeds to be equally divided between my loving brother, John Suydam, and my two loving sisters, Catherine Cornell and Phebe Suydam. I make my loving wife, Mary Suydam, and my loving brother, John Suydam, and my trusty friend, John Field, all of Flushing, executors.

Dated September 7, 1780. Witnesses, Isaac Smith, miller, and his wife, Haty Smith, Mary Divine. Proved, October 15, 1781.

Page 384.—In the name of God, Amen. I, SYLVANUS DAVIS, of Southold, in the County of Suffolk, being weak of body, but of sound mind and memory. All my just debts and funeral charges be paid out of my personal estate. I leave to my daughter, Phebe Goldsmith, £5; also one feather bed. To my son, Joshua Davis, £5. To my son James £5, and one feather bed.

All the residue of my real and personal estate to my son Benjamin, with all appurtenances. I make my son, Benjamin Davis, executor.

Dated November 17, 1771. Witnesses, Barnabas Terrel, yeoman, Parker Wickham, Joseph Wickham, yeoman. Proved, May 16, 1781.

Page 386.—In the name of God, Amen. I, THOMAS WENDOVER, of the City of New York, cordwainer, being in good health, and of sound and disposing mind and memory and understanding. All my just debts and funeral expenses be fully paid. I leave to my son Herculus my silver watch which I had of my brother, Peter Breastead. To my daughter Mariah, now the widow of John Shaw (late of the said city, mariner), deceased, £20, which sum is hereby intended to make her equal with her two sisters, Anatie and Elizabeth, for what they respectively received for their out-sets at their time of marriage. All the residue of my estates to go to my loving wife Elizabeth for and during her natural life for her better support and maintenance. To enable my wife to pay debts, which I do now owe, I empower her and my other executors to sell any one of my messuages or dwelling houses. After the death of my wife, all my real and personal estate unto my several children and grandchildren; viz.: one fifth to my son Herculus; a like part to my daughter Anatie, the widow of Henry Play, deceased; a like part to my daughter Mariah, the widow of John Shaw, deceased; a like part to my three grandchildren, Joseph and Robert Ketch, and Elizabeth Melvin the wife of Peter Melvin, mariner, being the children of my deceased daughter, Elizabeth Ketch; and the remaining one fifth part thereof to the children of my deceased son Peter; viz.: Thomas, John, Margaret, Mary, Peter, and Stephen, to be divided among them share and share alike. In case either of my six grandchildren, the children of Peter Wendover, shall happen to die before majority or marriage, then

I give the deceased child's share to the survivors.
The one fifth part given to the children of my son,
Peter Wendover, deceased, to be put out at interest
for their use, and paid to them as they respectively
arrive at the age of twenty-one years, or marry. I
make my loving wife Elizabeth, my son Herculus, and
my friend, Thomas Collister, of the said city, joiner,
executors.

Dated November 6, 1773. Witnesses, Augustus V.
Cortlandt, of Flatbush, esquire, Robert Towl, Isaac
Stymets. Proved, July 28, 1779.

Page 388.—In the name of God, Amen. The twenty-
fourth day of July, 1775, I, JOSEPH HINCHMAN, of the
Town of Southold in the County of Suffolk, "cir-
geion," being weak in body. All my just debts and funeral charges to be paid out of my book debts or accounts; and if they should be deficient, some of my
creature and household goods and outlands be sold by
my executors. All the remainder of my Estate I give
the use thereof to my wife Annar and my children
until they are brought up; then all my estate is to be
sold and the proceeds are to be equally divided between my wife Annar and all our children; only to
my oldest son ten shillings more than his equal proportion. I make my wife sole executrix, and her
brother, John Griffing, and Mr. Daniel Osmonjrher,
Assistants to execute this Will and Testament.

Witnesses, Joseph Griffing, yeoman, Prudence
Downs, spinstress, Israel Youngs. Proved, September 12, 1775.

Page 389.—In the name of God, Amen. I, HENRY
PIKE, of Southold in the County of Suffolk, being
weak in body. After my decease my body may be decently buried at the expense of my executors. I leave
to my beloved wife, all my Home estate, both house
and lands, as well as personal estate, during her widowhood. My executors are to sell a certain piece of

land, bounded by Jonas Tuthill on the east, and by John Corwin on the west and south, and the highway on the north. As to my mill, I order it sold by my executors when they think it necessary. Unto my wife, a certain tract of land bounded north by Timothy Corwin, west by Hannah Harvey, south by the highway, and east by the land of John Hubbard, deceased. My executors are to sell, within one month after my decease, three cattle and all my carpenter's tools. I make John Corwin, executor, and my wife executrix.

Dated November 13, 1780. Witnesses, Thomas Wines, yeoman, Jonathon Pike, yeoman, John Leveret Hudson. Proved, December 7, 1780.

Page 390.—In the name of God, Amen. I, Rutgart Van Brunt, of Brooklyn in Kings County, yeoman, being sick and weak in body. All my just debts and funeral charges to be paid. I leave to my two sons, John and Jacob Van Brunt, the farm on which I now live, with eight acres of woodland laying and being at the Narrows; with two acres of woodland laying in Bedford in the Township of Brooklyn. My son John keeps the house, barn, and all the buildings on the said farm to his own use. When my son Jacob comes to the age of twenty-one years, then the executors are to have the said house and barn valued, and the half of what they are valued at is to be paid by my son John to my son Jacob. My son John is to take his choice of one of the negroes and the choice of one of the best horses with a new bridle and saddel. My son Jacob shall have my negro boy named Joe. To my son John one silver-hilted sword and a pike; to my son Jacob, one silver-hilted sword. In case my son John should marry and have lawful issue before he comes to the age of twenty-one years, then in case of his death, his share to go to his lawful heir or heirs. My beloved wife, Lena Van Brunt, shall have two negroes to her sole use and benefit. My sons to have all the wagons, sleighs, plows, harrows, and horse tackling. My son John, further to have one good horse. All the residue of my personal estate unto my wife Lena and my two daughters, Lana and Jane Van Brunt. In case either of my daughters should die before she comes of age, without lawful issue, then her share is to go to the surviving sister. If they both die, then to my sons, John and Jacob. Whereas by the will of my grandfather I stand chargeable with the payment of the annual sum of £12 to my mother during her life, I do hereby order that the same be paid by my executors to my mother during her life; for the payment thereof I charge my whole estate. Further, that piece of meadow adjoining Nicholas and Fise Vandickes to be for the sole use of my wife and two daughters. My children to be maintained and supported by my whole estate until they arrive to the age of twenty-one years, or marry; and that my wife also live upon my homestead farm and be supported with them out of the Profits thereof, without committing any waste. I make my beloved wife Lena, my friend, John Rapleja, of Brooklyn, and Cornelius Van Vorst, of Bergen County, executors.

Dated January 20, 1781. Witnesses, Christopher Sweetland and Michael Grant, of Kings County, gentlemen; and Joseph Furmer, executors. Proved, December 18, 1781.

Page 392.—I, John L'homedieu, of Southold in the County of Suffolk, cooper, being sick. I leave to three of my children, John and Henry L'homedieu and Mary Reeve, five shillings apiece. To my well-beloved wife Mary all my moveables after my funeral expenses and legacies are satisfied; and the use and improvement of all my lands and buildings that shall remain unsold by my executors to pay all my just debts; so long as she remains my widow, and to be in lieu or right of dower. Unto my youngest daughter, Mary, £20; to be paid to her at the time my wife shall cease to be my widow, and not before. Unto my sec-

ond son, Benjamin, the reversion of all my lands and
buildings thereon erected, provided he shall pay the
legacy above mentioned to my youngest daughter,
Mary. If he shall refuse to pay it then my executors
shall sell so much of my lands as shall pay the legacy.
I make my well-beloved wife, Mary L'homedieu, and
my trusty, well-beloved friend, Micah Wells, executors.

Dated January 23, 1777. Witnesses, Ezekiel Pat-
tery, jr., Isaiah Wells, Youngs Wells, yeomen, all of
the County of Suffolk. Proved, April 25, 1777.

Page 393.—In the name of God, Amen. I, DAVID
FERRY, of Southold in the County of Suffolk, yeoman,
being of sound mind and memory. After my just debts
and funeral expenses are paid, I leave to my well beloved wife Mehetebel the use and improvement of all
my estate, both real and personal, so long as she remains my widow. To my oldest son, David, £30. To
my second son, Thomas, £5. To my three sons, John,
James, and William (after my wife's interest therein)
all my lands, buildings, stock, and farming implements
of all sorts. To my eldest daughter, Mehetable Edwards and my youngest daughter Bethiah, all my
household goods of every kind (after my wife's interest therein) equally between them. I make my
sons, John and James, executors.

Dated October 3, 1778. Witnesses, Jershom Al-
drich, Eli Corwin, Daniel Wells. Proved, June 26,
1779.

Page 394.—In the name of God, Amen. I, ABIGAIL
SEARY, widow to Mr. John Seary, of Huntington in
the Province of New York, being weak in body, but
of perfect mind and memory. I leave to Jonathan
Scudder my clock that now stands in my house. To
Jonathan Scudder's wife my horse and riding chair.
To Elizabeth Scudder, daughter to Jonathan Scudder,
my gold beeds and silver buttons. To his daughter,
Mary Scudder, my negro girl named Judah. To Abi-

gail Platt, daughter to Obadiah Platt, all the residue
of my estate, both real or personal. I make my three
friends, John Brush, Jonathan Scudder, and Joseph
Lewis, executors.

Dated August 5, 1779. Witnesses, Platt Wickes,
Ephraim Chichester, Moses Scudder, farmer. Proved,
May 12, 1781.

Page 395.—In the name of God, Amen. I, JAMES
HALLIOCK, of Southold in the County of Suffolk, being
weak of body. I leave to my son James the house and
land whereon I now live, bounded south on the road,
west on a lane, north on Daniel Alditch, and easterly
on Richard Howell and Micah Howell, containing about
one hundred and twelve acres. Also, another piece of
land containing thirty acres, bounded westerly by the
heirs of the late Capt. Conkling, easterly by Capt.
Richard Howell, southerly by Isaac Reeve, and northerly by the road. Also, all my meadow ground in
Southold or elsewhere, with all edifices, building,
fences, ways, easements, and appurtenances, provided
my son James shall pay to my two sons, Jeremiah and
Benjamin, £50 each when they arrive to the age of
twenty-one years. Unto my son William my lot of
land bounded westerly on Samuel Hudson and Daniel
Worner, southerly by Thomas Conkling, easterly by
the land late of David Horton, north by the road,
containing about ninety acres. My executors are to
sell ten or fifteen acres of the above piece of land for
the payment of my just debts. Unto my Son Thomas
one piece of land adjoining westerly to Zerobable
Halliock, south and east by Micah Howell, and north
by the road, containing about thirty acres. To my
two sons, Jeremiah and Benjamin, £50 each; to be
paid them by my son James when they shall arrive to
ye age of twenty-one years, respectively; or on his
neglect, by my executors. To my wife Mary three
cows, and to keep fifteen sheep of my stock until my
youngest child shall arrive to ye age of ten years,

after that six sheep; which I freely give her. All my indoor moveables (except my silver tankard) two fat cattle, my fatting hogs, and a sufficiency of grain and produce now growing, for an ensuing year. All which I freely give her during her widowhood. To my two daughters, Mary and Abigail, £5 each. To my son William my silver tankard. All the remainder of my personal estate to be sold. I make my wife, Mary Halliock, my two brothers, Zerobable and Joseph, executors.

Dated September 22, 1774. Witnesses, Parker Wickham, Mica Howell, yeoman, Richard Steer Hubbard, yeoman. Proved, December 14, 1775.

Page 397.—The will of the Lord Jehovah be done. My will is as follows: I leave all my moveable estate to my children; to my two eldest daughters, namely, Jerusha and Mary, each £100, with the use or interest of it after my decease. Also, to them, all their own mother's household goods. Then my whole estate to be equally divided between all my daughters, only that Abigail, Juliana, and Phebe have all their mother's household goods divided between them only. I make my brethren, Capt. Josiah Smith and David Howell, executors.

Dated December 24, 1773.

          (Signed)   MICAH MOORE.

Witnesses, John Bousseave, Nathaniel Bousseave, yeomen, John Pain. Proved, February 8, 1776.

Page 398.—Know all men by these Presents that I, JOSHUA BRUSH, farmer, of Huntington in Suffolk County, this fifth day of August, 1776, being sick and weak in body. My executors to pay all my just debts and funeral charges. I leave to my loving wife Margaret, one horse, saddle, and bridle, one cow, one bed and furniture as she shall choose, and the use of my cupboard, so long as she remains my widow. All except the cupboard I give to her free disposal. There

shall be flax, wool, and all other necessary provisions
for my family for one year after my decease. Unto
my daughter Susannah £10 and my cupboard after
my wife is done with the same. My wearing apparel
and two deer skins should be equally divided between
my two eldest sons, Abel and Philip. The £10 given
to my daughter should be kept at interest and paid to
her with interest when she is eighteen years of age, or
on day of marriage. My executors are to sell all the
remainder of my estate, and the proceeds to be divided
between my wife and my three sons, Abel, Philip, and
Jonathan. My executors to be guardians of my estate,
and bind out all my children to trades as they shall
think proper. If either of my children should die under age or without issue, then that part to be equally
divided between my surviving children. I make my
good friends, Jesse Brush, Esq., and Jesse Whitman,
executors.

Witnesses, Joseph Ireland, Pearesan Brush, Solomon Ketcham, yeomen. Proved, March 28, 1781.

Page 399.—In the name of God, Amen. I, JAMES
HALLETT, of New Town in Queens County on Nassau
Island, wheelwright, being at this time in a reasonable
state of health, and perfect understanding. All debts
and funeral charges to be paid out of my personal
estate. I leave to my beloved wife Lydia one bed and
furniture, six chairs, six knives, and forks, three
dishes, six plates, six spoons, a set of blue and white
china tea furniture, and tea kettle. Also, the choice
of the best room in the house, half of a good beef, one
fat hog, firewood cut and brought to the door for one
fire, a privilege in the garden and fruit in the orchard
as she shall have occasion of for her own use, one hogshead of good cider, the milk of one good milch cow,
and bread corn sufficient for her use, and the use of a
horse and chair, the sum of £20 yearly during her
natural life instead of her dower. Unto my son James,
£10 for his birthright. Unto my son, Stephen, the

whole of my real estate, and also the remaining part of my personal estate, on condition that he does faithfully and particularly provide for his mother the hereinbefore mentioned articles for her use and support. I make my loving sons, James and Stephen Hallett, and my brother-in-law, Nathaniel Moore, Sr., executors.

Dated July 21, 1781. Witnesses, Isaac Bragaw, yeoman, William Hallett, Moses Hallett. Proved, October 23, 1781.

Page 401.—In the name of God, Amen. I, Mary Vanderbilt, of Staten Island, in the County of Richmond, widow, being weak in body, do this twelfth day of December, 1781, make and publish this will and testament. I leave to my son Cornelius my house I now live in, with all my lands I now possess, on condition he paying six months after my decease to my [son?] John Vanderbilt, £100; unto my son Oliver £100. Unto my two daughters, Eloner Johnson and Doretea Garrison, all my wearing apparel to be divided between them, share alike. Likewise, to my said two daughters and my grandson, Jacob Vanderbilt, all my moveable estate (my funeral expenses first being paid). I make my two sons, Oliver and Cornelius, and my son-in-law, Nathaniel Johnson, my executors.

Witnesses, Christian Jacobson, yeoman, John Barbank, yeoman, Mary Barbank. Proved, December 18, 1781.

Page 402.—In the name of God, Amen. George Wizer, of Wine Common on Nassau Island, yeoman, being weak of Body, yet of a Perfect understanding, will and positively order after all my debts and funeral charges are paid, to my dearly beloved wife all the farming tackle, with one pair of oxen, the biggest pair together, with all my stock, to bring up his [sic] children, and to give all good learning together for the use of the farm. Unto my beloved son George all my land and meadow, with all its buildings, when at age; and my wife to give him a team of oxen and horses. Unto my dearly beloved daughter Rebeccah, three cows and calves, together with one good bed and bedding. Unto my beloved daughter Margaret, three cows and calves. I make my trusty true Friends, Elijah Wicks and Isaac Burr, executors.

Dated November 26, 1778. Witnesses, Samuel Bruce, Lemuel Roos, John Wickes, of Winocomack, farmer. Proved, March 21, 1781.

Page 403.—I, ESTHAR BRYAN, of Huntington in Suffolk County, this third day of July, 1780, being weak in body but of perfect mind and memory. I leave unto William Netherway, 80 shillings; unto Margaret Netherway the use and improvement of all my part of the homestead that did belong to my brother, John Bryan, so long as until it be sold by me or my executors, if she see fit to live there; and to have the use of my part of the building and firewood; and when sold it shall be equally divided between her and Esther Bennett, daughter of Joseph Bennett. Unto the said Margaret Netherway, one case of drawers, one table, and one bedstead, two wheels, one iron pot and one tea kettle, and one set of curtains. Unto Elizabeth and Esther Bennett, each, one chest. To Elizabeth Bennett, one bed. Unto all my sister's daughters, all the remainder of my moveable estate to be equally divided between them; after my debts and funeral charges are paid. If the said Margaret Netherway should die without any heir, her part should be equally divided between my sister's daughters and her sister's daughters, to their free disposal. I make my good friend, Henry Sammis and William Pleas, executors.

Witnesses, Thomas Sands, Mary Sands, Solomon Ketcham, farmer. Proved, May 12, 1781.

Page 405.—In the name of God, Amen. I, JEREMIAH RULAND, of Huntington Township, of Suffolk County, of Long Island, being weak in body. All my just debts and funeral charges to be paid. I leave to my dear wife, Dinah, £20; also one riding horse and chair; with the use and profits of all my farms, she making no waste or destruction thereon, until the full age of my son, Jeremiah Ruland, except she should brake her widowhood and marry. Then in that case my executors should take such profits of my farm for the use of bringing up and for a necessary education of all my children. Unto my two sons, Obediah and Jeremiah, all my lands and fast estate. Unto my wife, two milch cows with the use of all my household furniture during her natural life. To my wife, forever, one feather bed and furniture to dispose of them as she may think fit. Unto my three daughters, Experience, Keturah, and Amy Ruland, each £10; to be paid to each at their proper age. I make my worthy friends, Serjeant Vanbaclah Robbins and Mr. Moses Wicks, both of the Township abovesaid, executors, and my wife, Dinah Ruland, executrix.

Dated October 12, 1779. Witnesses, Nathaniel Brown, Lemuel Roos, Stephen Vedeto, of Huntington, schoolmaster. Proved, February 8, 1781.

Page 406.—In the name of God, Amen. This sixth day of November, 1776, I, JEMIMA WICKES, widow and relict of Eliphalet Wickes, Esq., deceased, of Huntington in Suffolk County, being of perfect mind and memory. I leave to my grandson, Eliphalet Wickes Close, £100; to my granddaughter, Elizabeth Close, one bed and furniture and likewise £10 in money; to my granddaughter, Hannah Brush, one bed and furniture and £5; to my granddaughter, Sarah Wiser, one bed and furniture and likewise the curtains belonging to the same, and £10; to my granddaughter, Vileter Allen, £5; to my granddaughter, Sarah Jarvis, £5, and likewise to her sister, Phebe Jarvis, £5; to my granddaughter, Sarah Wiser, one large cupboard and one round table; to my granddaughters, Rebecca Youngs,

Freelove, Phebe and Hannah Brush (the daughters of John Brush), each £5. Unto my daughter, Mary Close, the wife of the Rev. John Close, one silver tankard and six silver spoons. If any of the children above mentioned should die before they come of age, their legacy shall devolve upon the rest of the children, who must wait for their legacies until the land in the eastern purchase which was laid out upon the right held by Jonathan Scudder, is sold. I likewise order a certain lot of upland and meadow, that my husband bought of Oakley upon Santipague, to be sold, and all my other lands, cattle and sheep, and my negro woman named Rachel. One-fourth part of the proceeds in the eastern purchase to be equally divided between the children of my daughter, Margaret Allen. The rest unto my two daughters, Hannah Brush, the wife of John Brush, and Mary Close, the wife of the Rev. John Close, in equal shares. I make Captain John Wickes, Joseph Lewis, and John Brush, executors.

Witnesses, John Brush, Sr., Moses Rolph, yeoman, David Ruseo, yeoman. Proved, May 12, 1781.

Page 408.—In the name of God, Amen. I, JOSEPH COLES, of Oysterbay, Queens County, yeoman, being in good health and perfect memory, do this twelfth of January, 1780, make this will and testament. I leave to my beloved wife, Freelove Coles, one-third part of the incomes of the whole estate during her widowhood; and the best room in the house and the benefit of the household furniture, one horse and chair. All my debts and funeral charges to be paid. Unto my son Stephen, £110; to my daughter, Achsah Craft, £50; to my daughter, Elizabeth Feeks, £50; to my daughter, Anne Mott, £50; unto my daughter, Zipporah Coles, £50, and then as much more as to make her equal with the rest of her sisters in the outset and privileges in the house. Unto my daughter, Sarah Willis, £50. Unto my son, Robert Coles, one equal half of my fast estate; unto my son, Jesse Coles, the other half of it. If Jesse dies without any heir, then his estate to be divided equally between Stephen and Robert Coles. If my daughter Zipporah dies without an heir, then her estate to be divided equally between her sisters. I make my three sons, Stephen, Robert, and Jesse, my sole executors.

Witnesses, Daniel Albertson, David Doty, Caleb Cole. Proved, December 31, 1781.

Page 409.—Know all men by these Presents that I, Thomas Powell, in the Township of Hempstead in Queens County on Nassau Island, being this twenty-eighth day of the sixth month, 1781, very poorly in body, but of perfect mind and understanding. My just debts to be fully paid. I leave to my dearly beloved wife, Sarah, £100 and one silver tankard before any division be made out of my estate. Unto my daughter, Mary Powell, £60 and one good bed and furniture; when she comes of age, or day of marriage. The remainder of my estate, both real and personal, to be equally divided between my wife Sarah, and my sons, viz: Solomon, Samuel, Thomas, Richardson, David, and James Powell when they come of age. My children to have learning given to them at the discretion of my executors, and such trades as may appear best for them to learn. My wife and children (that arrive at age) to pay the schooling of my younger children. If my lands be sold, the executors are to pay the charges of schooling out of the legacies, but to be sure-minded that the division be as above directed in every part thereof. I make my brother, Stephen Powell, and my friend, Samuel Way, with my well-beloved wife, Sarah Powell, executors. But before I conclude, notwithstanding what is above written, I give to my son Thomas, one young sucking colt, before any division be made of my estate.

Witnesses, Mary Post, Sarah Hutchens, Henry Post, yeoman. Proved, December 21, 1781.

Page 410.—In the name of God, Amen. This twenty-sixth day of November, 1781, I, THOMAS BEADLE, of Hempstead Harbour in Queens County, being sick and weak in body. All my just debts and funeral charges be paid out of my moveable estate. I leave to William Beadle, my son, so called, five shillings. To my son Thomas all my real estate. All the remaining part I give to my wife and my daughters, Catherine and Mary, to be equally divided. I make my friends, Timothy Smith, Esq., and William Valentine, both of Hempstead Harbour, executors.

Witnesses, Charles Titus, yeoman; Susanna Titus, George Weeks. Proved, January 9, 1782,

Page 412.—In the name of God, Amen. I, WILLIAM SMITH, of Hempstead in Queens County, being sick and weak in body. All my fast estate, houses, land and meadow, to be sold the next spring. Likewise all my moveable estate, both within doors and without, except that shall hereafter be mentioned. All my lawful debts and expenses to be paid. I leave to my well-beloved wife Mary, £130; likewise, two cows, one horse, one cupboard, two beds and furniture, one table, two pewter platters, six pewter plates, six knives and forks, six chairs, my looking glass, two iron pots, one trammel, one tea-kettle, two keelers, one piggen; also my negro girl Sal, so long as she shall remain my widow. Unto my children all the remainder of my estate equally among them; my wearing apparel also, in like manner to be shared. My executors to put my children to trades as soon as they shall come to sufficient age. My father to take my son Jacob and bring him up until he shall be old enough to put to a trade. I make my brother, Isaac Smith, my brothers-in-law, Thomas Dorlon and John Pettit, executors.

Dated October 17, 1781. Witnesses, William Stilwell, Peter Thomas, Abel Southard. Proved, December 22, 1781.

Page 413.—DERICK ALBERTSON, of Mosquito Cove in Township of Oysterbay in Queens County, being advanced in years and under infirmity of body. All my just debts be paid. I leave my son Derick, £20; and to each of my daughters, viz.: Anna, and Mary, and my granddaughter, Mary Golding, each 40 shillings. Unto my son Daniel all my personal estate, provided he pay yearly to my wife the sum of £4 during her life, and maintain her, and my son John, comfortably during their lives, I make my sons Derick and Daniel Albertson, my wife Rebecca, and my neighbour, Charles Valentine, executors.

Dated July 17, 1781.

Added before execution.—Notwithstanding what has been done, my wife to have all the indoor moveables at her own disposal.

Witnesses, Obadiah Lawrence, Albert Albertson, Thorn Goldin. Proved, December 31, 1781.

Page 414.—In the name of God, Amen. I, WILLIAM HEWLETT, of the Township of Hempstead in Queens County, being weak in body. My executors to sell and dispose of all my real estate (except land and meadow at Near Rockway, laying the west side of the road that leads through the same), and pay all my just debts and funeral charges. I leave to my loving wife Phebe, all my moveables within doors and out, in lieu of her dower. Unto my sons Isaac and Samuel, and the child my wife is now pregnant with (if a son), my land and meadow above mentioned, equally to be divided between them, when my youngest son shall arrive at the age of twenty-one years. Unto my daughters, Rosannah and Hannah, and the child my wife is now pregnant with (if a daughter), the sum of £200 apiece; to be paid when they arrive to the age of eighteen years. Unto my sons, all the residue of my estate, equally between them. My wife to have the use or interest money of all children's parts or portions during their non-age for their maintenance and bringing

up. I make my brother, Richard Hewlett, Benjamin
Hewlett, Jr., and Samuel Way, all of the Township
and County aforesaid, executors.

Dated August 31, 1781. Witnesses, Samuel Townsend, yeoman, Oliver Willis, James Cornwell, yeoman.
Proved, December 21, 1781.

Page 416.—In the name of God, Amen. I, RICHARD
LAWRENCE, of New Town in Queens County, gentleman,
being sick and weak in body. I leave to my dearly
beloved wife Amy, £450, and my negro girl named
Phillis, my best bed and furniture, including three pair
sheets, and three pair pillow-cases, half a dozen fiddle
back chairs, half a dozen silver table and half a dozen
tea spoons. All to be in lieu of her dower. Unto my
brother, Samuel Lawrence, £7 a year; to be paid to
him by my executors yearly during his natural life.
All the remainder of my estate, both real and personal,
to be disposed of either at publick vendue or otherwise.
The proceeds to all the children of my brothers Joseph,
William, Thomas, Jonathan, and Daniel Lawrence, and
to the children of my sister, Anna Sackett, equally to
be divided. I make my brothers, William and Thomas
Lawrence, executors.

Dated December 15, 1780. Witnesses, Hendrick
Suydam, Richard Betts, Robert Hinchman.

Codicil. September 24. 1781. Whereas, I have given
unto Amy, my wife, £450, my executors are to pay her
instead £500. I leave to Melancton Lawrence, son of
Elizabeth Fowler, £200. All my negro slaves, ordered
to be sold, shall have a reasonable time to look out for
their own masters. In case my negro girl named Phillis, given to my wife, shall die with her present illness,
in lieu of her, I give to my wife my negro girl named
Mary. Unto my brother, William Lawrence, my lot
of land lying adjoining to the land of David Provoost
and Capt. Samuel Hallett, and the road leading
from New Town to Hallett's Cove, containing ten
acres, more or less, upon condition, that he pay to

my brother Thomas, for the use of my estate, £20 per acre.

Witnesses, Hendrick Suydam, yeoman; Richard Betts, Jacob Hewlett. Proved, December 24, 1781.

Page 418.—In the name of God, Amen. I, JOHN BELL, of the City of New York, carpenter and joiner, being aged, sick and weak in body, but of sound mind, do this twenty-fifth day of June, 1762, make this will and testament. My executors to pay my just debts and funeral charges out of my personal estate. I leave to my granddaughter, Elizabeth Rowe, of said City, spinster, all my messuages, lands, tenements, and hereditaments; also the remainder of my personal estate, upon condition that she shall cloathe, maintain and take good and proper care of my beloved wife Elizabeth, for and during the term of her natural life. I make my trusty friends, Abraham Anthony, ship carpenter; Thomas Brookman, and Elizabeth Rowe, executors.

Witnesses, Susanna Boskark, John Norris, Charles Morse, scrivener. Proved, October 11, 1775.

Page 420.—Know all men by these Presents that I, ELIAS DOUGHTY, of Flushing in Queens County on Nassau Island, yeoman, being this twenty-third day of January, 1764, well in health of body and mind. I devise all my land and rites to lands, houses, buildings, and improvements, and all my moveable estate, (except what is hereafter willed away), to be sold. I leave to my son Jacob, £50, to be paid at the discretion of my executors, and if my executors don't think proper to pay it unto Jacob, what remains shall be paid unto his children as they come of age. Unto my son William, £50; payable at the discretion of my executors; and if they don't think proper to pay it unto William, then it shall be paid unto his children as they come of age. Unto my two grandchildren, Mary and Sarah Doughty, daughters of my daughter Mary, deceased,

£20 each. Unto my sons, John, Charles, and Timothy
Doughty, and daughter, Sarah Doughty, all my estate
to be equally divided. Unto daughter Sarah, the two
best beds and furniture, and all my linen, my riding
chair, and large brass kettle, half dozen new pewter
plates, notwithstanding I have ordered all my estate
to be sold; my daughter Sarah shall have the things
mentioned, over and above her equal part, with the
deduction of £100 for a negro boy Ceasar, which I have
already given her. I make my sons, John, Charles,
and Timothy Doughty, executors.

Witnesses, Jan Hageman, Benjamin Hageman, yeoman, Gilbert Clement, yeoman. Proved, May 13, 1777.

Page 422.—In the name of God, Amen. I, HENRY
HARRISS, of the Town of Southampton in the County
of Suffolk, husbandman, being in health of body and
of sound mind and memory. All my just debts shall
be truly paid out of my moveable estate. I leave to my
loving wife Lydia, one-third part of all my moveable
estate. Unto my son George, the house, barn, and
home-lot where he now liveth; also, that piece of land
called the old " Pitte," which was formerly Joseph
Lupton's; also, a piece of land on Cow Neck, containing about fifteen acres, called the Indian Hedge; also,
one-half of a lot of woodland joining to Mattuck
Swamp; also, one-half fifty right of land in the lot
No. 44 in the Great North Division; also a piece of land
lying adjoining to the Fish Cove, which I bought of
Jackson Scott, containing about five acres; also, that
piece of land and meadow called Mitchel's meadow;
also, that piece of meadow called Indian Hedge
meadow; and that piece of sedge meadow called Cedar
Point; also, one-third part of all my woodland lying in
the Great South Division. Unto my son Henry, my
new dwelling house, barn and home lots; bounded north
by Joseph Rugg; east by the highway; south by David
Rose; and west by Joseph Ruggand, the lands of
Thomas Jennings, deceased; also, that piece of land

and meadow called the Swamp Pitte; also, a piece of
land and meadow lying on Cow Neck, containing ten
acres, which was formerly Samuel Clark's; also, a piece
of land on Cow-neck, lying by the west side swamp;
also, a piece of land and meadow lying at Cow-neck
Gate, called by the name of "the nearest way meadow"; also, that piece of land lying at the clay pits,
which was formerly Joseph Lupton's; also, a piece of
woodland adjoining to William Jones's land at the
fresh pond; also, one-half fifty right of land in the
lot No. 44 in the Great North Division; also one-third
part of all my woodland lying in the Great South Division; and one-half fifty right of commonage running
throughout, the Town Quogue purchase excepted. Unto my son Daniel, all my lands and meadows that I
have at the place called Little Noyack, running up
southward to a ditch called Randals Ditch; also, that
piece of land which I bought of Benjamin Foster, adjoining to Joseph Post on the west; also, one-half of
my right of woodland in the Lot No. 47 in the Great
North Division; also, one-half fifty right of commonage running throughout, the Town Quogue purchase excepted. Unto my three sons, John, George,
and Henry, one fifty and a half right of commonage within the north sea-line; also, one-half lot of
woodland within said line; to be equally divided between them; that half lot of land lying the eastward
of David Haines Forster's. The remainder of my
moveable estate to be equally divided among all my
five sons and three daughters. I make my son John
and my friend, Stephen Rogers, executors.

Dated December 23, 1769. Signed, Henry Haris.
Witnesses, Timothy Peirson, yeoman, Elias Cooper,
Abraham Fordham. Proved, December 10, 1781.

Page 424.—I, ELBERT HOOGLAND, of Flushing in
Queens County on Nassau Island, yeoman, being weak
of body, but of sound mind this thirteenth day of
March, 1780, make this will and testament. All my

just debts, with my funeral expenses to be paid. I
leave to my well beloved wife Catlinetie, £25 to be paid
yearly during her lifetime. Unto my wife, my best
bed and furniture, my cupboard, best dining table,
arm chair, half a dozen of my best other chairs, my
tea kettle and all my china ware, best looking glass,
riding chair, and a horse fit to draw the same; all
which said money and moveables to my wife, " Together my Beaufat," to be at her own absolute disposal, and in lieu of her Dower. I also allow my wife
the use of my best room in my house, during the time
she remains my widow. My son Elbert shall provide
for my wife, bread and meat and all other necessaries
that shall be judged reasonable and necessary for her
to keep house with by herself, if she shall choose it,
during her widowhood. Unto my son Elbert, all my
real estate, together with the remaining part of my
moveable estate, on his paying all legacies. Unto my
daughter, Phebe Monfort, £200. Unto my granddaughter, Catlinetie Schenk, (daughter of my son Cornelius,
deceased), £100. I have heretofore given to my son
John, deceased, in houses, cattle and other things, to
the value of £50, and also £300 in money; I do now
further hereby leave to my granddaughter Catharine,
daughter of my son John, deceased, £50; to be paid
when she shall arrive to the age of twenty-one years.
Unto my granddaughter Elizabeth, the daughter of
my son John, deceased, £100; to be paid in like manner. I make my well beloved wife Catlinetie, and my
son Elbert, executors.

Witnesses, Cornelius Rierson, Joseph Willis, Frederic Jahn, all of Queens County, yeomen. Proved,
November 9, 1781.

Page 426.—In the name of God, Amen. I, SARAH
HORSFIELD, of Jamaica in Queens County, widow, being sick and weak in body . My executors to pay and
satisfy all my just debts and funeral expenses. To my
daughter, Elizabeth Willett, my best bed and furni-

ture; all my wearing apparel and wrought plate. To
my son, Benjamin Whitehead, my next best bed and
furniture and £30. The remainder of my estate to
my daughter, Elizabeth Willitts, and my son, Benjamin
Whitehead; to be equally divided between them. My
executors to sell all such my estate as is not herein
before given away; the proceeds, together with all
other money, to be paid out to interest for the use of
my daughter and son, and paid to them as they respectively arrive to lawful age, or marry. I make my
brothers-in-law, Thomas Horsfield and Samuel Skidmore, and my nephew, Whitehead Cornell, of Rockway, executors.

Dated April 29, 1781. Witnesses, Abigail Cornwall,
Robert Hinchman, scrivener. Proved, November 3,
1781.

Page 427.—I, SAMUEL DENTON, of Jamaica in
Queens County, yeoman, being very weak and low in
body, but of sound mind, this ninth day of October,
1776, make this will. My just debts, and funeral
charges to be paid. I leave to Martha, my dearly beloved wife, £50, my best bed and furniture and two
cows, as also the pasture and fodder for said cows, for
so long a time as she shall continue my widow; also,
the use and choice of one of the rooms in my new dwelling house, as also bread, corn, and fireing wood sufficient for the said room; all to be provided and sup-
plied to her by my son Nathaniel for so long a time as
until my son Samuel shall arrive to lawful age, and
then by my two sons equally between them. Unto my
two daughters at " Gotion," Catherine, the now wife of
Henry Smith, and Phebe, the now wife of Abel Gale,
each five and thirty Pounds; to my other two daughters, Martha and Hannah, a hundred Pounds and all
my indoor moveables to be equally divided between
my wife and my two daughters last named. All the remaining part of my estate to my two sons, Nathaniel
and Samuel, except thirty pounds in money I give to

my son Nathaniel. I make Martha, my wife, my two sons, Nathaniel and Samuel, and my daughter Martha, executors.

Witnesses, Joshua Carpenter, yeoman, Obadiah Mills, Daniel Smith, yeoman. Proved, February 27, 1780.

Page 429.—In the name of God, Amen. I, JOHN WALKER, of His Majesty's ship *Carisfort*, mariner, being of sound mind and memory. After all my just debts be paid and discharged, I leave to my friend, John Jack, belonging to His Majesty's ship *Centurian*, of the Shire of Anguish, North Briton, all wages, sums of money, lands, tenements, goods, and chattels and estate whatsoever as shall be any ways due me. I make my friend, John Jack, my only and sole executor.

Dated January 11, 1782. Witnesses, Jno. Lawrence, surgeon; William Johnstone, of the City of New York, cordwainer; Thomas Cantillon. Proved, February 18, 1782.

Page 430.—In the name of God, Amen. The seventeenth day of February, 1781. I, EFFEE VAN VARICK, of the city of New [York], widow, being sick in body. All my just debts and funeral expenses be paid and discharged by my executors. They, as soon as convenient after my decease, to sell all my real estate at public vendue or otherwise, the proceeds therefrom, together with all my personal estate, I leave in manner following; one-third to my daughter, Effee Stout, wife of John B. Stout, of this city, baker; one-third to my daughter, Dinah Periam, wife of Thomas Periam, of said city, mariner; the remaining third to the children of my son, James Van Varick, deceased, to be equally divided between them; their share to be put at interest upon good land security, until he or she shall arrive to the age of twenty-one years, or marriage. I make my sons-in-law, John B. Stout, and Thomas Periam, and my nephew, John Walter, house carpenter, executors.

Witnesses, Jacob Durye, Andrew Ricker, Peter Thompson, bricklayer. Proved, February 18, 1782.

Page 432.—In the name of God, Amen. I, JACOB COLE, of Staten Island in the County of Richmond, being weak in body. My executors to take so much of my moveable estate as shall discharge all my just debts and funeral expenses; also, to take the sum of £25, and keep and apply it for the best use of my son David; it being a legacy given him by his uncle, David Cole. All the residue of my estate, both real and personal, I leave to my beloved wife Anne during her widowhood, upon condition she brings up my children. But if she marry, then my executors are to sell the whole of my estate, real and personal, at vendue or otherways and the proceeds to be equally divided, between my wife and five sons, John, Cornelius, David, William, and Jacob Cole. If my wife marry, my executors to take that part of my estate which falls to the children, and out of the same to support them so long as the youngest is no longer chargeable to my estate. I make my brother, Cornelius Cole, and William Lakarman, my brother-in-law, executors, and my loving wife Anne, executrix.

Dated October 28, 1781. Witnesses, Ephraim Johnson, Abraham Cole, Isaac Dooty. Proved, February 21, 1782.

Page 433.—I, CHRISTIAN JACOBSON, on Staten Island, the County of Richmond, being in good health and of sound mind, this fourth day of January, 1782, ordain this will and testament. I leave to my loving wife, Ann Jacobson, my house I now live in, with all the land now in my possession, and also my negroes, live stock, farming utensils, household furniture (except such articles as are given to each of my children); as

long as she remains my widow. After her death to go
to my son, John B. Jacobson. Unto my daughter Catharine, £1050; to my daughter Elizabeth, £1000; to be
paid to them when they come to age of twenty-one
years; or till then, so much of the interest as is necessary for their bringing up. To my son John the sum
of £400; to be paid when he is of age; till then to
have his maintenance on the place. To my loving wife
Ann, the sum of £600, in lieu of dower in case she
should marry again. I give to the Brethren's Church
on Staten Island, £20 and to the Reverend Mr. Gam-
bold, £10, also to him £20 for the use of the Mission-
aries amongst the Indians. The rest of my money
after the foregoing legacies are paid shall be divided
in equal shares between my wife and children. To my
son John, all my wearing apparel, my horse, clock, and
watch; to my daughter Catharine, my silver tea pot
and six silver table spoons; to my daughter Elizabeth,
my silver tankard and my little negro wench Suck, and
also one good feather bed with furniture. I make my
wife Ann, my brother-in-law, Cornelius Vandeventer,
and my good friends, Cornelius Cortelyou and Lewis
Ryersz, executors.

Witnesses, Catharine Ryersz, Richard Seaman,
Samuel Woodward. Proved, February 20, 1782.

Page 435.—In the name of God, Amen. I, ANN
VANHORN, of the County of Richmond, being weak in
body, doth this fourth day of February, 1774, make
this my only last will. I leave to my brother Hendrick
Demott's daughter Margaret, £25 (living in Morris
County and Province of East New Jersey). To the
eldest daughter of my brother-in-law, John and Mary
Van Wagenin, whose name is Margaret, £25, to the
second oldest daughter of the aforesaid, whose name is
Ann, all the remaining part of my estate. If she
should die without issue, then that part of my estate
shall be divided equally among the surviving children
of my aforesaid brother-in-law and Mary his wife. I

make my loving brother-in-law, John Van Wagenin, and Mary his wife, together with my trusty friend, Jacob Freeland, executors.

Witnesses, John Jacks, Anthony Fountain, yeoman, Vincent Fountain. Proved, February 21, 1782.

Page 436.—In the name of God, Amen. The twenty-fourth day of April, 1781, I, GABBIT COSINE, of the County of Richmond, yeoman, being weak in body. All my just and honest debts and funeral charges to be paid. I leave to my two sons, Jacob and Cornelius Cosine, a certain piece or parcel of land lying and being on Long Island at New Lots in Kings County, now in the possession of the said Cornelius Cosine, to be equally divided between them. Also, to my son Jacob, £3 in consideration of his being my eldest son. To my son James, £90. To my son Wilhelmes, £100. To my two sons, James and Wilhelmes, all my Farmer utensils of all kinds; also, all my cattle, horses, sheep and hogs, to be equally divided between them. To my son James, my brass " cittle," but order that he shall pay to my daughter, Altie Dougan, 40 shillings in lieu of the said cittle. To my daughter Altie, one pewter platter and three pewter plates. All my estate, real and personal, to be sold at publick auction or vendue at the expiration of one year after my decease. After all my estate shall be turned into cash the residue, after paying debts, shall be equally divided between all my children, viz: Jacob, Cornelius, James, Wilhelmes Cosine; Affie, wife of John Blaw; Altie, wife of Cornelius Dougan. My executors to deduct £33 out of the share of Affie, wife of John Blaw, in lieu of money as I have paid for her. My executors to retain in their hands the portions of my two daughters, Affie and Altie, and not pay their husbands, but distribute to my daughters as they shall have need or occasion for the support of nature; if their husbands shall die, my daughters to receive their remainder in full immediately. I make my dearly beloved sons Jacob, Cornelius, James and Wilhelmes, executors. Signed, Garret Cosyne.

Witnesses, Peter Houseman, William Kingston, yeoman, John Houseman.

Dated February 20, 1782.

Page 438.—In the name of God, Amen. The 27th day of November, 1781. I, BARNT SLEIGHT, of the County of Richmond, yeoman, being at this time very weak and low in body, but of sound mind. All my just debts and funeral charges to be paid. I leave to Elizabeth, my beloved wife, all my lands and all my stock of horses and cattle that is on my farm and my farmer's utensils and everything that belongs to me, so long as she remains my widow. If my wife marry then my three sons, Henry, Jacob and Barnt, should divide my estate equally between them, excepting Henry to have £5 more, and they to pay unto my wife £40 instead of her Right of Dower. My three sons each to have a negro boy; but not to be in their possession while my wife remains my widow. I make Elizabeth, my wife, and my son Henry, and my brother-in-law, James Seguine, all of the County of Richmond, executors.

Witnesses, Joshua Wright, yeoman, John Cole, Daniel Peatman, yeoman. Proved, February 21, 1782.

Page 440.—In the name of God, Amen. I, JOHN BURN, mate of the Brigantine *Nancy*, a Navy victualer, at present about to sail for Great Britain, being of sound mind and memory. After all my just debts be paid I leave to my loving friend, John Henderson, King's Pilot for the Harbour of New York, dwelling in New York, all my effects, real and personal. I make the said John Henderson, executor.

Witnesses, Daniel Wardrop, Wm. Glassell, at present of the City of New York, gentleman. Proved, February 27, 1782.

Page 441.—In the name of God, Amen. I, JOHN
SLOAN, being of sound mind and memory. After all
my just debts be paid, I leave to my brother, William
Sloan, baker, near Bow Church Yard, London, all
wages, debts, sums of money, goods and chattels, and
estate whatsoever. I make Thomas Clousedale, of New
York, trader, executor.

Dated August 10, 1779. Witnesses, James Fore-
man, Ranald McDonald, mariner. Proved, February
18, 1782.

Page 443.—In the name of God, Amen. I, THEO-
DORUS POLHEMUS, of Bushwick, in Kings County, being
sick and weak in body, but of sound mind and memory. All just debts and funeral charges to be paid
out of my moveable estate. I leave to my beloved
wife, in whom I am well pleased, £300; also my negro
woman named Peg, my riding chair, and the use of a
horse when she shall have occasion, and the use of two
of my milch cows and pasture and fodder for them,
which horse and two cows my two sons, Theodorus
and Jacob, are to find her during widowhood. I also
order my two sons, Theodorus and Jacob, to find my
wife and her family, grain sufficient and also beef and
pork and other vegetables for her family during her
widowhood; also, the use of my west dwelling room
and one of the rooms adjoining to it, and the use of
the kitchen, and also firewood delivered at the door;
as much of my household furniture as she shall have
occasion of. Unto my son Abraham, my house and lot
of ground and all the tenements thereon, situate in
the City of New York, which I bought of William
Taylor, also £300. Unto my sons, Theodorus and
Jacob, all my farm-house and tenements, which I have
in Bushwick, also the remaining part of my moveable estate to be equally divided between them. To
my son Jores, £600, which sum my executors are to
retain and keep in their hands for the use and support
of my son Jores during his life. After his death, what

is remaining of it, (if he should die without issue), is to be equally divided among my children. Unto my daughter Geartry, widow of Paul Vandervoort, £500. In case of her death before that time, to be paid to her children when of age. Unto my daughter Altje, £500; also, the sum of £60. If she dies then to her children. Also to her my negro girl named Dinah. Unto Altje Rapelye, daughter of John Rapelye, deceased, £40. Whereas, I have bought a house and lot of ground, situate in the City of New York, in Ferry Street, whereon I have paid £120, (the Title being vested in me), whenever my wife's sister, Mary Bloodgood, shall repay the £120 to my two sons, Theodorus and Jacob, then my executors are to give a deed to Mary Bloodgood, or to her executors, for the use of her children. I make my three sons, Abraham, Theodorus, and Jacob Polhemus, executors.

Dated December 23, 1781. Witnesses, Joost Durye, of Kings County, yeoman; John De Voo, Abraham Schenk, of Kings County, yeoman. Proved, March 4, 1782.

Page 446.—In the name of God, Amen. I, PAUL VANDERVOORT, of Bushwick, in Kings County, carpenter, being in good health of body and of sound mind. All my just debts to be paid and funeral expenses out of my moveable estate. I leave to my dear and loving wife Charity, with whom I am well pleased, and children named Peter, Antie, Elizabeth, Lettie, Paul, Matje, and my daughter Charity, all my real and personal estate to be equally divided amongst them after my wife's death or remarriage. Should my widow die or remarry, all my real and personal estate to be disposed of within two months, either at private sale or public vendue. Before any division is made I give £25 to my son Peter; my wearing apparel to be equally divided to my sons Peter and Paul; the residue of the estate to be divided as aforesaid. Should any of my children, after such division is made, die under age and without lawful issue, then their share to be my two sons', Peter and Paul. I make my dear and loving wife Charity, and my brothers-in-law, Abraham Polhemus, Theodorus Polhemus and Jacob Polhemus, to be executors.

Dated December 5, 1781. Witnesses, Burger Vandewater, cordwainer, Lettie Polhemus, Theodorus Colyer. Proved, March 4, 1782.

Page 448.—In the name of God, Amen. I, WILLIAM BOWNASS, Matross in the Royal Regiment of Artillery, being of sound mind and memory. All just debts to be paid. I give to my beloved wife Martha, all my real and personal estate. I make my wife and my worthy friend, Lieut. John Cockburn, of the Royal Regiment of Artillery, executors.

Dated December 4, 1780. Witnessed in the City of New York where no stamps are used. Peter Clopper, John L. C. Roome, Public Notary, Edward Greswold. Proved, March 5, 1782.

Page 449.—In the name of God, Amen. January the 13th day, 1779. I, BENJAMIN BARKER, of Hempstead in Queens County in Nassau Island, yeoman, being in good health and of sound mind and memory. My just debts and funeral charges to be first satisfied. I leave to my loving daughter, Catharn Laranace, wife of Edward Laranace, five shillings; to my loving daughter, Margaret Stuart, wife of John Stuart, five shillings; to my loving son, Samuel Barker, £5. All estate not given away in this will, such as horses, cattle, swine, beds and bedding, pewter, I give to my well-beloved wife Hannah. In case of her second marriage or death, what remains of my estate in her hands I leave to my two sons, John and William, equally. I make my friends, Samuel Pettit, Jr., and Christian Snetecor, executors.

Witnesses, James Wood, yeoman, Elijah Wood, yeoman, Harry Shaw. Proved, February 18, 1782.

Page 451.—In the name of God, Amen. I, JOSEPH REEVE, of the Town of Southold in the County of Suffolk, yeoman, being in a tolerable state of health and of perfect mind and memory. I give to my beloved wife, Bethiah Reeve, the privileges of one-half the rooms in my dwelling house that she may choose; to live in and to use as she thinks proper during the term of her natural life. Also, I give her yearly twelve bushels of wheat; ten bushels of Indian corn; thirty pounds of flax; one hundred-weight of beef; fifty weight of pork; twenty pounds of tallow; eight pounds of wool; ten pounds of hog's fat; her fire-wood, cut and carted, as much as she needs for fuel; two cows, which are to be kept for her, summer and winter; to be paid to her by my son James. I leave my wife all my household goods and £40 and a garden. To my daughter, Bethiah Conkling, £100; to my granddaughter, Elizabeth Reeve, £40; to my granddaughter, Sarah Conkling, £40; to my granddaughter, Wate Woodhull, £40. What my wife leaves after her decease shall be equally divided betwixt my granddaughters. I leave to my grandson, Ezra Woodhull, my rights in Indian Necks, so called in Southold, both lands and meadows; also, my rights in the common creek. To my son James, all the residue of my lands and meadows during the term of his natural life. Should he leave no son, then such residue shall be for my grandson, Ezra Woodhull. To my said son, James, all my farming tackling. The remainder of my personal estate I leave to my five grandchildren: Joseph, Benjamin, Zebulon, James, and Thomas Woodhull, to be equally divided betwixt them. All bequests to my grandchildren to be paid when they are twenty-one years of age. My negroes to have the choice of their masters without regard to the price. I make Zebulon Woodhull and Daniel Osborn, executors; and authorize my executors to sell my part of the wind-mill; the proceeds to be paid to my said grandson Ezra.

Dated January 12, 1782. Witnesses, Jeremiah Reeve, Mary Osborn, Mehetable Hornton. Proved, February 8, 1782.

Page 452.—In the name of God, Amen. I, SETH WORTH, of the Town of Southold in the County of Suffolk, yeoman, being weak in body, but of perfect mind and memory. My just debts and funeral expenses being paid I give to my daughter Abigail, my best and poorest bed with the bedding thereto belonging, my desk, my mother's wearing apparel, my hand irons, fire tongs and shovel and all my pewter. To my daughter Phebe, one bed and bedding, six pint-bowls, one two-quart one, one quart and pint glasses. To my daughter Anna, one bed and bedding, her mother's snuff-box, and ivory salt-cellar dyed red, the table-cloths, napkins, and other cloths not already given away. To my son Laban, all my wearing apparel, and carpenter's tools and oil-stone. To my son Seth all my books. To my son Stephen, £30. My sons to be bound out to learn trades, at the discretion of my executors, on arriving at suitable ages. My two youngest daughters to have schooling at the discretion of my executors. As much leather to be reserved for shoeing my children as my executors shall think proper. Also a piece of Rusha sheeting and a piece of red flannel to be reserved for clothing for the children. I leave to my six children: Abigail, Phebe, Anna, Laban, Seth, and Stephen, the whole of my estate not heretofore given away, to be equally divided betwixt them, the farm on which I now live, its appurtenances, my stock and moveables to be sold for this purpose. I make my daughter Abigail, my two brothers, Jonathan and Paul, Messrs. John Corwin and Thomas Wines, executors.

Dated March 19, 1781. Witnesses, Daniel Osborn, yeoman, John Case, yeoman, Mary Harvey, spinstress. Proved, January 10, 1782.

Page 454.—In the name of God, Amen. I, Timothy Wells, of Southold in the County of Suffolk, yeoman, being of sound mind and memory. All my lands, meadows, and buildings that I bought of Micah Wells and Jeremiah Wells shall be sold by my executors and my eldest son Timothy shall give a title for them when he is twenty-one years. My just debts and funeral expenses to be paid out of the price of the said lands; my son Timothy to have the remainder. I leave to my second son, Richard, the worth or value of £200 on attaining his majority. To my two sons, Richard and Elijah, my desk cabinet, concordance, and Great Bible, equally between them, on coming to majority. Should both die in non-age then my daughter, Deborah Wells, shall have £50 and the rest to my son Timothy. My two youngest sons, Richard and Elijah, shall be brought up to trades, and that what necessary charge there shall be to bring them to trades and learn them to write and cipher to ye Rule of Three, shall be paid out of the use of my lands and meadows. Anna Moor shall have the same privilege in my house and estate, as she has now, so long as she lives. I leave my daughter Deborah the use of my weaving shop so long as she shall live single; and also the use of back room and bed room; a privilege in kitchen and cellar so long as she shall live single after her mother's death. To my daughter Deborah, my loom, working bars, with all the implements belonging to them; moreover, an equal half part of all my whole moveable estate, not yet given away, (excepting my clothes, which I give to my well-beloved wife Martha and one ox called Bell, my yearling colt, and out-doors husbandry implements which I give to my son Timothy). To my wife Martha, all my weaving clothes and the other half of my moveable estate. To my eldest son Timothy all that shall remain of my estate.

Dated April 30, 1774. Witnesses, Israel Reeve, Nathan Goldsmith, Gershom Terry, yeomen; all of said County. Proved, January 28, 1782.

Page 456.—In the name of God, Amen. January the third day, 1774. I, NATHANIEL WELLS, of Southold in the County of Suffolk, yeoman, being of sound mind. After my just debts and funeral expenses are paid I leave to my eldest son James £5, to my second son Manly, all lands and meadows in Southold, with all the buildings and orchards thereon; also my husbandry implements of every kind. My well-beloved wife Mary shall have the use of the remainder of my moveable estate during her life for her comfortable support. After she shall have done with it, then to my three daughters, Mary Wells, Bethiah Luce, and Sarah Downes. I make my son Manly and my wife executors.

Witnesses, David Wells, Gershom Corwin, Timothy Wells, yeomen, all of said County. Proved, December 26, 1781.

Page 458.—In the name of God, Amen. I, WILLIAM DOWNS, of Southold, in the County of Suffolk, yeoman, being weak in body, but of sound mind. After my just debts and funeral expenses are paid, I leave to my eldest son, William, all my lands which my father purchased of Richard Sweasy, Jr.; and all my lands lying between the said lands and the North Road; also one-half of all my meadows lying northward of the neck called Little Neck. I leave to my second son, Nathaniel, that part of my lands lying northward of the North Road, bounded as follows: South by the Highway, west by the land of Samuel Wells, north by the Sound, and east by the land of Daniel Terry. Also, my meadow lying in Saw Mill Brook Neck, that I lately purchased of William Hallock. I leave to my third son, Benjamin, all my lands that I lately purchased of Colonel Phineas Fanning, lying northward of the North Road; also my part of Indian Island, so called, land and meadow; also my little island lying in the River. I leave to my fourth son, John, all the rest of my lands, meadows, and buildings not yet mentioned, except the land lying at the Batin Hallows that I lately purchased of

James Downs; which land my executors are to sell, if need be, to pay my debts. I leave to my two daughters, Anna and Sarah Downs, £100, when eighteen. Also two cows and calves, six ewes and lambs, to each of them. To my well-beloved wife, Sarah, two cows and calves, five ewes and lambs, with all the household goods she brought to me. Also, the negro girl. I make my trusty friend, Daniel Wells, and my brother-in-law, Manly Wells, executors.

Dated August 22, 1781. Witnesses, Joshua Corwin, Jr., Jonathan Raynor, yeomen, Temperance Corwin, spinstress. Proved, January 3, 1782.

Page 459.—In the name of God, Amen. April, the twenty-ninth day, 1774. I, JOSHUA WOOD, of the Township of Hunting and County of Suffolk on Nassau Island, being in health of body. My just debts to be paid. I leave to my well-beloved wife Ruth the use of all my land and meadow, buildings, negroes, and farming tackle until my son Selah arrive to age, and all my cattle for the bringing up of my children; and all my household goods; after that to have the use of one-third part of all my lands and meadows, two cows, one horse, and riding " cheir " and that part of my house, cellar, and barn, she pleases, so long as she remains my widow. Should she marry, she is to have the one-half of my household goods and £100. I leave to my son Samuel £200 and one-third of my land and meadow on the south side of this land, one-third of one hundred Right in the Baiting Place purchase, and one hundred Right in the Old Purchase, one-third of all my land in the Baiting Place that is laid out. I leave to my son Selah all my lands and buildings on the north side of this land where I now live, with one-third of my land and meadow on the south side of this land, and one-third of one hundred Right in the Baiting Place purchase, and one-third of the land laid out in that purchase, and the one-half of one hundred Right and a quarter in the Old Purchase. To my son Silas £700 when twenty-one; also, one-third of my land and meadow on the south side of this land, and one-third of one hundred Right in the Baiting Place purchase, and one-third of the land laid out in that purchase, and the one-half of one hundred Right and a quarter in the Old Purchase. The remainder of my moveable estate to my three sons, Samuel, Selah, and Silas. If either of them should die in non-age, then to the surviving brothers. My son Silas should be brought up to Learning, tho' it should take some of his portion, if my executors and Israel Wood shall think it best, whom I choose to be his guardian. I make my son Samuel and my brother, Israel Wood, executors.

Witnesses, Samuel Oakly (tanner), Selah Platt, John Oakley (tanner). Proved, March 11, 1782.

Page 461.—In the name of God, Amen. I, WAIT SMITH, of Jamaica, in Queens County, yeoman, being sick and weak in body. My just debts and funeral charges to be paid. All my estate, real and personal, be sold. I leave to my well-beloved brothers, Nehemiah, Noah, Nicholas, and Jonathan Smith, £10 each; to my well-beloved sisters, Phebe, Everitt, Rachel, wife of Thomas Reade, Priscilla, wife of William Ludlum, Jr., and Mary, wife of Elias Bayles, each £10. To my cousins, John and Nehemiah Bayles, sons of Elias Bayles, and Mary, his wife, each £5. To the Elders and Deacons of the Presbyterian Church and congregation in Jamaica, for the support of the Gospel, £10. To my well-beloved wife Jane all the residue of my estate. I make my wife and my well-beloved friend, Daniel Bayles, executors.

Dated May 29, 1765. Witnesses, Thomas Bayles, Patience Bayles, and Rob't. Hinchman, scrivener. Proved, May 11, 1781.

Page 463.—In the name of God, Amen. I, NATHAN SMITH, of the Town of Flushing, in Queens County, yeoman, being sick and weak of body. My just debts and funeral charges to be paid. I leave to Emelia, my dearly beloved wife, my best bed and furniture, my cup-board, half a dozen of my best chairs, my best looking glass, and as much other household furniture as my executors shall think necessary, for her comfortable keeping house. To my daughters, Elizabeth and Mary, a feather bed and furniture apiece. The remainder of my estate, real and personal, to be sold. My executors to purchase a house and land for the use and support of my wife and children so long as she remains my widow, or until my son Jacob shall arrive at lawful age. I give such houses and lands to my said son Jacob (reserving to my wife Emelia a descent room). To my wife £100 and two cows for the better supporting of herself and children during their non-age. To each of my above-named daughters £100. The remainder I give to my wife and daughters. To my wife a negro man named Low. My son Jacob, when of age, shall allow his mother a peaceable living in his dwelling, and provide her with fuel for her winter's fire as well as hay for her cows. I make my trusty and loving friends, James Mackrell my father-in-law, and Ambrose Fish, and Emelia Smith, my wife, and Samuel Fish, my friends and relations, executors.

Dated January 16, 1782. Witnesses, Herman Clark, yeoman, Benjamin Buckbee, and George Barwick. Proved, February 18, 1782.

Page 465.—In the name of God, Amen. I, JOHN FOSTER, of West Hills, Township of Huntington, and Suffolk County, on Nassau Island, being weak in body. I give to my eldest son Samuel my colt, saddle and bridle, and twenty shillings, when of age, as a birthright. I leave to my well-beloved wife Sarah £100. Should she marry before the children are brought up, then £50. To my wife my roan horse and my large Bible; also the use of two milk cows, as long as she remains my widow. I would have my wife live on my place until Spring, or till the place is sold, with all my personal estate, excepting as much as my wife will necessarily want for the use of the family, and one bed and furniture, and the household goods my wife brought with her. To my four sons, Samuel, John, William, and Henry Foster, £100 apiece, when of age. To my daughter, Glorianna Foster, £50, when eighteen or married. To my second daughter, Elizabeth Foster, £50, when eighteen or married. All debts to be paid after the sale of my estate, and the overplus to be put out at use for the benefit of my family and children underaged. I make my brother-in-law, Richard Wiggins, of Hempstead, and my brother, Henry Foster, and Richard Smith, of the West Hills, executors.

Dated October 10, 1781. Witnesses, Albertus Van De Water and Christian Tobias, both of West Hills, and Theodorus Vanwyck, tanner, of Oyster Bay. Proved, March 16, 1782.

Page 467.—In the name of God, Amen. I, GEORGE MITCHELL, belonging to his Majesty's ship *Iris*, Captain Dawson, commander, being of sound mind and memory. After all my just debts be paid, I give to my friend, William Pye, of his Majesty's ship the *London*, all such sums of money as shall be due me for wages, prize-money, or on any other account; as also my wearing apparel and personal estate. I make my friend, William Pye, executor.

Dated March 4, 1782. Witnesses, Jno. Lawrence, Daniel Cann, James Rippeth, mariner. Proved, March 18, 1782.

Page 468.—I, JOHN FELTHAUSEN, a native of the City of Hamburgh, in the dukedom of Holstein, now an inhabitant of the City of New York, being sick, but of sound mind. My just debts and funeral charges to be paid. I leave to my dearly beloved brother, Daniel Felthausen, £10 for his birthright. To my goddaughter Catherine, my brother Christopher's daughter, £100. Whereas, I have helped to build the meeting-house or church, commonly called the Moravian Meeting in the City of New York, and knowing there is yet some debt on the same, I give, towards discharging the debt, the sum of £200. All the remainder of my estate, real and personal, unto my dearly beloved brothers and sisters, whose names are as follows: Daniel, Henry, Christopher, Andrew, and Peter Felthausen; Margret Beekman, Catherine Seeme. I make my dearly beloved brothers, Henry and Christopher, and the Reverend Gustavus Shewkirk, executors.

Dated February 19, 1782. Witnesses, John Smith, Abraham Warner, and Richard Fletcher, shopkeeper. Proved, March 25, 1782.

Page 470.—In the name of God, Amen. I, HENRY LOWERRE, of Flushing, in Queens County, yeoman, this tenth day of April, 1771, being well in body and of perfect mind and memory. My just debts and funeral charges to be paid. I leave my dearly beloved wife Mary all my household furniture or moveable estate within doors and my best cow; also the benefit of all my dwelling house, a garden, and a yard before the door. Also the privilege of keeping a hog or two, and of raising poultry, as she used to do in my lifetime. Also the privilege of apples, peaches, pears, and of what other fruits there may be, for her own use. All the above privileges, and what I have herein given her shall be in lieu of her dower. To my loving son Thomas my small dwelling house, wherein he now lives, with a piece of land whereon it stands, as will make a half acre. The remaining part of my lands are to be equally divided between two of my loving sons, William and Thomas, and both to have the use of the barn; they to have my dwelling house at the time of my wife's death, or second marriage, upon condition that they pay to each of my son John Lowerre's children, £5, as they become of age, and also all the reversions of my moveable estate. I make my loving wife Mary my executrix, and my loving son Thomas, executor.

Witnesses, Christopher Robert, of New York, gentlemen, Christopher Robert, Jr., John Field, Jr.

Codicil. We give to our son, Henry Lowerre, a certain piece of land lying on the eastermost end of his land, and containing about three acres, being a part of a tract of land which my wife's father, Christopher Hopper, of Flushing, deceased, bequeathed to her.

(Signed)   HENRY LOWERRE.
MARY LOWERRE.

Witnesses, same as above. Proved, March 15, 1782.

Page 473.—In the name of God, Amen. I, ABRAHAM HENDRICKSON, of Jamaica, in Queens County, yeoman, being now far advanced in age, but of sound mind. I leave to Wynche, my dearly beloved wife, the use and profits of all my messuages, tenements, lands, meadows, and real estate, so long as she remains my widow. Also during her life my negro wench named Sarah, and three of my milch cows. At her death to be for my three sons, William, Hendrick, and Isaac. To my wife my best bed and furniture, all my linen, cupboard, warming pan, great chair, and half a dozen common chairs, two pewter platters, half a dozen pewter plates, and two iron pots. All to be in full of her right of dower. The residue of my personal estate to be sold at public vendue, to pay and discharge all my just debts and funeral charges; the overplus, if any, I give to my sons William and Isaac. After the death or remarriage of my wife my son William to have the dwelling house he now lives in and two acres of land adjoining; the land joining to the road, beginning by the land of Nehemiah Everit, then running along the road until it comes to the south side of the garden so as to take in his well; then easterly so far as to contain two acres. To my sons, William and Isaac, all real estate, excepting what I have

given to my son William. In consideration of what I
have above given to my three sons, William, Hendrick,
and Isaac, they shall pay to my son Aaron, £5; to my
son John, £60; to my son Abraham, £40; to my
daughter Altie, the wife of Peter Vangelder, £5;
to my daughter Mercy, the wife of Anthony Vannos-
trant, £5; to my daughter Heliche, £60; and to my
grandson, Simeon Hendrickson, £40. I make my sons,
William, Hendrick, and Isaac, executors.

Dated December 28, 1776. Witnesses, James Everit, Samuel Mills, Barnardus Hendrickson, all of
Queens County, yeomen. Proved, August 10, 1778.

Page 475.—In the name of God, Amen. I, NICHOLAS
DEPUY, of the County of Richmond, being in a weak
state of health, but of sound mind. My executors to
take of monies arising out of my moveable estate sufficient to discharge all my debts and funeral expenses.
All my moveable estate to be sold and the balance
of the proceeds to be equally divided in four parts
for my daughter Catharine, my other daughter Elizabeth, the children of my son, John Depuy, deceased;
the other part to the children of my son, Moses Depuy, deceased. All my real estate of lands, meadows,
and buildings to be equally divided between my two
sons, Aaron and Peter Depuy. I make my trusty
friends, Richard Conner, Esq., and Barnet Simonson,
both of Richmond County, executors.

Dated June 26, 1781. Witnesses, Richard Conner,
Barnet Simonson, and Isaac Doty. Proved, March 25,
1782.

Page 477.—In the name of God, Amen. I, JOHN
JOHNSTON, of Monmouth County, being of Peace of
body and mind. I leave Joseph Hancock and his wife
Rachel, my executor and executrix to all my estate,
both real and personal, all that tract of land lying
and being Boylsis Mill upon Manolopin River, and
running from thence along the old Indian path, or

Burlington road to William Parents; being one thousand acres more or less; as also several acres of wheat left in Samuel Sprouls's care; and a large sow, with Daniel Osborn, for half her increase. Joseph Wilson, £1, two shillings, hard cash. My estate, real and personal, together with everything appertaining thereto, to be divided in manner following: I leave to my grandchildren, John Johnston, William Hancock, and William Johnston to share part and share alike; yet nevertheless the above-mentioned three boys to share double with my grandchildren as follows: Mary Hancock, Ruth Johnston, and Martha Johnston; yet nevertheless out of all these shares must be paid to my daughter, Jean Fitchet, and her children, £30; the boys to pay double as much as the girls.

Dated October 13, 1781. Witnesses, Joseph Hancock and Charles Fleming (soldiers in the First Battalion, New Jersey Volunteers), and Rachel Hancock (wife of Joseph Hancock). Proved, March 26, 1782.

Page 478.—THOMAS HENDRICKSON, SR., of Huntington, Suffolk County. Dated June 14, 1776. Wife Dorcas, sons Daniel, Thomas (and his wife Margaret), and Steven; daughters Hephzibeth and Elizabeth Waters, grandsons, John, Thomas, John (son of Daniel), Carman, and Hendrickson Waters; granddaughters, Sarah (daughter of Thomas), and Sarah Waters; Uncle Steven. Also mentions Dyer Valentine, Mr. Bolden, Mr. Hulit, Mr. Burcham, Jotheny Woods, Mr. Brush, Abijiah Ritchman, Jecomya Roggers, Thomas Dennis, Richard Rogers.

Executors, Tise Lain, and sons Daniel and Steven. Witnesses, John Concklin, Alexander Denton, Israel Titus, yeoman. Proved, March 4, 1782.

Page 480.—On the 22d day of July, 1775. I, ANNE PETTIT, of Hempstead, in Queens County, being of sound mind and memory. I leave unto my son John, £14. The remainder of the money that is in anyways

due me I will to my three sons, Joseph, Samuel, and
Isaac, to be equally divided. Unto my daughter, Anne
Smith, all my linen, wearing apparel, my warming pan,
and my best coverlet. The remainder of my household
goods of what kind soever I give to Jacob, Samuel,
and Solomon Seaman, my grandchildren, to be equally
divided. My four sons, Joseph, Samuel, Isaac, and
John, to pay all my just debts and funeral charges.
I make my sons, Joseph and Samuel, executors.

Witnesses, Elizabeth Batty, Ezekiel Mathies, David
Batty, yeoman. Proved, March 15, 1782.

Page 481.—I, WILLIAM SEAMAN, JR., of Jerico, in the
Township of Oysterbay, in Queens County, being this
20th day of the fourth month, 1779, weak in body but
of sound mind. My executors to pay all my just debts
and funeral charges. To my well-beloved wife Mary
£600, and one of my horses, saddle, and bridle, and the
desk that was her father's, also six silver tea spoons
and six silver table spoons, one bed and furniture, also
the privilege of living in my house so long as she remains my widow, all to be in lieu of Dower. Unto my
mother, Esther Seaman, the use of £100, but if she
should not need the money it should be equally divided
between my three children, viz: David, Mary, and Hannah. Unto my son David, half of all my lands, meadows, and buildings. Inasmuch as my wife is like to
have another child, if she have a living child and a son,
I give to him the other half of all my lands, meadows,
and buildings. If a daughter, then I give £400 to be
paid to her at the age of eighteen, or time of marriage,
and the half of my lands, meadows, and buildings that
I intended for said child had it been a son, I give to
my son David. Unto my daughter Mary the £400 to
be paid when eighteen, or time of marriage. Unto my
daughter Hannah £400 to be paid when of age. My
children to be brought up and educated in a decent
and commendable manner. My executors to sell my
moveable estate and pay all the legacies. I make my

two uncles, John Willis and Fry Willis, and my friend, Elias Hicks, all of Oysterbay, executors, and to divide the land with Zebulon Williams, which now lies unsettled between us.

Witnesses, Joseph Doty, William Valentine, Jacob Willets, yeoman. Proved, March 15, 1782.

Page 483.—In the name of God, Amen. I, CORNELIUS VAN DER VEER, of Flatbush, Kings County, yeoman, being in perfect health of body and of sound mind. All my just debts and funeral expenses to be paid. I leave to the children of my son John, deceased, viz: Garret, John, Peter, Hendrick, Jannitie, and Beletie, the bonds and money lent, I have of their father. My son Cornelius shall have my silver Tinker. Unto my grandchildren above named, one fourth of my estate; my son Cornelius, one fourth; my son Peter, one fourth; and my daughter Catrina, deceased, her children, Ejda, Jannetie, and Abigail, one fourth part. I make my loving brother, John Vander Veer, Engelbort Lott, Jacob Leffertze, and my son, Cornelius Van Der Veer, all of Flat Bush, executors.

Dated June 7, 1775. Witnesses, Jacob Suydam, yeoman, Petrus Heegeman, weaver, Hendrick H. Suydam. Proved, April 8, 1782.

Page 485.—In the name of God, Amen. The 22d day of October, 1776. I, JAN VAN DER VEER, of the Township of Flatbush, in Kings County, yeoman, being in good health and perfect of mind. After my lawful debts are paid, and my funeral charges are defrayed, I give, before any division is made of my estate, unto my loving son Joan, my negro man named Philip. Unto my beloved wife Cornelia, £30 yearly, during the time she remains my widow; also two bedsteads with the furniture thereunto belonging and as much household furniture as she shall have occasion for; also the use of one of the rooms in the house where I now live

in, and to pass and repass through my whole house;
also liberty to use the fruits out of my gardens and
orchards, as she has done in my life time. The £30
shall be paid, out of the portion of my son John, £10;
out of that of my daughter Femmetye, the wife of
Guliam Cornell £10; also out of that of my daughter
Catharine, the wife of John Stryker, £10. If my wife
should remarry, my executors shall pay out of the portions of my children, £6 during her natural life; also
my large cupboard with her linen and wearing apparel
and one bedstead with the furniture thereto belonging,
and therewith shall quit all pretensions of Dowery.
Unto my son John all my real estate, with the farm I
now live on, with the houses, barns, and all appurtenances. Unto my two daughters, Femmetye and Catharine, all my money which I have in cash, with my
bonds and notes. My executors shall keep in their
hands my daughter Femmetye's share and put it at
interest, to be paid to her during her life. £100 out of
the share of my daughter Femmetye unto my grandson, Abraham Wykoff, son of my said daughter Femmetye, when twenty-one, under the express condition
if his brother, John Wykoff, and all the heirs of their
father, Wilhelmus Wykoff, should refuse to give him
an equal share with them out of the estate of their
father, Wilhelmus Wykoff, deceased. Otherwise the
£100 shall remain in the hands of my executors with
the other part of my daughter Femmetye's portion;
which, after her decease, shall be equally divided
amongst all her children. My personal estate, not before bequeathed, shall be sold, and my negro slaves
shall have liberty to choose masters for themselves. I
make my loving son, John Van Der Veer, my loving
son-in-law, John Stryker, my loving cousin, Cornelius
Van Der Veer, and my loving cousin, Johannis E. Lott,
my executors.

Witnesses, Engelbart Lott, Rem Hegeman, cordwainer, Andrew Suydam, yeoman. Proved, April 8,
1782.

Page 488.—I, HULDAH VALENTINE, of the Township of Hempstead, on Nassau Island, being this 10th day of November, 1781, weak in health of body, but understanding sound, altho ancient in years. I leave unto my two sons, Richard and Phillip, three cows, paying all my charges of sickness and funeral charges. Unto Phebe Crooker, daughter of my daughter Ruth, my best cupboard and stand and two brass candlesticks, one small trunk, a half a dozen silver tablespoons, silver tea tongs and milk pot. The rest of my estate that was given to me by my husband, to Phebe Hendricks, Sarah Crooker, Anna Smith, wife of James Smith, and Phebe Crooker, and Martha Forster's children as much as either of my above-mentioned daughters, and Black Sarah and the rest of my money and clothes to be equally divided between Phebe Hendrickson, Sarah Crook, and Anna Smith, wife of James Smith, my three daughters, and Phebe Crook and Martha Forster's children equal with either of my three daughters. Unto David Valentine's, deceased, two sons, George and Phillip, £50, to be in their uncles' (Richard Valentine and Phillip Valentine) hands till the boys come of age. Unto Abigail Valentine, daughter of David, £10; to James Valentine's four daughters, £20. I make James Smith, Hendrick Onderdonck, John Williams, executors.

Witnesses, John Williams, Samuel Searing, Richard Smith, yeoman. Proved, March 25, 1782.

Page 489.—In the name of God, Amen. The 17th day of September, 1781. I, DANIEL BRINKERHOFF, of the Township of Hempstead, in Queen's County, yeoman, being sick and infirm, but of perfect mind. All my just debts and funeral charges to be paid. My wife Anne shall be in full possession of my estate, real and personal, as long as she remains my widow. If she should marry, then an equal proportion with all my children (except £30, 5 shillings, which I give to my son Hendrick, and £30, which I

give to my son Abram, is likewise excepted). The
residue of my estate, to my sons, Hendrick, Abram,
Jacob, Daniel, and Peter, and to my daughters, Alche
and Sarah, to be equally divided. If any of my children die under age, such part shall be equally divided
among my surviving children. I make my brother-
in-law, Peter Monfort, and my brother, Isaac Brinkerhoff, and my two sons, Hendrick and Abram, executors.

Witnesses, Elbert Adriance, John Schenck, Luke
Cummins. Proved, March 12, 1782.

Page 491.—I, ELEANOR MOODE, of the City of New
York, being weak in body but of sound mind. All my just
debts to be paid. I leave to my beloved sister, Hannah
Haydock, one third of an undivided lot of ground in
the City of Philadelphia, the whole containing one hundred feet, fronting Mulberry Street, and is about two
hundred feet deep, formerly the property of my great-
grandfather, William Hudson, of Philadelphia, and
bequeathed by him to my dear mother. Also my household furniture, wearing apparel, and plate of every
kind. My dear father, William Mood, deceased, left
me by will the dwelling house in which he lived, in
Chestnut Street, Philadelphia, and the ground thereunto appertaining, which house and ground I order to
be sold whenever my executors may think proper. The
proceeds and all other monies shall be equally divided
as follows: To my nephew, Samuel Emlen, one eighth;
my niece, Mary Haydock, one eighth; my niece, Rebecca Haydock, one eighth; my niece, Hannah Haydock, one eighth; my nephew, Henry Haydock, one
eighth; my niece, Elizabeth Moode Haydock, one
eighth; my niece, Eleanor Haydock, one eighth; my
niece, Jane Haydock, one eighth. I make my loving
brother-in-laws, Henry Haydock and Samuel Emlen,
junior, my executors.

Dated in New York, this 15th day of sixth month,
1779. Witnesses, Thomas Pearsall, watchmaker, John

W. Haydock, Quaker and Merchant, Eden Shotwell.
Proved, March 25, 1782.

Page 493.—In the name of God, Amen. I, NICHOLAS
LAMBERSON, of Jamaica, in Queens County, being of
sound disposing mind. All my just debts and funeral
charges to be paid. I leave to my son John, £10, out of
the bonds I have at interest. Unto my son Simion the
house wherein he now lives with the tract of land ad-
jacent, which he has now in possession, containing ten
acres. The money which I have out at interest unto
these four of my children, viz: John, Catharine, the
wife of Gerrit Nostrand, Judith, the wife of George
Watts, and Mariche, the wife of Aron Hendrickson, to
be equally divided. Unto my two granddaughters-in-
law, Sarah Lamberson, who was the wife of Nicholas
Lamberson, and Latticia Lamberson, who was the wife
of Cornelius Lamberson, both of them my grandsons,
my dwelling house where I now live in Springfield, in
Jamaica, with all my lands and meadows, as long as
these two widows shall live, and to maintain and bring
up Nicholas and Sarah Lamberson, the two children of
my grandson Cornelius, and at the decease of Sarah
and Latticia Lamberson, what remains shall fall to
Nicholas and Sarah Lamberson, the son and daughter
of Cornelius Lamberson. Unto my said great-grand-
children all my moveable estate, indoors and outdoors,
such as horses, cattle, waggons, ploughs, and all my
farming utensils, and all my household goods, to be
equally divided, after the decease of Sarah and Latticia Lamberson. There is a certain quantity of paper
money, the sum not known, I give to my son Simion
and to my two·granddaughters, Sarah and Latticia
Lamberson, to be equally divided. It is my mind
and will to live in my own dwelling house till my decease, and that Sarah and Latticia Lamberson shall
provide for me the necessaries of this life, such as I
shall have occasion for, both bed and board or anything else. I make my well-beloved friends, Sarah

Lamberson, Christopher Rider, and John Bremner, executors.

Dated November 7, 1781. Witnesses, Daniel Smith, yeoman, John Mills, yeoman, Mary Ramsen, spinster. Proved, January 4, 1782.

Page 495.—In the name of God, Amen. The 7th day of September, 1781. I, JOHN MUNSEY, of Hempstead, in Queens County, being in a reasonable state of health, I give to my well-beloved son Hendrick, all my lands and building in Hempstead, except my lot of meadow near Rockaway. Also all my horses and horse-kind, my wagon, plow, and all my utensils for farming business. All the bread corn and meat, together with all the green corn that I shall happen to have on the ground or in the house, of the dry corn and meat to my family for their support. All the moveable estate not disposed of, together with my lot of meadow, near Rockaway, Hempstead South, to be sold, and out of the proceeds all my just debts and funeral charges are to be paid. To my daughter, Mary Munsey, £15. To my daughter, Hannah Munsey, £15, and to my daughter Ginney, £15. The overplus of money I give to my daughters, Elizabeth Bedle, wife of Daniel Bedle, and Greche Cornwell, wife of Stephen Cornwell, and Alcha Burtis, wife of Benjamin Burtis, and Mary Munsey and Hannah Munsey and Ginney Munsey, to be equally divided. My executors to pay the money to my daughter, Greche Cornwell, as they think that she shall have real occasion of it. The money to be paid to each of them, when they arrive to the age of twenty-one. I make my trusty son Hendrick and my loving wife Stinche my whole and sole executors.

Witnesses, Paul Cunningham, Caleb Southard, Isaac Denton, yeoman. Proved, April 1, 1782.

Page 497.—In the name of God, Amen. I, ADOLPH BRAS, of the City of New York, shoemaker, being at present sick and weak in body, but of sound mind. All my just debts and funeral expenses to be paid. I leave to my eldest son Adolph, £5, for his birthright. The remainder of my estate, both real and personal, I give to my beloved wife Maritie, during her widowhood, to bring up and educate our children until they shall severally attain the age of twenty-one or marry. After the death or remarriage of my wife, then among my six children, to wit: Adolph, Gerret, Catherine, Mary, Jannetie, and Gertie, and the child my wife now goes with, when born. I make my wife sole executrix during her widowhood; after her death or remarriage then I appoint my brother, Hendrick Brass, and my son Adolph (when he shall come of age), executors.

Dated April 3, 1751. Witnesses, Amos Pain, John Vredenburgh, cordwainer, Lambert Moore. Proved, October 1, 1765.

Page 499.—In the name of God, Amen. On the 24th day of August, 1781, I, JOHN STEVENSON, of Hempstead, in Queens County, being in a reasonable state. All my real and personal estate to be sold and my just debts and funeral charges to be paid. I leave to my well-beloved daughter, Mary Burtis, wife of John Burtis, blacksmith, £20, 8 shillings. Unto my daughter, Nancy Frost, wife of Nathaniel Frost, £20, 8 shillings. Unto my daughter Charity, wife of John Burtis, £20, 8 shillings. Unto my granddaughter, Margaret Cornwell, daughter of James Cornwell, £20, 8 shillings. The remainder of my estate to be divided equally among my three daughters and two grandchildren, Mary Burtis, Nancy Frost, and Charity Burtis, John Hendrickson, son of John Hendrickson, and my granddaughter, Margaret Cornwell. I make my trusty son-in-law, Nathaniel Frost, and my trusty cousin, Hendrick Eldert, both of Queens County, executors.

Witnesses, Daniel Van Nostrand, Benjamin Mott, Isaac Denton.

Codicil. Over and above what I have given to my

grandson, John Hendrickson, I give him the sum of £20, 8 shillings.

Dated November 24, 1781. Witnesses, Hezekiah Pearsall, Daniel Van Nostrand. Proved, April 1, 1782.

Page 501.—Know all men by these Presents that I, THOMAS ALLEN, near Jerusalem, the east part of the Township of Hempstead, in Queens County, yeoman, being this twenty-first day of March, 1776, in middling health of body, and of sound mind and memory. My loving and well-beloved wife Elizabeth shall have all my moveable estate. My executors to sell my dwelling house and all my lands and meadows. My just debts and funeral charges to be paid out of the proceeds of such sale. Unto my wife the use of £200, and so much of the principal as she shall have need of, for her support during her life. The remainder, if any, to be equally divided amongst my daughters, Freelove Bedle, Letishe [Letitia] Seaman, and my granddaughter, Jerusha Powell. Unto my grandson, Benjamin Lawrence, £40, when twenty-one. Unto my two daughters and granddaughter the remainder of my estate, not disposed of, equally divided amongst them. My wife Elizabeth shall have all the rents and profits of my houses, lands, and meadows, after my decease, until they shall be sold. I make my loving wife, my son-in-law, Amos Bedle, my trusty friends, Thomas Seaman, of Jerusalem (son of Thomas), and Richard Ellison, all of Hempstead, executors.

Witnesses, George Wright, yeoman, Zebulon Wright, Anthony Wright. Proved, March 18, 1782.

Page 503.—Philadelphia. In the name of God, Amen. I, JAMES BROWNE, of Moyne, County of Galway, the Kingdom of Ireland, late resident in the Island of Jamaica, being weak of body. All my just debts and funeral expenses to be paid. I leave to Elizabeth Browne, alias Brady, my natural daughter, begot in the body of Betty Brady, £30 sterling; to be paid to Valentine Browne, of Moyne, Esquire, for her use. Unto my loving brother, Dillon Browne, and my loving sister, Frances Jordan, wife of Walter Jordan, and to my two loving sisters, Ann and Mary Browne, the residue of my estate equally to be divided. I appoint Valentine Browne, Esq., guardian of my said Brother. I make Mathias Hanly, late resident of the Island of Jamaica, now of this City, Esquire; Mr. Michael Dillon, of Guanaboa, Practitioner in Phisick and Surgery, and Edmund Betagt, of the Parish of St. John's in said Island, planter, my lawful executors.

Dated September 12, 1777. Witnesses, Alfred Clifton, Lieut. Col. Commandant; John Lynch, Major of the R. C. Volunteers. Proved, May 10, 1779.

Page 504.—I, JOHN SEAMAN, of Jerusalem, Township of Hempstead, Queens County, being weak in body. My estate to be sold, and all my just debts and funeral expenses to be paid. The remainder, if there be anything left, I leave three-quarters to my two sons, John and David, in equal shares; the rest or one-quarter to my three daughters, Mary, Elizabeth, and Sarah, equally divided. I make my brother-in-law, John Birdsall, and Thomas Seaman, schoolmaster, executors.

Dated October 21, 1777. Witnesses, Solomon Seaman, Israel Seaman, of Hempstead, yeoman, Amos Powell. Proved, April 9, 1782.

Page 505.—In the name of God, Amen. The thirteenth day of March, 1782. I, WILLIAM MERRELL, of Staten Island, Richmond County, yeoman, being in a low state of health, but in perfect senses. My funeral charges and other debts to be paid. I leave to Mary, my dearly beloved wife, all my estate, personal and moveable, except my gun and one pair of silver clasps. Them to my cousin, Richard Decker, my sister, Margaret Decker's son. I make my dear and beloved wife Mary, executor.

Witnesses, James Grover Garrison, Charles Decker, farmer, Richard Merrell. Proved, April 19, 1782.

Page 506.—In the name of God, Amen. I, ROELEF VOORHEES, of Flat Lands, in Kings County, being of sound and perfect understanding. All my just debts and funeral charges to be paid. I leave to my son Peter, all my estate, real and personal, for him to possess and receive the incomes for fifteen years, and sold at expiration of said term. The proceeds to be distributed as follows: Unto the children of my son Peter, £250; unto my grandchildren, the children of my daughters, Maria, Deborah, and Dorothy, £200, to be divided among the children of each of my daughters. The remainder of my estate shall be divided between my grandchildren, who are to have equal shares in the rights of their fathers or mothers. I make my son, Abraham Voorhees, and Jerome Lott, executors.

Dated April 11, 1782. Witnesses, Barant Johnson, Folkert Sprong, of Kings County, yeoman, John Voorhees, house carpenter. Proved, April 17, 1782.

Page 508.—In the name of God, Amen. I, JOHN VER MILLIE, of Yonkers, County of Westchester, farmer, being far advanced in years. All my just debts and funeral charges to be paid. I leave to my son Abraham my dwelling house and homestead, lands and improvements, which I bought of William Betts, containing about one hundred acres; upon condition that he pays to my daughters, Antie, Maritie, Sarah, and Rebecca, £35, to be equally divided. The lands which I bought of Roger Barton, containing about ninety-nine and a half acres; also a piece of land, which I bought of Samuel Betts, containing about forty acres; also, a piece of land, which I bought of Benjamin Betts, containing about forty acres; to my two sons, Joshua and Frederick; upon condition that they each pay to my four daughters, £60. Unto my three sons, Abraham, Joshua, and Frederick, a piece of Salt Meadow, which

I bought of Nicholas Koertright, lying [on] Harlem River. Unto my son Johannis, all my Lands, which I bought of Anthony Basley; upon Condition that he pays unto my four daughters, £340. Unto my two sons, Gerardus and David, all that my piece of Land, which I bought of Benjamin Betts, containing about 231 acres, they to pay £140 to my four daughters. Unto my wife Maritie, all my household goods and furniture; also, £70, to be paid out of my moveable estate, moreover, the liberty and use of any room in my house, which she shall choose, as long as she remains my widow; also, the use of my garden. My son Abraham to see this performed; and do subject the estate I have given him to the same. My sons, Abraham and Frederick, to provide for my wife a sufficient quantity of meat, wheat, and firewood at her door, during her widowhood. Unto John Kortright, £20, also, a certain debt that he owes me, as he is my grandson, and the debt was originally due to me from his father, John Kortright. All my stock, horses, hogs, and sheep, and the rest of my personal estate, to my four daughters and my son Benjamin, equally to be divided. What I have given to my daughter Rebecca and her children to be kept at interest, and paid occasionally as my executors think fit. I make my sons, Abraham and Frederick, and my wife Maritie, executors.

(Signed)   JOHN VERMILYA.

Dated June 11, 1776. Witnesses, William Betts, Peter Bussing, jr., of West Chester County, yeoman, Peter Bussing, son of Peter. Proved, April 23, 1782.

Page 510.—In the name of God, Amen. I, GEORGE GILLESPIE, of Bristol Township, County of Bucks, Pennsylvania, but late of St. Mary's in the Island of Jamaica, planter, being of sound and disposing mind. All my just debts and funeral expenses to be paid. My temporal estate to be disposed of; and I leave it to my dear beloved wife Elizabeth and my three sons, Denormandie, James, and George. My executors are to sell all my personal estate, except my negroes and such part of my household furniture as may be necessary for the use of my wife. Also, to sell, at publick vendue, my homestead farm whereon I now dwell, containing about 120 acres, and my small farm in Amwell Township, County of Hunterdon, containing about 79 acres. The proceeds to be put out at interest on good land security; one third to be paid annually to my wife during her life; the other two thirds to be applied towards the maintenance and education of my three sons. As I have £5,200 sterling money of Great Britain in the hands of Hibbert Purrier and Horton, merchants, of London, for my special use, some part of which has been drawn out, as will appear by my Books, what may be found due to me from them on a just settlement is to remain in their hands, they giving sufficient security and paying the interest thereof, until my three sons shall arrive at the age of twenty-one; interest to be paid annually to my executors for the use and benefit of my wife and children. My desire being to make as ample a provision for my dear wife while living, and for my children after her death, as my estate will admit of. Moreover, unto my loving wife, the use of all my negroes, to wit: Sam, Matilda, and Rosetta. The principal and remaining part of my estate, to go to my three sons, when twenty-one, on condition, that my sons arriving at age shall pay unto their mother, annually during her life, one-third part. If all should die in nonage, and without lawful issue, then to my five brothers and sisters, equally. Although my negroes are only given to my wife during life, yet if they misbehave, and she should be inclined to part with them, she to make sale of all or part of them to any purchaser, she being accountable to my children for the original sum of the purchase money. I make my loving wife Elizabeth executrix, and my father-in-law, Doctor John Abraham Denormandie, now in Europe, Doctor Samuel Bard, in New York, my friends, John Clifford and John Lawrence, of the City of Burlington, executors.

Dated December 1, 1781. Witnesses, Thomas Riche, Joseph Baldwin, a Quaker, Samuel Allen. Proved, May 6, 1782. On the same day, Samuel Bard appeared and qualified as executor.

Page 512.—In the name of God, Amen. This tenth day of April, 1782. I, GERRIT WILLIAMSON, of the Township of Gravesend, Kings County, being weak in body. After all my lawful debts and funeral charges are paid, I leave to my eldest son Peter, £5 for his birthright. And to Peggy, my wife, £100; and the little negro girl named Bet. Should there be any overplus of the £700, now in the hands of Samuel Stryker, for which sum I have put the said Samuel Stryker in full possession of my real and personal estate, lying and being in the Pattent of Gravesend, for which I have given a deed, bearing date to this my last will and testament, to take the same in his possession directly after my decease, such overplus to be divided among my four youngest daughters, as follows: My two youngest, Jeny and Anny, each £15 before any division is made; the remainder to be divided equally among the four, Charity, Moica, Jeny, and Anny. Should any die without any lawful issue, the legacy to be equally divided among the survivors. I make my neighbours, Samuel Stryker and Samuel Hubbard, executors.

Witnesses, Koert Jansen, Stephen Hubbard, of Kings County, yeoman, William Vander Voort, of Kings County, schoolmaster. Proved, April 29, 1782.

Page 516 (should be 514).—In the name of God, Amen. I, THOMAS EMMANS, of the Little or Lower Yonkers, West Chester County, yeoman, being indisposed in Body. All my just debts and funeral expenses be paid. I leave to my daughter Elizabeth, widow of James Henderson, deceased, £500. Like-

wise, to my said daughter, my negro girl named Sook
or Susannah. Unto my only son Abraham, £1,000;
also, my negro boys, Peter and Pompey. Unto my
daughter Frances, wife of Isaac Green, the interest of
£100, to be paid to her yearly during the lifetime of
the said Isaac Green; should she survive her husband,
then the said £100 to be at her disposal. Unto my
daughter [Sarah], wife of Joshua Ver Millye, the interest of £100, on like conditions as to her sister Frances. The residue of my estate to my son Abraham and
the children of my daughters Frances and Sarah. The
share of each of my grandchildren to be placed out at
interest and paid to them as they come to full age, or
marry. I make my friends, Frederick Van Cortlandt,
Isaac Vollentine, and George Briggs, executors.

Dated September 6, 1781. Witnesses, Elizabeth
Sallee, Rev. Charles Morgan, of the City of New York,
Augustus Van Cortlandt. Proved, April 9, 1782.

Page 516.—In the name of God, Amen. I, ROBERT
COLES, of Mamarneck, being in a weak state of health.
All my just debts and funeral charges be paid. I leave
to my son John, 10 acres adjoining the lands of Reuben Bloomer's, on the west side of the road. Unto my
daughter Elizabeth, the use and privilege of my largest room to live in, she and child, as long as she
remains single; with privilege of keeping a cow summer and winter; and of firewood, and a garden where
she shall choose; the privilege of fruit, for summer and
winter, of all sorts; and of making a hogshead of sider
yearly; the use of the oven to bake in; and to be made
equal with the rest of my daughters, what they have
already had. To my five daughters, Jennie, Sarah,
Mary, Anne, and Elizabeth, £520 each. Unto my
grandson, James Secor, £10, when twenty-one. Unto
my son Joseph all the rest of my estate, real and personal. I make Benjamin Griffen, Joseph Griffen, and
my son, Joseph Coles, executors.

Dated November 1, 1776.

I also give unto my granddaughter Hannah, Elizabeth's oldest daughter, £10, when of age; if she dies, then among Elizabeth's surviving children.

Witnesses, Reuben Bloomer, of West Chester County, saddler, Mercy Bloomer, John Rushton. Proved, May 6, 1782.

Page 517.—In the name of God, Amen. The twenty-fifth day of August, 1780. I, PETER VAN DE WATER, of Bedford, Township of Brooklyn, Kings County, yeoman, being very sick and weak in Body. All my just debts and funeral charges to be paid. My loving wife to remain in my dwelling house along with and to the care of my grandson, Peter Harper, during her natural life or remarriage, she to have a decent maintenance out of my estate, so long as she remains my widow; also, a Christianlike and decent burying in case she dies my widow. Unto my wife, one negro wench named Fann. Unto my daughter, Sarah Keys, wife of Joseph Keyes, £200, payable the day my grandson, Peter Harper, is twenty-one. Unto my said grandson, all my estate not given here before. I make my brother, Barnardus Van De Water, and my neighbor, Leffert Lefferts, executors.

Witnesses, Jonathan Van der Voort, of Kings County, schoolmaster, Barrent Lefferts, of Kings County, yeoman, Lambert Andress. Proved, May 6, 1782.

Page 519.—April 26, 1782. It is the request of the subscriber that after my just debts are settled that Mr. Benjamin Swain for his humane kindness and attention to me enjoys the remainder of my effects.

Signed, GEORGE SWANSON.

Witnesses, Thomas Walker, of the City of New York, cooper, Henry Stevenson, Surgeon B. Legion. Proved, April 30, 1782.

Page 520.—In the name of God, Amen. I, DANIEL DURYEE, of Hempstead, Queens County, yeoman, being at this time unwell, and still of sound disposing mind. All my funeral charges and just debts be paid. I leave to my son Jacob, £5, when of age. Unto my daughter Catharine, my best bed and furniture thereunto belonging, my cupboard and half the linen that ·is therein. Unto my daughter Mary, one bed and its furniture, and the value of a cupboard, and the other half of the said linen. The residue of my estate, to be sold by my executors. The proceeds to be equally divided amongst my children, namely: Catharine, Jacob, Abraham, and Mary, when of age. I make my loving brother, John Duryee, my cousin, Cornelius Montfore, jr., of Flushing, my friend and neighbour, John Hendrickson, merchant, executors.

Dated February 9, 1782. Witnesses, Nathaniel Box, John Demot, Garrett Nostrand, both of Hempstead, yeomen. Proved, April 11, 1782.

Page 522.—The seventh day of August, 1780. In the name of God, Amen. I, NICHOLAS BLOOM, of Bedford, Kings County, yeoman, being very sick. I give all the remainder of my estate, real and personal, unto my wife Mattie, and all my children, so long as my wife and children shall be able to maintain, keep good, and make satisfaction to all my present creditors. If my wife and children should neglect or not be able to make full satisfaction to all my creditors, or if my wife shall remarry, or after her death, then my executors are to sell and dispose of all my estate, for my wife and children, and the monies thence arising to be divided amongst my wife and children in manner following: Unto my eldest son Barrent, £10, for his birth-right; also, unto my wife an outset of household furniture, or, in lieu thereof, £50, also, the remainder of my estate or monies, which was not given herebefore, unto my wife and all my children, Barrent, Peter, Jacob, and Phebe, to be equally divided. The portion of each of my children under age to be put out, to the best advantage, till they become twenty-one years. I make my well-beloved wife Mattie, executrix, my beloved brother, Jacob Bloom, and my brother-in-law, Paul Van Der Voort, executors.

Witnesses, John V. D. Voort, schoolmaster, Wm. V. D. Voort, yeoman, both of Kings County, Lamberth Vandervoort. Proved, May 6, 1782.

Page 523.—In the name of God, Amen. I, Silas Lawrence, of White Stone, Township of Flushing, Queens County, yeoman, being weak in body. At my decease my body shall be interred in the burying ground of David Roe, close adjoining the said Roe. My funeral debts and other charges against me shall first be paid out of my moveable estate. All my personal and real estate to be sold for the benefit of my wife and children, except £50 and my best breeches, which shall be given to my son William. Unto my son William, all that charge of my nephew named Jacob Lawrence, who has an estate called Cooky Hill, which was left to me until he arrives at the age of twenty-one years, to support him during the said time. In case the said Jacob Lawrence shall die in minority, the estate befalls to me. It is my will and pleasure that my son William shall be heir to the same, and support him decently during his minority from the benefits of the Cooky Hill estate. My executors to sell all my estate. The proceeds to be equally divided between my wife and children. Concerning such of my children not at age at my decease, such shares to be put out to interest to support them until they arrive at majority, or marry. My sons to receive their fortunes at the age of twenty-one, and my daughters at the age of eighteen. I make my trusty and loving friends, Edmond Penfold and David Roe, called by name of Constable Roe, and my beloved son, William Lawrence, executors.

Dated October 2, 1781.

It is my will that my executors reserve of the stock to be sold for the benefit of my wife Deborah to support

my youngest children, two cows, one horse, and a sufficiency of furniture and bedding to keep house with,
and the negro girl named Jude.

Witnesses, Samuel Goldthwaite, jr., of the City of
New York, gentleman, Joseph Roe, Robert Lawrence,
of Queens County, yeoman. Proved, March 23, 1782.

Page 525.—In the name of God, Amen. This eighth
day of June, 1776. I, John Cheshire, of Oysterbay,
Queens County, being sick and weak in body. My
executors to pay my just debts and funeral charges.
All the remaining part of my estate, I leave to my
worthy friend, Cornelius Hooglant, gentleman. I make
the said Cornelius Hooglant, together with his son
Tunis, executors.

Witnesses, Solomon Freligh, V. D. M., Daniel Duryee, Jacob Rhinehardt, both of Queens County, yeomen. Proved, December 23, 1777.

Page 526.—Know all men by these Presents, that I,
Richard Smith, Sr., of Huntington, Suffolk County,
yeoman, this twelfth day of May, 1779, being in
reasonable health of body. All my just debts and
funeral charges to be paid. I leave to my son-
in-law, Jecamiah Brush, £30. Unto my daughter,
Sarah Brush, wife of Smith Brush, £30. Unto my
two sons, Richard and John, all the remainder of
my real and personal estate (not disposed of), both
in the Townships of Huntington and Oysterbay, with
all my rights in the undivided lands, plains, beaches,
and marshes within the Township of Hempstead, to
be equally divided between them. I make my son-in-
law, Jecamiah Brush, and my two sons, Richard and
John, executors. Witnesses, Nathaniel Whitman, John
Oakley, Solomon Ketcham, of the same place, farmers. Proved, March 27, 1782.

Page 527.—In the name of God, Amen. I, Micajah
Townsend, of Oysterbay, Queens County, yeoman, be-

ing in health and of sound mind and memory, this thirtieth day of April, 1781. My just debts and funeral expenses to be paid. My executors to fulfill and perform a certain covenant which, on the nineteenth day of January, 1764, I executed to Joseph, Daniel, and Caleb Coles as Trustees for their sister, my wife Ann. I leave to my eldest son, Platt Townsend, £210; which, with £1,590 that I have already given him, makes $1,800. Unto my son Epenetus, £430; which, with £1,370 that I have already given him, makes £1,800. If my son Epenetus shall be dead, without leaving any children, then what is given him is to go to my other sons, equally. Unto my son Micah, one feather bed and its furniture; also the choice of one negro slave (having already given my son Micah £1,800). Unto my son Jotham, the Farm of Land where I now live (and all the buildings thereon), bounded on the west by the highway leading from Musqueto Cove to Hempstead; on the north by Hulett Townsend's land and partly by land in the possession of William Laton; on the east by the highway leading from Jericho to Mosqueto Cove; and on the south partly by John Liester's land, partly by Samuel Prier's land, partly by Albert Van Nostrandt's land, and partly by Sampson Crooker's land, containing about 220 acres. Unto my son Jotham, all my salt and fresh meadow lying at a place called Beaver Swamp, on the east side of the brook in the Township of Oysterbay, the same being in two parcells or lotts, both of which were conveyed to me by my brother, John Townsend, and are particularly butted and bounded in the records of the Town of Oysterbay in Book B, page 5th. Likewise to my son Jotham all my farming utensils. Unto my four sons above mentioned all my rights in the common privileges in the Town of Oysterbay or Township and all the residue of my estate, to be equally divided. I make my four sons above mentioned, executors.

Witnesses, Sampson Crooker, of Oysterbay, yeoman, William Laton, Jeremiah Tappen.

Codicil. I make my nephew, John Wright, an executor of equal authority with my sons.

Dated May 15, 1781. (Same Witnesses.) Proved, May 6, 1782.

Page 529.—In the name of God, Amen. I, SAMUEL SCIDMORE, of Huntingdon, Suffolk County, being weak in body, but of perfect memory and understanding. My wife to have the use of one third of my lands as the law directs. I leave to my son John, one half of my lands, lying south of the road that leads from Platt's farm to Lemuel Bryan's and adjoining Smith Town line on the east; also, 20 acres of land lying in the Eight teer lots; likewise 25 acres of land lying in Sqwa Pit Purchase, with all the rights in said purchase; also, all my lands in the Beating Place Purchase; likewise one half of my meadow lying by Isaac Bunce's. Unto my son Samuel, one half of the land by the road that leads from Platt's farm to Lemuel Bryan's, and on the east by Smith Town line; also, one equal half of my meadow lying by Isaac Bunce's; also, all my lands and buildings north of the line fence that runs between my brother Isaac and I, to Joseph Bunce's land, bounded on the east by Smith Town line, with all my rights in the Eastern Purchase. All the manure that shall be made on the land I have given to my son Samuel shall be used on the said land, or at least not carried off. Unto my son .John, two third parts of all my moveable estate. Unto my daughter Elizabeth, the other third part of all my moveable estate. All my lands to be hired out by my executors till my son Samuel is twenty-one. Such part of the money that shall arise from the hire, as necessary, to go to the support of my children, and the remainder, equally between my son John and daughter Elizabeth. I make my friend, Jonathan Sammis, jr., and David Ketcham, executors.

Dated March 14, 1782. Witnesses, Seth Jarvis, farmer, Phebe Stenins, Jonathan Stratton, farmer. Proved, March 25, 1782.

Page 531.—In the name of God, Amen. I, JACOBUS LUISTER, of the Township of Oysterbay, Queens County, yeoman, being weak of body, but of perfect mind and memory, this ninth day of May, 1777, make this will and testament. After my just debts and funeral charges are paid, I leave to my sister's son, Albert Van Nostrant, £20. Unto my brother's son, Jacobus Luyster, £20. Unto the following persons the sum of £20 each: My brother John's daughter, Maria Luister; my sister Ida's son, Abraham Monfort; my sister Sarah's son, William Bennett; my sister Jannetie's son, Charles Simonson; my sister Altie's daughter, Jannetie Wortman; my wife's brother Lucas's daughter, Mary Nostrant; my wife's brother George's son, John Nostrant; my wife's sister Anne's daughter, Rentie Luister; all of which to be paid out of my personal estate. The remainder of my estate, both real and personal, be left to the care of my executors for the use of my beloved wife Maria; and after her death, to go to my brother John's son, Peter Luister, and to my wife's sister's daughter, Rentie Monfort. I make my brother, John Luister, Jost Monfoort, Esq., and John Schenck, of Cedar Swamp, executors; and for their trouble they shall have £10 out of my estate.

Witnesses, Rem Hegeman, Samson Crooker, both of Oyster bay, yeomen, Alchee Wortman. Proved, April 29, 1782.

Page 532.—Know all men that I, GARRET VANWICKLEN, of Woolverhollow, Oysterbay, Queens County, yeoman, being this seventeenth day of May, 1774, well in health of body. All my just debts and funeral charges to be paid. I leave to my loving wife Helena the use of my household goods within my house, and the use of the best rooms of my house, and the use of one third of my lands, and the one third of the use of my farming utensils during the time that she remains my widow; and to be in lieu of her Dower. Unto my three youngest sons, John, Jacob, and Abraham, all my lands in the Township of Oysterbay, together with all my houses, barn, buildings, and improvements, to be equally divided. My daughter Mary to have the privilege to live and dwell in my house so long as she remains single. Unto my eldest son Garret, two bonds which I have against him; one for £200 and the other for £70, both principal money out of which there was £20, his own money that he had from his uncle, John Vanwycklen. As to my son Paul, I have heretofore given unto him his full share in my estate, which shall satisfy for his part. Unto my seven daughters, viz.: Corneto, Catherine, Elizabeth, Sarah, Alchey, Helena, and Mary, all money that I have at interest, to be divided equally. My three sons, John, Jacob, and Abraham, shall pay unto my seven daughters, £60 apiece. If my three sons or either of them should neglect to pay them, my executors are to sell so much of my lands as will fully pay those legacies. Unto my three sons, John, Jacob, and Abraham, all my horses with my waggons and plows to be equally between them divided. Unto my four sons, Garret, John, Jacob, and Abraham, and my seven daughters, all my stock of cattle and household goods to be equally divided after my wife's decease. I make my son-in-law, John Monfort, of Wheatly, and my friends, Isaac Boget and Anthony Van Noorstrand, all of Oysterbay, executors.

Witnesses, Jane Seaman, Jane Willis, James Blonchfill, of Oysterbay, yeoman, Samuel Willis. Proved, April 29, 1782.

Page 534.—In the name of God, Amen. The twelfth day of July, 1779. I, WILLIAM GARRERD, of Brook Haven, County of Suffolk, cordwainer, being in health of body and of perfect memory. I give to my three sons, William, Azael, and Zophar, 20 shillings each.

Unto my son Joseph, all my house, lands, meadows, &c., even all my estate, real and personal; he paying the several legacies hereinbefore mentioned. I make my friend, Benjamin Woodhull of this place, sole executor.

Witnesses, Philip Leek, Benjamin Woodhull, and John Leek, both of said County, yeomen. Proved, March 8, 1782.

Page 535.—In the name of God, Amen. I, JOSIAH PEIRSON, of Bridgehampton, County of Suffolk, being of sound and perfect mind. I give to my son Silas, 5 shillings. Unto my son Matthew, my house and all my buildings and my Pickle, and the one half of my lot of land on the north side of my home lot, and the land lying on the east side of the land of Silvanus Topping and Peter Hildrith; and one-half of my lot of land, called my Narrow lot, on the south end; and one half of my lot, called Sayre's lot, on the west side; and one-third part of my woodland lying in the lot Number 102; and one half of my Fifty throughout the Township of Southampton. Unto my son Silvanus, my buildings and my lot of land called Norrise lot; and one half of my lot, called my home lot, on the South side; and one third of my woodland in lot 102; and one fourth part of my Fifty Right as far as the Canow place. Unto my son Timothy, my building and the lot of land bounded by David Hand's land on the west, and on the north, and Lemuel Peirson on the east, south by the road; and one half of my lot of land, called Sears lot, on the east side; and one third part of my wood-land in lot 102, in the South Division; and one fourth part of a Fifty Right as far as the Canow place; and all my commonage beyond the Canow place. Likewise unto my son Timothy, one piece of land bounded west by John Gibson land, north by the road, east by Ezekel Howell land; and one half of my lot, called the Narrow lot, on the north end. Unto my son Paul, 5 shillings; unto my son Josiah, 5 shillings; unto my son Joseph, 5 shillings; unto my son Benjamin, 5 shillings; unto my daughter Susannah, £30. I make my three sons, Matthew, Silvanus, and Timothy, executors, who are to sell my land lying in the Lots No. 1 and No. 2 in the North Division, and one eighth part of a share at Mantoak, and my moveable estate, and pay my just debts and legacies; what is left to be equally divided between Matthew and Silvanus and Timothy and Susannah.

Dated November 1, 1776. Witnesses, Elazar Stanbrough, Silvanus Topping, yeomen, and Annanias Cooper. Proved, March 25, 1782.

Page 537.—In the name of God, Amen. I, STEPHEN TOPPING, of Southampton, County of Suffolk, tanner, being in a weak state of health. I leave to my loving wife Abigail all the goods and effects she brought to my house. Also the east half part of my dwelling house with the use of part of the Linter Well, and, if wanted, part of the barn. Likewise £20 in cash to balance what money she brought; and the use of the third part of all my lands during the time she remains my widow. Unto my son Stephen the dwelling house he now lives in, with about eight acres of land, and all the buildings and privileges thereunto belonging. Also half my upper lot called Wainscot Lot, and half a fifty in the Great Division; and one half fifty in the commonage; and one half of a lot of land by John Norris, containing about eight acres; likewise, the liberty of part of the fruit in my home orchard; and one third of my orchard by Crooked Pond. It is to be observed the liberty of four years is granted in my home orchard to my said son, and no longer. Unto my son Henry, four acres of land, which I bought of Paul Peirson; and the half of my Wainscot Lott; and one quarter and one-half of one quarter of the Great Division; and one quarter of commonage. Unto my son Jeremiah, my Beach Lott in partnership with Ebenezer White, Esq., and David Topping; and a piece of land, about 4 acres, in partnership with Peter

Hildrett; and the one half of a lott of land by John Norris; and the one quarter and one half of a quarter of the Great Division; and one quarter of commonage. Unto my daughter Hannah, £5. Unto my daughter Abigail, £40. Unto my son Charles, all my lands and buildings, with the privileges thereunto belonging, not given away. After my just debts are paid, all my moveable estate (except my team and tackling, plows, harrows, and farming utensils, which I leave for the use of my sons in general), to be sold, and equally divided between my sons and my daughter Abigail. I make my sons, Stephen and Charles Topping, executors.

Dated February 11, 1780. Witnesses, Joseph Gibbs and Ebenezer White, yeomen, and Phebe Peirson. Proved, March 25, 1782.

Page 539.—In the name of God, Amen. I, RICHARD BROWN, of Oyster ponds in Southold, County of Suffolk, yeoman, being sick in body. I leave to my beloved wife Hannah, all my moveables (except what is hereafter excepted). Unto my daughter-in-law, the widow Zipporah Brown, the use and improvement of the land, herein given to my grandson, Richard Brown, during her widowhood, she making no waste in the same. Unto my grandson, Richard Brown, if he arrives to the age of twenty-one (and provided he make no demand of what his great-grandfather gave his father), a house and one acre of land at the Oyster Ponds, bounded east on the lands of Henry Tuthill. Also, all my lands southward of the country road in the Oyster Pond Upper Neck. If there are no heirs of his body, after his decease, then to my son Christopher and in default of his heirs the lands to go to my grandson, Samuel Brown. Unto my son Christopher, all my other lands and meadows, provided he shall have heirs male of his body lawfully begotten. Unto my said son Christopher, all my farming utensils and implements, and one pair of oxen and a horse; which oxen

and horse he may choose out of my stock. Unto my
daughter-in-law, the widow Zipporah, six bushels of
wheat and six of corn yearly during her widowhood,
to be paid by my son Christopher. Unto my grandson,
Thomas Vaill, jr., £10 when of age, which my son
Christopher is to pay. Unto my grandson, Samuel
Brown, £10, to be paid in like manner. Unto my
daughter, Hannah Vaill, two cows and six sheep. In
case my son Christopher shall refuse to pay unto my
daughter-in-law Zipporah the wheat and corn yearly,
and to my grandsons £10 each, then my executors shall
sell a square lott of land at Oysterponds, bounded west
on the lands of Joseph Youngs, east on the lands of
Jeremiah Tuthill, north upon the road, and south by
my other land called a Ten Acre Lott; and with the
proceeds pay the above legacies. I make my wife
Hannah, executrix, my son Christopher and my trusty
friend, Asa King, executors.

Dated June 3, 1772. Witnesses, Ezekiel Glover, and
John Tuthill, jr., and John Racket, jr., both yeomen.
Proved, April 1, 1782.

Page 541.—In the name of God, Amen. I, Lemuel
Howell, of Southampton, County of Suffolk and Colony of New York, farmer, being in perfect health of
body. I leave to my loving wife Abigail, £50 in lieu
of her Dower, if she choose to accept it, out of my
moveable estate. Also, the use of a negro wench called
Jane, as long as she is my widow. Also, two young
cows, such as she shall choose; also, the use of the
north half of my dwelling house. Unto my daughter,
Charity Hedges, £5. Unto my son Moses, my home lot
with all the buildings thereon; also, my part of Charles
Lott that lies southerd of the Bridge; also, one piece of
wood-land in the Great Division in the South end of
the lot No. 16; likewise, one piece of woodland being
in said lot east of Jonah Sandford's house; also, half
of my north lot No. 10; also, half my orchard and half
my orchard lands lying at the Brick-Kilns; also, all my

lands in Paun Quaog; also, the half of a piece of land adjoining to Matthew Halsey's land, called Silas Sandford's lot; also, one fifty of commonage throughout the bounds of Southampton; also, my Fulling Mill and the land and Damm belonging thereto; and all my clothier's tools also, my weaver's loom, with the tackling and wool combs; also, my negro boy named Elymas; also, my horse and one yoke of oxen. Unto my son Caleb, that part of my Charles Lott that lies northward of the Bridge; also, my lot of land in the Wind Mill Lane; also, my lands in Brush Plain lying northward of the highway that goes to Jeremiah Brown's No. 14 in the last division; also, half my orchard and half my orchard lands at the Brick lins; also, half my north lot No. 10; also, my northermost lot of land in No. 16 in the Great Division; likewise, the half a piece of land adjoining Matthew Halsey's land, called Silas Sandford's lot; also, one half of my land in lot No. 11 in the Great Division, which I bought of Henry Pierson; likewise, three quarters of a fifty in the bounds of Southampton and Topping's Purchase; also, my negro boy Titus. Unto my daughter, Ruth Peirson, £40, to be paid out of my moveable estate. After my debts and legacies are satisfied, if any of my moveable estate remains, one third be given to my son Caleb, and the other two-thirds to be equally divided between my wife Abigail and my three children, Moses, Caleb, and Ruth. I make my son-in-law, David Hedges, and my son, Moses Howell, executors.

Dated September 3, 1779. Witnesses, Joshua Hildreth, yeoman, Sarah Hildreth, Joseph Gibbs, yeoman. Proved, March 25, 1782.

Page 543.—JONATHAN JONES, of Brook-Haven, County of Suffolk, yeoman, being this twentieth day of April, 1782, weak in body. All my just debts and funeral charges to be paid out of my moveable estate. I leave to my loving wife Jeany, all that she has brought to my estate; also, all that she can make in the house and poultry too, as long as she remains my widow. Unto my only son Jonathan, all my real and personal estate. Further, my wife shall have the best room in my house where I live now; a cow to milk, a horse to ride, when she thinks proper, and a girl to waite at any time, and to be clothed and keep horse, cow, and girl on my estate, and have every other necessary of life. I make Gesham Brown, Joseph Rainer, and Jeany Jones, executors.

Witnesses, Samuel Satterly, William Davis, yeomen, Phebe Clark. Proved, May 7, 1782.

Page 544.—In the name of God, Amen. The twenty-first day of May, 1774. I, Samuel Hudson, of the Town of Southold, County of Suffolk, yeoman, being weak in body. I leave to my son Nathaniel, one half of all my land lying northward of the highway commonly called the North Road, which land I bought of Youngs Wells; also, one half of all that my meadow lying at the island called the Collonel's Island. Unto my son Henry, all that land and building where he now lives, which I bought of Capt. James Fanning; also, the land bought of David Horton; also, the land bought of Nathanael Worner, being about 30 acres; also, one short lot of meadow lying at the Broad Meadows. Unto my son Samuel, 5 shillings. Unto my grandson, Thomas Hudson, all that land and buildings where I now live, which I bought of Mr. John Tuthill; also, all my land bought of Eleazor Luce; also, all my land bought of Mr. David Howell; and all my meadows bought of David Reeve, lying at the Deep Creek so called. After all my just debts and funeral charges are paid out of my moveable estate, all the remainder to be divided between my two daughters, Sarah Hudson and Elizabeth Tuthill. Whereas I have given my daughter Elizabeth a fitting out at her marriage, my daughter Sarah shall have the same value out of my moveable estate; and the remainder shall be equally divided between my two daughters, excepting my silver Tankard, I give to my daughter Sarah over and above her division. My negro wench Florah shall have her choice which of my daughters she shall live with after my wife's decease; which wench I give to my wife during her life. I make my son Henry and my son-in-law, Nathan Tuthill, executors.

Witnesses, Nathan Corwin, of Suffolk County, yeoman, Mary Corwin, Israel Youngs. Proved, April 12, 1782.

Page 546.—In the name of God, Amen. I, James Jeanes, of South Haven, County of Suffolk, being weak in body. All my debts to be paid. I leave to my dearly beloved wife Deborah for ever, this house where I now dwell and the land belonging to it, and my other house in Coram and land belonging to it; and all my money, household goods, and furniture and tenements to me belonging; with all my estate, both real and personal, at home and abroad, moveable and unmoveable, excepting what I give to my three eldest sons. To my sons, Tinkenson, Shadrack, and Mesheck, each 5 shillings sterling in money. The rest of my estate, I give to my wife forever, but only 5 shillings sterling money for her to pay to each of my and her younger children, Abednigo, James, and Onne. I make my loving wife Deborah and Samuel Tobey, executors.

Dated September 5, 1781. Witnesses, Samuel Tobey, yeoman, Robert Satterley, Amos Addams. Proved, October 8, 1781.

Page 547.—In the name of God, Amen. I, Thomas Conkling, of Shelter Island, County of Suffolk, this fourth day of June, 1770, being weak. My just debts and funeral charges to be paid out of my moveable estate. I leave to my son Thomas, two cows: Unto my son Shadrick, all the lands and buildings on Shelter Island where I now live, except 20 acres adjoining to the new house where my son Thomas liveth, with the reserve hereafter to be mentioned, and two thirds of all my stock; also my desk and half my apparel. Unto my son Benjamin, the house where my son Thomas dwelleth and 20 acres of land lying north of the house, joining easterly to West Neck Farm, and so to go up to a square body until it make 20 acres; also, all the lands I have in Southold; also one-third of my stock and half of my wearing apparel. If either of my sons, Shadrick or Benjamin, should die without lawful issue, his part to go to the survivor. Unto my daughter, Mary Conkling, all my household goods and £100 in money. My daughter Mary to have the privilege of living in the westermost room of my now dwelling house so long as she remains unmarried. Likewise, one cow and the privilege of keeping it on my farm during her single state; also, some firewood, a sufficiency during said term. Unto my son Shadrick all my farming implements and moveables of every kind not before disposed of. I make my two sons, Shadrick and Benjamin, executors.

Witnesses, Mahittable Sawyer, Phebe Havens, Robert Hempsted. Proved, March 23, 1782.

END OF LIBER 34.

LIBER 35.

Page 1.—In the name of God, Amen. I, JESSE
SAMMIS, of Huntington, in Suffolk County, being weak
in body, do this day, in the year of our Lord 1781,
make this will. I leave to my son Platt 20 shillings.
Unto my son Jacob my loom and all my Weaving
Tackle. My house and lands, with my stock and
all my household furniture to be sold. My executors
not to pay out any money to the Legatees until the
charges are paid for the bringing up of the children.
After that, when Jacob comes of age, to give one-
third of the whole to him. Unto my son Daniel, when
he comes of age, one-third of the whole. Unto my
four daughters, Mary, Elizabeth, Rhode, and Pene,
the other one-third in equal shares. If any of them
die without lawful issue, then their parts to be equally
divided amongst the surviving brothers and sisters.
My executors to put the money out upon interest;
and the children to be bound out as soon as possible
after my decease. I make these loving friends, Annanias Carlle, Philip Smith, and Micael Hart, executors.
Dated September 12, 1781. Witnesses, Nathaniel
Harrisen, Nathaniel Sammis, Job Sammis. Proved,
January 30, 1782.

Page 2.—In the name of God, Amen. I, BENJAMIN
HORTON, of Southold, County of Suffolk, being in a
weak state of bodily health. I leave to my nephew,
John Case, all my lands and meadows. Unto my two
nephews, Benjamin Horton and Joseph Horton, £5
each. The residue of my personal estate to my three
nieces, Martha Overton, Mary Harvey, and Unice
Wines. I make Thomas Overton and Daniel Osborn,
executors.
Dated October 31, 1781. Witnesses, Wines Osborn,

Noyes Wickham, Mary Osborn. Proved, April 29, 1782.

Page 3.—In the name of God, Amen. I, Samuel Youngs, of Southold, County of Suffolk, husbandman, being weak in body. All my just debts and funeral charges to be paid. I leave to my three sisters, for sundry good causes, my two home lots, including my house, barn, and orchard, and all things pertaining thereto, viz.: to Mehitable, Hannah, and Dorothy. Also, the one-half of my woodland and a lot of land, known by the name of the Old Ground, adjoining my meadow, which is about 13 acres; also, the one-half of my salt meadow and my fresh grass, equally alike, as long as they remain unmarried. The rest of my lands and meadows unto my nephew, Jeremiah Youngs, for the love and respect I do bear to him. If either one or two of my sisters die and leave the two or one unmarried, their parts to the surviving and unmarried sister. At her death to go to my nephew Jeremiah. If one or two marry, to go to the unmarried one; if all marry, to go to my nephew. Unto my brother, Jonathan Youngs, 30 shillings, for the love and good will I do bear to him. The lands and meadows given to my nephew Jeremiah to be let out by the discretion of my executors until his majority. I make my trusty friends, Christopher Tuthill and Daniel Tuthill, executors.

Dated June 2, 1777. Witnesses, Amon Taber, Jr., carpenter, Fred Taber, John Racket, Jr. Proved, March 18, 1782.

Page 5.—In the name of God, Amen. The fifth day of October, 1781. I, Zacheriah Hawkings, of Middle Town, in Brook Haven, being weak in body, but having my usual understanding. All my just debts and funeral charges to be paid out of my moveables. I leave to my son Joseph my house, barn, and all my land lying southward of a certain piece of woodland which joins the mowing lot where a line running from the south side of said woods west to the river and east to the "manner" line shall be his north bound; with all the buildings and improvements thereon. Unto my son Zacheriah the remaining part of my land lying north of said line; with the improvements thereon. Unto my youngest son, Brewster, £100, out of my moveable estate, payable at the discretion of my executors when he comes of age. Also, that he be put to such suitable trade as he shall choose, and they think proper. Unto my daughter Ruth £100, payable in like manner when she comes of age if required. Unto my loving wife Sarah the use and improvement of all my estate, real and personal, for the purpose of bringing up the family until they come of age; provided she remains my widow. Likewise, all my household furniture; she to dispose of at her discretion. At my youngest son's majority my land to be divided between my two sons as above directed. The whole family to be brought up and supported on the place until they come of age; and after that my wife to be provided with everything necessary for her comfortable maintenance by my two sons that hold the land, so long as she remains my widow. I make my loving wife and my two brothers, Gershom and William, executors.

(Signed) Zachirah Hakings. Witnesses, Gershum Hawkings, Benjamin Woodhull (yeoman), John Leek (yeoman). Proved, March 8, 1782.

Page 7.—I, BENJAMIN BREWSTER, of Brookhaven, County of Suffolk, having my understanding good and being of perfect mind and memory, do this ninth day of January, 1782, make this will. All my just debts and funeral charges to be paid by my executors. I leave to my wife Mehetable a living in my new dwelling house as long as she remains my widow. Unto my son Benjamin that tract of land called my Home Lot, with my house building and orchards, and all other improvements thereon; also, my tract of land

lying the west side of the road that leads from my
barn to Nessekeig as far south as the sheep pasture
path; also, my tract lying on the east side of Nessekeig road leading from my barn, commonly called
Old Nassekeig; together with the lot joining to the
same, commonly called the East lot; also, my share
of meadows at the West Meadows, lying on the east
side of said meadows; together with the uplands or
spreading yard joining to the same as it is now within
fence; also, the equal one-half of my share of meadow
lying in the northward part of the said West Meadows,
to be equally divided, and the equal one-half of the
spreading yard joining to the same as it is now within
fence. Likewise, my farming tackling. Unto my son
Caleb one whole right and one-third part of a right
of commonage throughout the Township; also, all my
rights or lotts of meadow on the South Beach; also,
one-third part of a lot in the old man's sheep pasture
drawn on the right of Thomas Biggs, Jr.; also, a lot
and one-third part of a lot in the sheep pasture at the
southeast part of the town; also, a lot and one-third
part of a lot in the little division near Nassekeig
Swamp; also, the one-third part of a 20-acre lot lying
on the hills at the southwest part of the town, drawn
on Thomas Biggs's, jr., right; also, a lot on the little
division at South; also, the equal one-half of my
share of meadows lying in the northward part of the
West Meadows, to be equally divided; together with
the equal half of the spreading yard. My executors
to sell my moveable estate (except what is given to
my son Benjamin), and to pay all my just debts and
funeral charges out of the proceeds. Any balance to
be equally divided between my two daughters, Peninah
and Orpha, or their children. Should either die leaving no issue, then her part to go to the surviving sister or her children. I make Nathan Woodhull, Elnathan Satterly, and my son Benjamin, executors.

Witnesses, Elijah Smith, yeoman, John Tyler, Amos
Smith, yeoman. Proved, March 14, 1782.

Page 8.—Southold in the County of Suffolk, October 4, 1771. The last will and testament of Captain Daniel Osborn. In the name of God, Amen. I, Daniel Osborn, of Southold, above mentioned, being at this time in perfect health. My debts and my funeral charges be first paid. I leave to my dearly beloved wife Hannah, during widowhood, the possession of the east room in my house, which is my dwelling room, with the chamber over it, and the bedroom joining to the said east room; also, the garden to the east of my house; together with all such privileges as she needs in the cellar, and the well which I now use and enjoy. I render back, of my own mere motion, to my beloved Hannah all the household stuff which is yet remaining of what she brought to me by marriage. Likewise to her, the use of the feather bed on which I sleep; during her widowhood, with the usual furniture, and the sole use of my negro maid named Peg during the same term. Unto my wife, to be her sole property without term, such two of my milch cows as she shall choose, and one pig, together with the side saddle she now rides. Unto my oldest son, Wines Osborne, meadow from the lower end of my meadow up to Daniel's Hole, so called, and so to the corner of Major Wickham's land joining to my meadow. Unto my son Daniel the remaining part of my meadow, and all my other real estate in Southold; he to provide for and bring to the custody of my wife, yearly, the following necessaries of life, in consideration of her having no dower of thirds in my estate: 15 bushels each of wheat and Indian corn; 30 weight of flax dressed; 20 loads of firewood; 10 pounds weight of wool after shearing; 120 weight of beef; and 20 weight of tallow; and he shall keep the above mentioned two cows yearly, and such other cows as may succeed them in my wife's possession, and allow my wife to keep one swine during the term of her widowhood after me, only. Unto my only daughter, Elizabeth, all my undisposed of personal estate. Should she die without children, then said personal estate is to be divided between my two sons. I make my two sons, Wines and Daniel, executors.

Witnesses, Richard Hudson, Gains Gardiner, Timothy Allen.

Codicil. Be it known unto all men that I do recall the appointment of my son Wines as Executor, and do appoint Daniel (my son) to be sole executor. I further leave to my beloved wife Hannah £40; and after the decease of my son Wines I give the meadow (in my will given to him) to my grandson, Wines Osborn.

Dated August 2, 1779. Witnesses, Barnabas Terrel, Phinehas Fanning, Elizabeth Corwin. Proved, April 29, 1782.

Page 11.—I, JOHN BILES, at present of the City of New York, master ferryman, being sick and weak in body. My just debts and funeral expenses to be paid. My executors to sell my estate, real and personal, and the proceeds, after deducting debts and charges to be put out at interest on real estate security; the principal and interest thereof to be applied as follows: I leave to my son William two full sixth parts, payable on his demand; or, in default, within twelve years after my decease. If proof be made of his death within that time, without leaving lawful issue, then the said legacy to go to my daughters. The other sixth parts unto and equally among my daughters, Hannah, Ann, Sally, and Elizabeth, payable as each attain twenty-one years of age. Should any die in non-age without lawful issue, then the legacy of her so dying to be equally divided among the survivors. The four sixth parts to be put at interest on real estate security; the interest, or such parts of the principal as the executors may think necessary, to be applied for the maintenance and education of said daughters until they shall severally come of age. The remainder of my estate to my children, to be equally divided among them. I make my friends, Thomas Pearsall, watchmaker, and John Bissonnett, of the City of New York, executors.

Dated May 2, 1782. Witnesses, John O'Brien, innkeeper, John Grigg, tanner, both of the City of New York. Proved, June 3, 1782.

Page 12.—In the name of God, Amen. I, STEPHEN WOOD, County of Richmond, cordwainer, being sick, do this 20th day of November, 1781, make this will. I leave to my son Jacob 10 shillings; unto my son John 5 shillings; unto my son James £50. The remainder of my estate to be equally divided amongst my four children, namely, Phebe, Mary, Joseph, and James. Should James die under age, or without issue, then his part is to be equally divided among the other three children after paying out the above legacies, all my just debts, and funeral charges. All my real and personal estate to be sold by my executors. I make my loving friend and brother, Silas Bedell, jr., and Stephen Bedell, both of Richmond County, executors. Witnesses, Timothy Wood, shoemaker, John Wood, James Grover Garrison. Proved, May 22, 1782.

Page 13.—In the name of God, Amen. I, JEREMIAS REMSEN, of the Wallabought of the Township of Brooklyn, Kings County, being sick and weak in body. All my just and lawful debts and funeral expenses to be paid. I leave all my personal estate to my widow; also, the use of all my real estate, while my widow. Should she remarry, she is to have no more than the personal estate; and that in lieu of dower. At her death or remarriage all my real estate is to go to Barrent Johnson; he paying for seven years running, £50 yearly, to my seven brothers and sisters, or to their children; to be divided between them. Also, £12 to my brother, Rem Remsen's grandson, Jeremias Remsen, the first year. In case the said Barrent Johnson does not appear to take possession of the estate, then all my real estate in the Township of Brookland is to go to the eldest son of said Barrent, to wit: Jeremias

Johnson, he paying all the legacies in the same manner which his father was ordered to do. Also, in such case, all the real estate which I have in the Township of Bushwick to go to the wife of the said Barrent while his widow; at her death or remarriage to go to the three youngest children of said Barrent, to wit: John, Jeromis, and Catelina, in equal shares. I make my loving wife executrix, and my friends, Abram Remsen, Jeremias Remsen, and Martin Schenk, executors.

Dated September 26, 1776. Witnesses, John Alstyne, of the City of New York, blacksmith, Martin Schenk, Kings County, yeoman, Nicholas Couwenhoven. Proved, May 14, 1782.

Page 15.—In the name of God, Amen. This eight and twentieth day of October, 1760, I, NICHOLAS STILLWELL, of Gravesend, Kings County, being weak in Body, but of perfect mind and memory. I give to Altey, my beloved wife, an equal part of my real and personal estate with my sons and daughters; she to remain in full possession of all my estate while my widow. After her death or remarriage my estate shall be disposed of amongst my sons and daughters. Unto my son Richard £25, to be levied out of my estate before any division be made. The remainder to my four sons and three daughters, parts alike; all my lands, tenements, goods and chattels to my sons Richard, Jost, Nicholas, and Rutgart, and to my daughters Jannetey, Ida, and Catharine Stillwell. If any of my negroes or wenches should have a mind to be sold, it shall be in the discretion of my executors to dispose of them as they shall think fit. I make my loving wife Altie and my four sons, Richard, Jost, Nicholas, and Rutgart, and my brother, Richard Stillwell, executors.

Witnesses, Jacobus Ryder, Johanis Gerritsen, and Barnardus Ryder, of Kings County, yeoman. Proved, May 21, 1782.

Page 17. In the name of God, Amen. The third day of October, 1781, I, THOMAS HENDRICKSON, of

Hempstead, Queens County, yeoman, being sick and weak in Body. All my just debts and funeral charges to be paid by my executors out of my personal estate. I give to Ame, my dearly beloved wife, the whole use and benefit of all the farm that I now live upon, with my house, and the one-half of fresh and salt meadow at South; and the equal half of the Great Woods, with all things appertaining to the said farm, for the bringing up of my children, while my widow, excepting 2 acres, joining the woodland of Joseph Oldfield, which is to go to my dearly beloved daughter Anche, the wife of John Nostran; to be freely possessed and enjoyed. Unto my dearly beloved son Hendrick, my farm at Foster Meadow and all things appertaining; with the equal half of my fresh and salt meadow at South; and the equal one half of the Great Woods; likewise, my long gun and riding chair and half of the Boat. If my wife sees cause to marry before her decease, my son Hendrick is to have all my houses, lands, and meadows, with all my horses, waggons, and farming utensils. Unto my wife Ame and my son Hendrick, all my neat cattle and sheep equally divided between them; with all my negroes that I shall be entitled to at my decease. Unto my wife Ame, my tea-kettle, all my household furniture not heretofore given away. Unto my daughter Ame Nostrand wife of James Nostran £28, to be paid out of my estate by my executors. Unto my daughter Elizabeth, £40, payable in like manner when she is eighteen or at her marriage day. Unto my daughter Sarah £40 when 18. I make my beloved wife Ame, my son Hendrick, and Timothy Cornell, executors.

Witnesses, Samuel Hicks, Benjamin Burtis, Hendrick Muncy, all of Hempstead. Proved, May 22, 1782.

Page 18.—In the name of God, Amen. The twenty-fourth April, 1780. I, ZACHEUS VAN DYKE, of the County of Richmond, being weak in body. All my

just debts and charges to be paid and satisfied out of
my moveable estate. I leave to my beloved son John
all the lands and meadows that I now possess, together with two horses and one waggon, plows, harrows, and tackling belonging thereto; and two negro
boys named Jack and ·Bob; he to have full possession
at the age of twenty-one. If he die without lawful
heir, then his portion is to be equally divided to my
two daughters, Elizabeth and Catharine. Unto the said
daughters, all my moveable estate (except the above
mentioned) to be equally divided when my son John
is twenty-one; my daughters to have their option to
make their home with my son John on the homestead
farm during his non-age. My two daughters' portions shall not be sold immediately after my decease,
but shall remain on the farm until my son John is
of age, and then be delivered to them in equal shares
agreeable to the inventory that shall be taken at my
decease. My daughters shall so share with my son
John in all the increase of my stock and every other
emolument that may arise from the place during the
same period. Should either of my daughters marry,
then the executors to pay unto her one equal half of
what money there may be at my decease. If ever
my beloved brother, Cornelius Van Dycke, should return, my son John shall maintain him during his life
with victuals and Cloath upon the homestead farm.
In case the lands should be confiscated, my son John
shall share equally with my beloved daughters Elizabeth and Catharine to the contrary notwithstanding.
I make Cornelius Cole, Isaack Praul, and my son John,
executors.

Witnesses, Jacob Cole, John Marshall (farmer),
Obadiah Browne. Proved, May 31, 1782.

Page 19.—In the name of God, Amen. I, DANIEL
DOWNS, of the Manor of St. George, County of Suffolk, yeoman, being sick and weak in body. After all
my just debts and funeral expenses be paid and sat-

isfied by my executors, I leave to my well beloved wife
Desire, all my household goods, my negro girl called
Zipora, my brown horse and riding chair, and two
cows; all which she is to dispose of as she shall think
proper. Unto my eldest son Daniel £20. Unto my
four sons, namely: Nicols, Parshall, John, and Ira,
all my lands, meadows, and buildings (except my right
in the undivided lands) to be equally divided between
them. Likewise all my moveable estate (except that
given to my wife). Unto my eldest daughter, Desire
Rogers, £20; to my second daughter, Joanna Wells,
£20; to my youngest daughter, Huldah Downs, £100,
payable when she is eighteen years old. My said four
sons shall pay all my just debts and legacies above
mentioned, equally between them. Unto my five sons
above mentioned, the use and improvement of my
right in the undivided land before mentioned until it
is laid out, and to go to my son Daniel after it is laid
out. I make my endeared wife Desire, my son Nicols,
and my trusty friend, David Hallock, executors.

Dated April 12, 1782. Witnesses, William Penny,
John Havens, yeoman, Daniel Wells, yeoman. Proved,
June 4, 1782.

Page 21.—I, EDWARD PRICE, of Shrewsbury, County
of Monmouth, in New Jersey, being this seventeenth
day of May, 1779, weak of body. I leave to my wife
Anne my two negroes called Lucy and Sarah, and £50
to be paid in Spanish milled dollars at the rate of eight
shillings the Dollar, or in other money equal in value
thereto; Also, the use of all my household goods, while
my widow, to be in lieu of her Dower. Unto my only
child and son Edward, all the remainder of my Estate; £10 to be paid to him when twenty-one years
of age, the other payable in whole or in part thereafter from time to time as my loving Kinsmen, Michael Price and Jacob Dennis (whose honesty I rely
on) may think him entitled to by his prudent behaviour; and in the meantime to be put out to use at his

risk and for his benefit, if by his conduct he may [be] thought fit as above to receive and enjoy the same. I make my wife Anne and my Kinsmen, Michael Price and Jacob Dennis, executors.

Witnesses, Timothy Russell, of the City of New York, house carpenter, William Hoffmire, Richard Lawrence. Proved, June 10, 1782.

Page 22.—In the name of God, Amen. I, PHILIP LEEK, of Brookhaven, County of Suffolk, being weak in body. I leave to my well beloved wife Mary, all my buildings, lands, and tenements, while my widow; and then to my son, John Leake. Likewise unto my wife, one cow. After her decease the cow to go to my son Philip. One chest and all my wearing clothes and a bed that was called his. The remainder of my cattle and household goods unto my two daughters, Submit Bartlett and Mary Homan, equally divided between them. I make Stephen Sweney and Gershon Brown, executors.

Dated February 12, 1781. Witnesses, John Turner, Samuel Turner, Samuel Satterly, yeomen. Proved, March 8, 1782.

Page 23.—In the name of God, Amen. I, DANIEL MUNROE, of H. M. S. *The Carisford*, Captain Peacock, commander, being of sound mind and memory. After all my just debts be paid I leave to my friend, Archibald Colbreath, of H. M. S. *Adimant*, Captain Graves, commander, all such sums of money as shall be due and payable to me for wages, prize-money, or on any other account; Also, my wearing apparel and personal estate. I make my friend, Archibald Colbreath, H. M. S. *Adimant*, executor.

Dated April 26, 1782. Witnesses, Jacob James, Jeremiah Fennhorn, Cormick McHugh, William Pye, of the ship *London*, schoolmaster. Proved, May 27, 1782.

[NOTE.—Cormick McHugh, steward on board H.M.S.

Assurance, assignee of Archibald Galbreath, sole devise, and executor of Daniel Munroe, was granted letter of administration on June 8, 1782.]

Page 24.—In the name of God, Amen. I, JOHN PELL, of the City of New York in America, mariner, being sick and weak in body. All my just debts and funeral charges to be paid within a convenient time after my decease. I leave to my eldest son Samuel £1, because he is my eldest son. My beloved wife Sarah shall have the possession and profits of all my estate, real and personal, while my widow, for her own support and for the maintenance and education of the younger children not of age. Should she remarry, then the one full third part of my real and personal estate to be given to my wife during her lifetime. All my real and personal estate to go to my son Samuel and to my other children, John, William, Anthony, Frances, Sarah, and Margaret Pell in equal shares. Should any die unmarried and without issue, then their parts to go to my surviving children. Should my wife depart this life before my youngest child is of lawful age, then no division shall be made until my youngest child shall have attained its full age. If any of my children have had any sum of money or goods advanced over and above to each of the others then the amount of such money or the price of such goods at the time of advancement shall be deducted from the share of such child. All my children to be provided for without preference, except as above. Whereas Mrs. Hester Pell, late of New York, " spinster," who died in the month of November last, was related to me, and by which means I became her heir at law, and whereas she did leave at the time of her decease considerable real estate, and which estate I conceive to be mine of right; now therefore I do direct that my executors do commence, prosecute, or defend any action in law or equity that may be effectual to the full recovery of said real estate as may and did descend to me; except they shall think it desirable upon good grounds and solid reflection to give up my claim. Should any part be recovered then it is to be disposed of as if it was part of my real estate herein before mentioned. I make my beloved wife Sarah and my good friends, Lawrence Kortwright, John Thurman, and William Depeyster, of the City of New York, merchants, executors.

Dated April 4, 1782. Witnesses, William Kenyon, merchant, John Brade, clerk to Wm. Kenyon, both of the City of New York, and William Cock. Proved, June 17, 1782.

Page 26.—In the name of God, Amen. I, JOHN DE BEVOIS, of New Town, Queens County, yeoman, being in a reasonable health of body. All debts to be paid. I leave to my dearly beloved wife Jannietie, my best bed and furniture, riding chair and horse, cupboard, and her choice of my negro wenches; £20 per year, payable during her natural life by all my children, each in their proportion; the same to be in lieu of her Dower. Unto my son Karel, £10 for his birthright; Also, my homestead that I had of my father, and the one half of my woodland near New Town Spring; Also, the one half of the woodland that I had of Nathan Smith, he and his heirs rendering and paying £200 in two equal payments. Unto my son George, the farm that I bought of Bernardus Van Zant, and the one half of my woodland near New Town Spring, one half of the Nathan Smith woodland; he and his heirs to pay £200 in two equal payments. Unto my son Jacobes, the farm he now lives on at Bushwick, with the woodland; Also, two thirds of my meadow at Seller's Neck, he to pay £100 in two equal payments. Unto my son Johannes, the farm that I bought of Culver, with the woodland and meadows; Also two acres and a half of woodland that I bought of Duryo in the Hills; Also the one third of my meadow at Seller's Neck; he to pay £100 in two equal payments.

The payments of my sons to begin at two months time after my decease, and the other payment to be one year after that. Unto my son Daniel, £600; one half payable in two months after my decease; the other in one year's time after that. After my debts, funeral charges, and these legacies are satisfied the remainder of my moveable estate unto all my above-named children in equal shares. I make my sons Karel and George and my brother-in-law, Jacob Rapelje, executors.

Dated October 1, 1774. Witnesses, Jacob Palmer, Samuel Lawrence (yeomen), Peter Rapelje. Proved, June 25, 1777.

Page 28.—Know all men by these presents that I, GILES SEAMAN, of the Township of Oysterbay, Queens County, being this 26th day of November, 1780, in a weak and infirm state of health of body. My wife Letitia to have the use of one gentle horse, one good cow, during life; Also, one of the best of my rooms to dwell in, bread and meat for her own use; hay and pasture for her horse and cow and barn-room for her horse; one of the best beds and bedsteads, furniture throughout; and privilege of all fruit trees for her use, and one half of the garden. Unto my son Jordan, all that land he has in possession that I bought of Nicholas Alberson, and had in exchange from Isaac Doty, lying on the north side of the highway that leads from Jericho to Muskete Cove. My two sons, Giles and Richard, to have all my land and plantation that I now live upon, that I bought of Abraham Seaman and of the Townsends, and a piece that I bought of Jonathan Pratt, lying on the East side of Muskete Cove road. All my meadows and upland and rights in the marsh at South; all my plain land and proprietor's rights in Hempstead and Oysterbay plains (the place where Jacob Hawxhurst now lives excepted), shall be equally divided between my three sons above mentioned, they paying £100 to my wife, a like sum to each of my daughters, Mary Hawxhurst and Hannah Oakley. My two sons, Giles and Richard, to have the privilege of taking the rails that they have carried on the plains at the southward of Daniel Lutter's house, and convert the same to their own use, before any division be made. All my household goods within doors to be equally divided between my wife and five children, Mary, Jordan, Hannah, Giles, and Richard. My two sons, Giles and Richard, shall have the effects arising from the sale of the farm that Jacob Hawxhurst lives upon, and two patent rights lying at New Hampshire, all my horses, cattle, sheep, hogs, farming utensils, all other living creatures upon the farm or land, and all other lands, and writings and money that hath not been mentioned, to go for the estate and use of my said two sons, in equal shares, with the paying of all my just debts and funeral charges. My executors to be reasonably paid for their trouble. I make my neighbor, Adonijah Underhill, and my three sons, Jordan, Giles, and Richard Seaman, executors.

Witnesses, Charles Clement, of Hempstead (yeoman), George Duryee, Sarah Clement, of Hempstead (spinster). Proved, June 1, 1782.

Page 30.—In the name of God, Amen. I, SAMUEL TREDWELL, of the Township of Hempstead, Queens County, farmer, being sick and weak in body. All my just debts and funeral expenses to be paid out of my personal estate. I leave to my son William, all my farm lands, messuages, dwelling house and homestead situate at Success in the Township of Hempstead where I now live, together with a piece of salt meadow at Hungary Harbour, at South, containing about ten acres. Likewise, my negro boy named Harry, to his own disposal upon condition that he allow his mother such a competent support and maintenance during her widowhood, (her wearing apparel excepted), as shall be thought sufficient and necessary; which I order my executors to pay particular attention to, and see amply done. In case of neglect or default of my son, they are to take such part of my farm as will yield sufficient for the purpose. Also, unto my son William, all my farming utensils and tools when he shall arrive at lawful age. My personal estate not herein disposed of to go to my wife and two daughters, Elizabeth and Susannah, in equal shares. My executors to keep on my farm so much stock of every kind and negroes, as they shall judge necessary; until my two daughters arrive at the age of eighteen years or marry. My executors to take on themselves in conjunction with my wife and son the management of my farm and business, to be at their direction during the infancy and non-marriage of my daughters. I give the use and privilege of such part of my dwelling house with kitchen and cellar room assigned her by my executors, while my widow, for my wife to live in; Also, one horse and my riding chair. Should my son William die under age without lawful issue, my farm and meadows and other legacies devised to him to go to my daughters, Elizabeth and Susannah, in equal shares. I make my father-in-law, Benjamin Hewlett, my brother, Benjamin Tredwell, and my brother-in-law, Uriah Platt, executors.

Dated August 28, 1781. Witnesses, Cornelius Cornell, John Mitchell, yeoman, George Hewlett. Proved, June 18, 1782.

Page 33.—In the name of God, Amen. I, JANNETJE REMSEN, of the Township of Brooklyn, Kings County, widow of Jeremiah Remsen, late of Brooklyn, being in perfect health of body and of perfect mind and memory. All my just debts and funeral charges to be paid. I leave to my brother, Luke Schenck, £300, my largest silver tankard, my silver cup or Beeker, and six silver table spoons. Unto my three nephews, sons of my sister Susanna, deceased, viz.: Martin, Johannes, and Abraham, £75 each. Unto the children of my nephew Peter, deceased, son of my said sister

Susanna, viz.: Jannetje, Margaret, and David, £25 each. Unto the children of my nephew, Barent Johnson, son of my sister Catalina, to wit: to Jeremiah, my brown chest; to Catalina, my largest bilstill cupboard and my great Dutch Bible; to Johannis, my small silver tankard; to Jeromus, my largest copper kettle; to Martin, my clock. Unto the daughters of my cousin, Johannes Lott (son-in-law of my sister Catalina): to Antje, my small Dutch Bible; to Catalina, my scissors with a silver chain; to Jannetje, two silver table-spoons. Unto Antje, my cousin (wife of said Barent Johnson), my silver teapot. Unto Jeremiah (son of my brother-in-law, Abraham Remsen), my flowered cupboard. Unto Martin (son of my nephew, Marten Schenck and grandson of my brother, Martin Schenck, deceased), my small brown cupboard. Unto Antje (daughter of my nephew, Martin Schenck), my Dutch New Testament, silver bound. Unto Jannetje, now the wife of Peter V. D. Bilt; Willempje, daughter of Abraham Casyon, deceased; Jannetje and Jeremiah, children of said Abraham Remsen; Jeremiah and Catalina, children of said Barent Johnson; John Rubel, son of Domini Rubel; Jeremiah, son of Jeromus Remsen; to each of them, £50. Unto the children of my cousin, Abraham Ditmas (son-in-law of my sister Catalina), viz.: Abraham, Catalina, Johannes, and Dowe, each an equal share of £50. Unto my five nieces, viz.: Jannetje, the wife of Johannes Lott; Elizabeth, the wife of Peter Onderdonck; Elizabeth, the wife of Joris Rapalje; Susanna, wife of Luke Bergen; and Maria, the widow of Douwe Ditmars, deceased; all my wearing apparel equally to be divided amongst them. Unto the said Barent Johnson, all my horses, cattle, hogs, wagons, sleighs, and all other farmer's tools and utensils, and all my hogsheads and other casks, all my corn and grain growing on the farm or being elsewhere. The remainder of my estate to be disposed of as follows, to wit: one third to my nephew, Martin Johnson; like part

to my nephew, Martin Schenck; the remaining part to
the children of the said·Barent Johnson. I make my
nephews, Barent Johnson and Martin Johnson and
Martin Schenck, executors.

Dated, February 7, 1780. Witnesses, Elizabeth Als-
tin, Hendrick Lott, of New Lotts, yeoman, Johannes
Lott. Proved, June 28, 1782.

Page 34.—In the name of God, Amen. I, CORNELIUS
RAPALIE, Sr., of New Town, Queens County, yeoman,
being sick of Body. All my debts and funeral charges
to be paid. I leave to my two daughters, Mary and
Adrina, all my bonds and cash in equal shares; which
division is to be made as soon as decency will permit
after my decease; and that which belongs to my youngest daughter, Adrina, to be put at interest by my
executors for her benefit until she is twenty-one. Unto
my eldest daughter, Mary, a negro girl named Isabell,
my best bed and furniture, and three best cows. Unto
my youngest daughter, Adrina, a negro girl named
Darcys, one best bed and furniture, and three best
cows. ·Unto my dearly beloved wife, Cornele, my cupboard, with all my linen, my tea-table, and all my tea
tackle, my negro wench named Marye, and one best
bed and furniture. Unto my executors, my arms and
wearing apparel to be equally divided among them.
The remainder of my estate, real and personal, to be
for the use and benefit of my wife Cornele while my
widow. In case of her remarriage or death, then unto
my two daughters, my gold watch, to be divided between them in such manner as they may think best,
but my farm and other part of my estate left for the
use and benefit of my wife to be sold at public sale.
Out of the proceeds, in case of my wife's remarriage,
£500 to be paid to her and the remainder to be divided
into three equal parts: one third part to my wife in
lieu of her Dower, the remaining two thirds unto my
two daughters, Mary and Adrina. Should my wife
Cornele die while my widow, then the whole proceeds

of sale to go to my two daughters. In case either of my servants which is left with my plantation should misbehave, then I authorize my executors to sell said slave or slaves and to purchase others, and replace them for my wife's benefit. I make my brother, Martin Rapalie, my brother-in-law, Jeremiah Remsen, and my friend, Nathaniel Moore, executors.

Dated October 24, 1781. Witnesses, Samuel Riker, Jacobus Riker, of New Town precinct, yeoman, Nathaniel Moore.

Proved, June 26, 1782.

Page 37.—In the name of God, Amen. I, JEROMAS REMSEN, Sr., of New Town, Queens County, yeoman, being sick of body. All debts to be paid. I leave to my son Jeremiah, £10 for his birthright. Unto my daughter, Hanachs Johnson, a negro girl named Abigill. Unto my daughter, Janneche Hadenbaruch, a negro girl named Molly, now in her possession. The remaining part of my real and personal estate to be sold by my executors within some convenient time after my decease, either at private or public sale. Unto my daughter, Hanachs Johnson, £200 out of the proceeds of the sale of my estate. Unto my daughter, Janneche Hardenbarach, £200. Unto my nephew, Abraham Remsen, son of my daughter, Brackey Remsen, £100, payable at his majority; in the meanwhile put at interest, which shall be for the maintenance of the child. Should it be not sufficient, my executors must make such other provision for him as he shall want provided his father should not return. Should he return, his father must make such other necessary provision for the child. Should the child die in non-age, then the above £100 shall be equally divided amongst my three sons and two daughters. Unto my son Jeromas all the remainder of my estate. I make my two sons, Jeremiah and Jeromas Remsen, and my son-in-law, Barent Johnson, executors.

Dated December 15, 1777. Witnesses, Samuel Riker,

Joseph Denton, James Morrell, of New Town, cordwainer. Proved, June 26, 1782.

Page 39.—In the name of God, Amen, 1782. I, NATHANIEL JARVIS, of Huntington, County of Suffolk, farmer, being sick and weak in body. My just debts to be paid by my executors. I leave to my beloved brother John all my lands and buildings and appurtenances that were given to me in my father's will; with all other land, buildings, rights and privileges that I have purchased, and all my moveable estate. My brother to pay out of it, £100, to be divided equally between William Jarvis, Austin Jarvis, Stephen Higbee, Hezekiah Weekes, Isaac Dennis, Benjamin Dennis, and Anna Jarvis. I make my brother, John Jarvis, Abraham Jarvis, and Nathaniel Bunee, executors.

Dated —— , 1782. Witnesses, Daniel Higbee, Nathaniel Udell (yeoman), Phebe Wickes. Proved, June 27, 1782.

Page 40.—Know all men by these Presents, that I, JOSEPH CONKLING, of Huntington, Suffolk County, farmer, February 12, 1779. All my just debts and funeral charges to be paid. I leave to my loving wife Judith my riding chair and chair horse, and two beds and furniture, and all the household goods she brought to me, which I give to her free disposal, with the use and improvement of the west part of the dwelling house where we now live, while my widow; likewise of the one third part of my farm. Also, two cows and one swine. All to be hers in lieu of Dower. Unto my two sons, Jonah and Joseph, all my lands, meadows, marshes, and buildings lying in Huntington, West Neck, in equal shares, with all the remainder of my moveable estate, except what I dispose of or order to be sold. Unto my son Joseph, one cow and my writing desk. Unto my daughter, Martha Long, £5. Unto my two daughters, Sarah and Rebecca Conkling, each of them, one bed and furniture, and each £25.

The linen in the house to be kept for the use of the family. If either of my two younger daughters, Sarah or Rebecca, should die under age or without issue, her part shall fall to my two surviving daughters. My two sons, Jonah and Joseph, shall each of them pay unto my son Ebenezer £75 in one year after my decease; also to my son John £50 when twenty-one. My executors to put my son John to a trade as they shall think proper, and pay the legacies to my three daughters out of my moveable estate. My wife to have the one third part of the grain on the ground for the use of the family. I make my brother-in-law, Philip Conkling, and my cousin, Richard Conkling, executors.

Witnesses, Frederick Dibble, Jesse Sammis (farmer), Solomon Ketcham. Proved, July 11, 1782.

Page 42.—I, John Colyer, of the Township of Huntington, Suffolk County, yeoman, the tenth day of the third month called March, 1778, being low and weak of body. All my just debts to be paid by my executors. I leave to my well-beloved wife Sarah all that she had from her father's estate, and the use of one third of my real and personal estate, while my widow. All the rest of my estate to go to my only son Charles; Also, that part which my wife has the use of, after her marriage or decease. Should my son live to lawful age, then he shall pay unto my sister Sarah's son, John Powell, £10, or the value of it. Should my son die before he comes to lawful age, then my executors shall (after my wife's decease) turn my whole estate into money and divide it in the following manner, viz.: £20 to my sister Sarah's son, John Powell; the remainder of my estate shall be equally divided between my brother, Abraham Colyer, and all my sister's children. I make my friends, John Whitson and Amos Whitson, executors.

Witnesses, Theodorus Van Wyck of Oysterbay (farmer), Richard Robbins (farmer), Martha Van Wyck of Oysterbay. Proved, June 6, 1782.

Page 44.—Know all men by these Presents, that I. WHITHEAD SAXTON, of Islip, being sound in mind and memory though mortally wounded in body, do this 24th of May, 1782, make this will. My just debts to be paid by my executors out of my personal and real estate. I leave to my mother, Elizabeth Saxton, and to my three sisters, Pheby, Ruth and Elizabeth Saxton, all my real and personal estate in equal shares. I make Isaac Thompson, Esq., of Islip, executor.

Witnesses, Nathaniel Oakly, Isaac Young, Paul Huff of Islip, yeoman. Proved, June 12, 1782.

Page 45.—In the name of God, Amen. I, SAMUEL BELL, of the City of New York, blacksmith, the 4th December, 1767, make this will. After my just debts and funeral expenses be paid I leave to my eldest son, Andrew, one shilling for his birthright. My beloved wife Jane shall have the full management of my whole estate, real and personal, while my widow. After my wife's decease my whole estate to be equally divided among my children in equal shares, viz.: my sons, Andrew, Robert, and Samuel, and my daughters, Mary, wife of Robert Leonard, and Jane. If any of my aforesaid children should die before the age of twenty-one, that share to go to my children then living. My executors to take a true inventory of my whole estate after my wife's decease, and sell the same at public vendue or otherwise. I make my beloved wife Jane. my son Andrew, and my son-in-law, Robert Leonard, executors.

Witnesses, Jacobus Stoutenburgh, George Walgrove, of the City of New York, cooper, Samuel Johnson. Proved, July 22, 1782.

Page 47.—In the name of God, Amen. I, ISAAC FARRIER, late of Philadelphia, now of New York City, mariner, being in bodily health. I leave to my worthy friend, David Gregg, of the City of New York, innkeeper, all and several my wages, sums of money, lands, tenements, goods, chattels, and estate whatsoever, as shall be anyways due, or belonging unto me at the time of my decease. I make David Gregg my sole executor.

Dated July 24, 1780. Witnesses, John Welsh, innkeeper, Jacob Bennett. Proved, July 15, 1782.

[NOTE.—David Gregg died before this will was probated. In his stead, letters of administration were granted to John Fegan, of the City of New York, on July 16, 1782.]

Page 48.—In the name of God, Amen, May 24, 1782. I, JOHN BRAGAW, of New Town, Queens County, being very sick and weak of body. All my just debts and funeral charges to be paid. I leave to Margaret, my dearly beloved wife, in lieu of her Dower, my whole estate, real and personal, while my widow. Should she marry again, then she is to have £300, payable out of my estate by my executors; and likewise, one of my best feather beds, with the furniture thereunto belonging, and then to quit the remainder of my estate. After my wife's marriage or decease, unto my three sons the following sums to be raised out of my estate, viz.: to my son Isaac £105; to my son Andrew £100; to my son Abraham, £200. Also all my estate, real and personal, unto my three sons, Isaac, Andrew, and Abraham, and my three daughters, Nelly, wife of Abraham Rapalje; Hile, wife of Jeromus Rapalje, and Jane, wife of Tunis Brinckerhoff, jr., in equal shares. I make my sons, Isaac and Andrew, and my son-in-law, Abraham Rapalje, executors.

Witnesses, George Brinkerhoff and Jacob Rapelje, both of New Town, yeomen, Richard Alsop. Proved, July 24, 1782.

Page 50.—In the name of God, Amen. I, MARY DENNY, of the City of New York, widow, being of sound mind and memory. After my just debts be paid, I leave to my worthy friend, Margaret Waterman, wife of William Waterman, of said City, all my estate, real and personal, together with all debts, dues, and demands due to me at my decease, in trust for the sole use of my son, John Denny, mariner, to be delivered to him at the discretion of my executors. Should he die before me, then the whole estate to go to said Margaret Waterman; whom I make executrix.

Dated August 3, 1782. Witnesses, Friederick Bausier, of the City of New York, cooper, Coleman Fisher, Nehemiah Field. Proved, August 12, 1782.

Page 52.—To all Christian people to whom these presents shall come or any ways concern. Know ye that I, WILLIAMPE DURYE, widow of Joost Durye, late deceased, of the Township of Oysterbay, Queens County, being this 2d day of August, 1781, in a good state of health. All my just debts, funeral charges and expenses to be fully paid before any division be made. I leave to my son Charles's son George, the lame boy, £10, to be put at interest until he arrives at lawful age. Should he die before majority, then his legacy to be equally divided between his brothers and sisters. Unto my daughter Willempey, one of my best cows, six pewter plates, three platters, two basons, six knives and forks, with all the tea tackling and china ware. Unto Mary Bennet, one large pewter platter marked M. R. T., which was my mother's. The remainder of my estate unto my three daughters, namely: Cornelia Nostrand, Mary Bennet, and Willempey Durye, in equal shares. I make my two sons-in-law, Garret Nostrand and Nicholas Bennet, both of the Township of Oysterbay, and my daughter, Willempey, executors. Unto my daughter Willempey my side saddle and brass kettle, before signing.

Witnesses, Isaac Wright, Jordan Wright, John Wright, all of Oysterbay, yeomen. Proved, July 22, 1782.

Page 53.—These Presents witnesseth this 16th day of the 10th month, 1775, that I, JACOB MOTT, of Hempsted, Queens County, do make this will. I give to my wife, one bed and furniture, 2 cows, 6 sheep, 6 chairs, one round table, one square table, one looking glass. Unto my daughter Kehia, one bed and furniture, but the use of it to my wife until my daughter Kehia is 18 years old. Unto my four daughters £30 apiece, payable as they are respectively eighteen years of age, or on the day of marriage. Unto my three daughters, Rachel, Phebe, and Amy, in equal shares, the remainder of my beds and bedding not yet given away. Unto my wife and four daughters the remainder of my moveable estate, except what is hereafter given away, but the use of my riding chair to my wife during her widowhood. Unto my son Jacob my great Bible; my daughter Rachel, Sewet's History, my daughter Phebe, George Fox's Journal; my son Samuel my little Bible, Thomas Choakley's Journal, and William Penn's Travels in Holland and Germany; my daughter Any, Samuel Bownne's and John Richardson's Journal in one volume, and John Fethergil's Journal. The remainder of my books unto all my children equally. Unto my two sons, Jacob and Samuel, one pair of oxen, my mare and colt, and all my farming utensils, which I order to be left on the farm; my wife shall have an equal right to use them until Samuel is twenty-one years old, in order that my wife and son Jacob may bring up and support my children therewith. Also, to all my sons, my writing desk, carpenter's tools and wearing clothes, equally; also, all my houses, lands, rights of land, meadows, marshes, and beaches in the bounds of Hempstead, divided or undivided; but my wife to have the use of the cleared land and meadow, and so much timber as shall be necessary for firewood and fencing until my son Jacob is twenty-one years old; and then to have the use of one-half of my land and meadows until my son Samuel is twenty-one years old, if she remains my widow; for the bringing up of my children, my wife to have the liberty to keep two cows, one horse, and one swine on the farm, and the use of the west fire-place and rooms of that house during her widowhood; my sons to supply her with such other necessaries for her support and bringing up of my young children. What is given to my wife to be in lieu of Dower. Each of my daughters to have the liberty to dwell in the west room of my house so long as they remain unmarried. I make my wife, my brother Jehu Mott, and my son Jacob, executors.

Witnesses, Silas Hicks, Phebe Wright, Rachel Hicks, of Hempstead, widow. Proved, August 5, 1782.

Page 55.—In the name of God, Amen. I, JACOB DURYEE, of the City of New York, being of sound disposing mind and memory. All just debts and funeral charges to be paid. I leave unto my dearly beloved wife Sarah the full and sole use and benefit of my estate to be by her enjoyed so long as she remains my widow, she maintaining and providing for my young and unmarried children, and committing no waste therein; should she complete a second marriage, in that case she to have the interest of £200; Also one complete bed and furniture, one silver milk pot, one silver sugar pot, one tea table, one set of china, six silver teaspoons, four silver table spoons, one large looking glass, one cupboard or clothes press, during her natural life, this to be for her right of dower. To my son Jacob, for his birthright, £100; Also my silver tankard, silver watch and all my wearing apparel; Also my negro boy Jack. Whereas my eldest daughters, Catherine and Mary, have each had an outset of the value of £130, everyone of my children that are unmarried at my decease may have £130 for their outset, each paid to them out of my estate by my executors at their marriage or at the age of twenty-one years. To my daughter Sarah (after the death of my wife), my negro wench Clarin, also one clothes press; should she die without heir, the said negro wench and clothes press to be sold. If my son Jacob should want money to put himself into business, my executors are to give him every prudent assistance out of my estate. All my estate, real and personal, to be sold and the proceeds divided into seven equal parts. My daughter Sarah to have a double portion; this I give her in consideration of her helpless condition. To my beloved children, Catherine, Mary, Magdalena, Jacob, and Jain, each one equal seventh part. Whereas, I have paid or advanced for my daughter Catherine, £40, this sum to be deducted from her portion. I make my dearly beloved wife Sarah, my son-in-law, Thomas Stagg, my beloved son Jacob, my nephews, Johannis Norestrant and Harry Peters, executors.

Dated January 28, 1782. Witnesses, Abraham Polhemus, Daniel Van Vlack, of the City of New York, cordwainer, Richard Fletcher. Proved, August 12, 1782.

Page 58.—In the name of God, Amen. I, STEPHEN SCHENCK, of the Township of Bushwick, King's County, being weak in body, do this 4th day of May, 1782, make this will. All my lawful debts to be paid. My beloved wife or widow (*name not mentioned*) shall have the management of my estate, real and personal, during her widowhood. Should she remarry, or after her death, all the estate to go to my son John. Should he die without heirs, then Antye Schenck, my niece, daughter of my brother, Adrian Schenck, to have £50 out of my estate for the love and good will I bear her. The rest of my estate to be equally divided between Jacobus De Bevois, and Nicholas Schenck, my brother, or their heirs. I make my wife sole executrix.

(*Signed* STEPHEN SCHANK.)

Witnesses, Michael Vandervoort, Harman Andresse, William Covert; all of King's County, yeomen. Proved, August 9, 1782.

Page 60.—These Presents witnesseth that I, SILAS HICKS, of Hempstead, Queens County, weaver, this 9th day of the second month, 1773, make this will. I leave to my wife Rachel one bed and furniture, also, a bedstead. My negro man Stephen to be free at my death, provided he will return to my executors yearly the sum of £3 for the use of my wife and children. Nevertheless if the negro man never becomes chargeable to my estate, then he shall give that money (which he puts into the hands of my executors) to whom he will at his death. My executors to sell all the rest of my estate and pay all my just debts; what remains to go to my wife and four children, Benjamin, Willit, William, and Martha Hicks, and all such children that my wife may have within nine months after my decease, in equal shares, payable to my sons when twenty-one and to my daughters when eighteen. My wife to have the use of what I have given to my children to bring them up. What is given to my wife is in lieu of her Dower. If she refuses to release the same, then that part to go to all my children equally in manner above. My executors to put out my children to such trades and to such places as they think best. I make Jehu Mott and my brother, Benjamin Hicks, executors.

Witnesses, Ruth Mott, Mary Mott, and Jehu Mott jr., of Hempstead, yeoman. Proved, August 5, 1782.

Page 62.—In the name of God, Amen. I, JOHN HYLTON, of the City of New York, being weak in body. My executors as soon as conveniently after my decease to sell all my real and personal estate, except such parts hereinafter mentioned, and immediately to pay my just debts. I leave to my son Ralph my negro boy named Harry. Unto my son Thomas my gold watch; unto my sister, Mary Hylton, for her attention to me during my illness, my negro girl called Mary. Whereas I stand seized in right of my late wife, Ann Hylton, of part of the estate of John Combs, late of Jamaica, on Long Island, deceased, I do give all my right in said estate, as also £40 to be divided equally between Sarah and Mariam Combs, daughters of my late wife, Ann Hylton. Also, unto them, all the wearing apparel of my late wife in equal shares. The remainder of my estate unto my two sons, Ralph and Thomas Hylton, in equal shares, payable when twenty-one. My executors to apply such parts of my estate as they shall think requisite to the bringing up of my sons, charging each with the sums so advanced them as part of their portions of my estate. I make my son Ralph, my friends, Thomas Braine and Stephen Skinner, executors.

Dated May 18, 1782. Witnesses, Sally Byvanck, Edward Laight, Mary Hylton.

Codicil. I appoint my sister, Mary Hylton, joint executrix with my son and friends above named. Unto my said sister Mary, in token of her tenderness and care of me during my illness, £50, to be paid out of the monies due me by virtue of a certain bond or obligation from Robert Randolph and Daniel L. Hylton, of Virginia.

Dated July 29, 1782. Witnesses, Edward Laight, of City of New York, merchant, Catherine Skinner, Margaret Gautier, of the City of New York, widow. Proved, August 20, 1782.

Page 64.—In the name of God, Amen. I, ANN COVENOVEN, of the Out Ward of the City of New York, widow of Jacob Covenoven, being in health of body. I leave to Jacob, Cornelius, Marite, Cornelia, and Annatie Harse, the children of John Harse, lately deceased, £10 each. Unto Ann Loy, £10; to Gouda Easterly, £10; to Tieunis Somerendike, one full and equal eighth part of my estate (after above legacies are paid); to the three children of Egbert Somerendike, a like part in equal shares; to the children of Volkert Hereman, one fourth part of my estate in equal shares. Unto the children of Gesse Van Hosen, deceased, who was the daughter of Egbert Hereman, one other like fourth part of my estate in equal shares. Unto Antie Hosen one eighth part of the remainder.

Unto the children of Volkert Somerendick, the remaining like eighth part in equal shares. I make my friends Tieunis Somerendick of the Out Ward of the City of New York, yeoman, and John Van Cortlandt, of the said city, gentleman, executors.

Dated April 19, 1775. Witnesses, Philip Van Cortlandt, Benjamin Vandewater, William Hoghland. Proved, September 2, 1782.

[NOTE.—Richard Fletcher, of said city, shopkeeper, and Tieunes Somerendike, of Bloomendale in the Out Ward of said city, yeoman, identified the signatures of the testator and witnesses.]

Page 67.—On board the ship *Tarter,* this 17th December, 1780. In the name of God, Amen. I, THOMAS C. WILLIAMS, of the City of New York, merchant, being in perfect health. I leave to my beloved wife Sarah all my household furniture and all my real estate in the City of Philadelphia, that is, one house or store between Chestnut and Walnut Streets fronting Water and Front Street; Also, one third of all my other real and personal estate wheresoever. Unto my brother, John Williams, in New York, £1,000. The remainder of my estate in this country unto my father, Samuel Williams, for life. After his death, the same to go to my brothers, William Williams, Samuel, and John Williams, and unto my sisters, Jane, Hanah, Esther, and Susan, in equal shares. I make Samuel Shoemaker, Esq., now of New York, my wife Sarah and my brother John, of New York, executors. All my affairs to be wound up, all my debts paid, and the legacies distributed in two years from the above date.

Witnesses, Eben^r. Putnam, Abr^m. L. Smith, Robert Rollo, Captain in His Majesties American Legion.

Codicil. New York, October 14, 1781. As I am now about going again to Virginia, do make this codicil. As I have a great property at risque on the Seigh at York Town and may be lost, do make this further provision for my beloved wife Sarah. Should my estate turn out deficient to what it is rated on the other side, she is to have my house as mentioned in Philadelphia on the other side, and £1,000 sterling, paid her out of my personal estate before any division be made; with all my household furniture. She to be at liberty to take the £1,000 sterling or the one-third of the personal estate as may be most agreeable to her.

Witness, Bartlee Smyth, of the City of New York, gentleman. Proved, August 26, 1782.

Page 69.—In the name of God, Amen. The 29th day of August, 1781. I, JOHANNES BRIT, of West Chester, County of New York, farmer, being very sick and weak in body. All my just debts and funeral charges to be paid. I give to my well beloved son William, whom I make my sole executor, all the lands, messuages and tenements. Unto my six daughters, namely: Agnes Steddal, Hannah Brit, Catharine Williams, Christianna Britt, Sarah Pim, and Elizabeth Brit, all the household goods and whatever remains of the above estate in equal shares.

Witnesses, Charles Shipman, Paul Chris^r Lentz, and James Foshay, of the City of New York, storekeeper. Proved, August 9, 1782.

Page 70.—In the name of God, Amen. I, MOSES MARDEN, of the City of New York, tavernkeeper, being weak in body. I leave to my daughter, Isabel Marden, about three years of age, £150, payable at my decease. When she is eighteen years of age the money with interest may be demanded and left entirely to the prudence of my daughter. Unto the infant that is now in the loins of my wife, £100; to be paid by my wife at the expiration of three years from the birth of the child. In case it should be a male child, the money may not be demanded until he is twenty-one; if a female, it may be demanded as by my daughter Isabel. If neither of them survive to majority, their portions

to go unto the prudent care of my loving wife Isabel.
All my book accounts and outstanding debts and the
remainder of my cash, stock in trade and household
furniture, land, and tenements unto my wife Isabel.
I make James Webb and my wife Isabel, executors.

Dated July 13, 1777. Witnesses, David Thompson,
James Ettredge, of the said city, saddler, Jacob Tyler.
Proved, July 22, 1782.

Page 72.—In the name of God, Amen. I, BENJAMIN
TREDWELL, the elder, of Madnans Neck, otherwise
Great Neck, in the Township of Hempstead, in full
and perfect health of body. All my just debts and
funeral expenses to be paid. I leave to my son Benjamin all that my farm, lands, and homestead where
I now live, with the appurtenances thereunto belonging, he paying in consideration thereof, £800 within
one year after my decease, for the purposes hereinafter mentioned, provided always in case my son Benjamin should refuse to pay the same sum, then my
farm and premises to go to my son William, he paying a like sum within one year next after such refusal.
Should William also refuse, then my farm, homestead,
etc., to go to my grandson, Thomas Tredwell, son of
my deceased son John, under the same conditions.
Should my grandson also refuse, then my executors
are to sell and dispose of the same by any means to
the best advantage; the proceeds to go as follows:
One equal fourth part to my son Benjamin; a like part
to.my son William; a like part equally to all the children of my son John, deceased; the remaining part
equally to all the children of my son Samuel, deceased.
Unto my two sons, Benjamin and William, all my
other lands, messuages, meadows, marsh, and beach,
rights in common of the undivided lands, in the Township of Hempstead or elsewhere, as tenants in common, in equal shares. Unto each of my three daughters, respectively, to wit: Peggy, Phebe, and Sarah,
£300, out of my monies, and personal estate; together

with all and singular my household furniture, plate,
beds, bedding, and linen, in equal shares. All my
cedar shingles lying on my farm and homestead to
such of my sons as shall possess and enjoy my said
farm in virtue hereof for the purpose of covering my
dwelling house or such other houses as he shall think
proper. My executors to sell my outdoor moveables,
negroes, stock, utensils, tools, and implements of farming (except those herein mentioned), with all my
other personal and moveable property. The proceeds,
together with the £800 charged on my farm, to go as
follows: In case either of my sons Benjamin or William shall take the farm and homestead, then the one
full and equal third part of such residuary part of my
estate to my other son, Benjamin or William, as shall
not possess the farm; a like part to the children of
my son, John Tredwell, deceased, to wit: Thomas,
Benjamin, Phebe Wooley, Sarah Tredwell, John,
Elizabeth, and Richard Tredwell in equal shares, to be
paid as they come to lawful age. The remaining equal
third part unto the children of my son Samuel, deceased, to wit: William, Elizabeth, and Susanna Tredwell in equal shares, to be paid when of age. In case
my grandson, Thomas Tredwell, should possess the
farm, then the residuary part of my estate is devised
in manner following: one equal fourth part to my son
Benjamin; a like part to my son William; a like part
to said children of my deceased son John (Thomas
excepted); and the remaining fourth part to the children of my deceased son Samuel. Unto Abigail Bennet, who has lived with me many years, and carefully
attended to my interests, in consideration thereof, and
as a recompense therefor, £20. Unto my two sons,
Benjamin and William, all my wearing apparel.
Whereas it is the desire of my two old negro slaves,
Peter and Jenny to live with my children after my
decease, viz.: Peter with such of my sons as shall
possess my farm, Jenny with my daughter Sarah;
therefore, in consideration of the legacies so be-

queathed to them, I desire they respectively suffer my two old slaves to live with them, and to maintain them comfortably in their old age during their lives for their past faithful services to me; if they shall choose the same. The rest of my slaves to be given the liberty to choose masters for themselves, provided it can be done without too great disadvantage and injury to my estate. I make my said son Benjamin, my son-in-law, Hendrick Onderdonck, and my respected friends, William Thorne and John Allen, jr., the son of Henry Allen, deceased, executors.

Dated August 3, 1782. Witnesses, William Mott, James Mott, Daniel Kissam, all of Hempstead, Queens County, yeomen. Proved, September 2, 1780.

Page 76.—In the name of God, Amen. January 29, 1782. I, MARY REEVES, of Southold, County of Suffolk, spinster, being weak and sickly in body. I leave to my grandchild, Mary Reeve, all the clothes that have been made for her since she has been with me. Unto my son, Ebenezer Reeve, my negro man named Reuben. Unto my son-in-law, John Gardiner, and to my son-in-law, William Corwin, and his wife all the remainder of my estate, consisting in money, goods, and chattels, to be equally divided. My executors to take proper care for the suitable maintenance of my two old negroes, Titus and Jude, and keep a sufficiency of my estate in their hands for that purpose. I make my beloved friends, Deacon Thomas Reeve and Daniel Osborn, executors.

Witnesses, Mary Gardiner, spinster, Harmony Reeve, James Reeve, Esquire, yeoman. Proved, June 11, 1782.

Page 78.—In the name of God, Amen. I, THOMAS DOWNAN, of H. M. S. *Austrea*, Captain Square, commander, being of sound mind and memory. All my just debts to be paid. I leave to my friend, John Whitegar, belonging to H. M. S. *Austrea,* all such sums of money as shall be due me and payable for wages, prize money, or on any account whatsoever; as also my wearing apparel and personal estate. I make my friend, John Whitegar, executor.

Dated June 10, 1782. Witnesses, William Pye of the City of New York, schoolmaster, Cormick Mc-Hugh, Alexander Elmslie. Proved, September 9, 1782.

Page 79.—In the name of God, Amen. I, ALEXANDER ELMSLIE, of H. M. S. *Quebec*, Captain Mason, commander, being in bodily health. After all my just debts be paid, I leave to my friend, William Pye, belonging to H. M. S. the *London*, all my prize money, wages, and sums of money, lands, tenements, goods, chattels, and estate whatsoever, as shall be anyways due unto me at the time of my decease; whom I make executor.

Dated July 3, 1782. Witnesses, John Thursby, of the City of New York, mariner, Charles Johnson, Daniel Cann. Proved, September 9, 1782.

Page 80.—In the name of God, Amen. I, ICHABOD SAYRE, of Town of Southampton, County of Suffolk, husbandman, being in health of body. All my just debts to be paid by my executors in a convenient time after my decease. I leave to my son Ichabod my house, buildings, and home lot adjoining that which I bought of Samuel Wick. Unto my son Stephen my house and home lot where I now live. The remainder of my lands, woodlands, meadow, and common land to be equally divided between my said two sons; Also, all my farming tackling in equal shares. The remainder of my moveable estate to be equally divided between my loving wife Elizabeth and my daughter Elizabeth. Unto my son Joshua, six shillings. Unto my daughter Eunice, £6. Unto my daughter Mary's children £6 in equal shares. My executors shall sell land and pay my just debts and legacies out of the proceeds. My daughter Elizabeth shall have the privilege to live in the house with my son Stephen while unmarried. I make my two sons, Ichabod and Stephen, executors.

Dated June 1, 1776. Witnesses, Isaac Post, James Post, yeoman, and Jane Post, of said county. Proved, July 3, 1782.

Page 82.—In the name of God, Amen. I, DANIEL McINTYRE, being sick in body but sensible in mind. I leave to Cornelius Mynihan my wages and prize money due to me from H. M. Ships the *Renown* and *Irish*. Given under my hand and seal at Martinico Hospital in Fort Royall this eleventh day of January, 1782.

Witnesses, T. M. De Kland, Patrick Gibland, Jn°. Malone. Proved, September 23, 1782.

[NOTE.—Cornelius Mynihan, legatee, deposed that he saw the testator make his mark, and the witnesses sign. Letters of administration were granted to said Cornelius Mynihan, mariner, on board H. M. S. *Barflour*, September 27, 1782.]

Page 83.—In the name of God, Amen. I, THOMAS STEPHENS, of Southampton, being in a poor state of health. I leave to my son Thomas, my now dwelling house, barn, and home lot, together with my lands and meadows that I have in Southampton; he paying to his brother Matthias £150, and also to his younger brother, Silvanus Halsey Stephens, £100; when they are twenty-one years old. Unto my son Thomas two oxen and two horses. Unto my son Matthias one colt. Unto my son, Silvanus Halsey, one small cow. Unto my two daughters, Ann and Mehetable Stephens, £50 each, when they are eighteen. Unto my son Thomas all my team, and farming tackling. Unto my loving wife, Mehetable, one mulatto boy named Hira; together with the residue of my moveable estate after the legacies, my just debts and funeral charges are defrayed. I make my friend, Hugh Gelston, and my loving wife, Mehetable, executors.

Dated March 16, 1782. Witneses, Henry Herrick, of said county, Nehemiah Scott, Stephen Rogers, of said county. Proved, July 3, 1782.

Page 85.—In the name of God, Amen. I, JOSEPH RUGG, of Southampton, County of Suffolk, presser of cloth, being infirm of body. I leave to my beloved wife Debory, all my lands and buildings, to be improved by her, while my widow; with all the grain that shall be in the house and on the ground; Also, the best cow on the farm, the best bed in the house and its furniture. Unto my eldest daughter, Sary, all those things that were her mother's; Also, £5 in hard cash. Unto my daughter Mary one feather bed and furniture and one chest with a double-spring lock. Unto my daughter Agnes my clothier's press with all belonging unto it. Likewise, unto my beloved wife all the moveables remaining in my house. My moveables out of the house, except the cow, shall be sold to defray charges. Should my wife decease or marry again, all my lands and buildings to be sold and proceeds divided equally between my five daughters, namely: Mary, Agnes, Phile, Phebe, and Jerusha. I make my beloved wife Deborah, and my brother-in-law Henry Hudson, and my friend, David Haines Foster, of Southampton, executors.

Dated February 1, 1781. Witnesses, Stephen Jennings, and David Lum, David Haines Foster, of said county, yeomen. Proved, July 3, 1782.

Page 87.—In the name of God, Amen. I, JAMES BUTCHER, late of London, but at present of New York, and master of the ship *Raynham Hall*, being of sound mind and memory. I leave all my estate unto my beloved wife Sarah, whom I make sole executrix.

Dated September 13, 1781. Witnesses, David Mathews, of the City of New York, Esq., William Wiseham, of same city, merchant, James Griffith. Proved, September 16, 1782.

Page 88.—In the name of God, Amen. I, BETHUEL REEVE, of Southampton, Suffolk County, shoemaker and tanner, being infirm of body. I leave to my well-beloved wife Mary, two thirds of my lands and buildings; to be improved by her three years after my decease, then the improvement of one half of my lands and buildings to be improved by her while she is my widow; Also, one third of all my moveable estate; one feather bed with a reasonable furniture. Unto my eldest son, Joel, one third part of my lands and buildings; to improve the same from the last of next March to the term of three years following (if he improves it personally) and then the improvement of one half my lands and buildings as long as his mother remains my widow; otherwise, to be void; and further, on consideration of these above improvements fulfilled, then I give to him the one half and one sixth part of all my lands and buildings. Unto my two sons, Jeremiah and Silas, all the lands and tenements remaining, in equal shares. If they should ever sell they are to give their brother Joel the first offer. Unto my other two sons, Daniel and Zebulon Reeve, £20 each. Unto my two daughters, Keturah and Bethiah Reeve, £20 each. I make my son Joel and David Haines Foster, of Southampton, executors.

Dated July 25, 1776. Witnesses, John Lum and David Lum, David Haines Foster, of said county, yeoman. Proved, July 3, 1782.

Page 90.—In the name of God, Amen. I, MICAIAH HERRICK, of Southampton, County of Suffolk, being in a very poor state of health. All my just debts to be paid out of my moveable estate. I leave to my son James my now dwelling house, and barn, at Second Neck; together with all my lands, meadows, and commonage that I have lying to the westward of Cannoe place; Also, one half fifty of commonage lying eastward of said place; Also, ten shillings out of my moveable estate. Unto my son Edward, my now dwelling

house and home lot; together with all my lands and
meadows that I have in Southampton lying to the
eastward of said place; Also, one half fifty of commonage lying eastward of said place; Also, ten shillings. My two said sons shall pay to their brother
Hiram, each of them, £100 when he is twenty-one.
Unto my son Hiram, £20. Unto my daughter Clar-
issa £20, payable when eighteen. After my just debts,
funeral charges and the legacies be paid, the residue
of my moveable estate to go to my loving wife Martha,
to her free disposal; Also, the use and improvement
of all my lands, meadows, and tenements, while my
widow and beareth up my name. I make my cousin,
Henry Herrick, and my loving wife Martha, executors.

Dated September 13, 1781. Witnesses, Nathan Jaggar, jr., of said county, yeoman, James Post, Stephen
Rogers, of said county, yeoman. Proved, July 3, 1782.

Page 92.—In the name of God, Amen. I, SAMUEL
JENNINGS, of Southampton, Suffolk County, husbandman, being in health of body. I leave to my loving
wife Rachel the use and improvement of the west half
of my now dwelling house, while my widow; Also one
good feather bed and furniture. My two sons, Samuel
and James, shall provide for their mother all the
necessaries of life while my widow and beareth up my
name. Unto my son Samuel, the house in which he
now lives, together with the barn and all the home lot
of land; Also, that piece of land lying before his door
on which the wind-mill formerly stood; Also, the piece
of land lying on the east side of the Major's path,
which I bought of my brother-in-law, Samuel Randall;
Also, the whole of that piece of land and meadow lying at a place called the Island, which I bought of
Captain William Jones; Also, one lot of land lying
toward the Fish Cove within the North Sea lines,
which I bought of John White and Thomas Scott;
Also, one half lot adjoining to it lying with Henry

Harris's; Also, that piece of meadow lying at Jeffries Creek with the upland adjoining, that is within fence; Also, the one equal half of that piece of woodland that I bought of John Haines and Thomas Scott, which lyeth at or near the Island; Also, one equal half of my commonage. Unto my son James, my now dwelling house, barn and home lot with the meadow adjoining; Also, all my right of lands that I have in Cow Neck; Also, all that piece of meadow that I bought of Captin Elias Pelletreau; Also, that piece of land and meadow lying at or near the Island, which was formerly my father's; Also, the one equal half of that piece of woodland that I bought of John Haines and Thomas Scott lying at or near the Island; Also, that piece of woodland lying within the North Sea line which lyeth on the west side of what we call the straight path; Also, the woodland that I bought of Joseph Hildreth and Stephen Jennings; Also, the one half of my commonage. If there be any land not mentioned I give it to my sons in equal shares. If one or both of my sons should die without male heir, then his or their portion to be equally divided between the surviving brothers. Unto my son Silas £20. Unto my son Joshua £20. Unto my two younger sons, Caleb and Annanias, each £50. Unto my daughter, Phebe Schellenger, forty shillings. Unto my two sons, Caleb and Annanias, each a feather bed and furniture. I make my loving wife Rachel, my two sons, Samuel and James, executors.

Dated June 19, 1776. Witnesses, Caleb Cooper, Abraham Fordham, jr., Stephen Rogers. Proved, July 3, 1782.

Page 94.—In the name of God, Amen. I, JOHN HAINES, of Southampton, Suffolk County, being in health of body. I leave to my loving wife Mary the use and improvement of all my lands, meadows, and tenements during her natural life; Also, one third part of my moveable estate, together with all the provisions in the house and all the grain upon the ground; Also, my great Bible and my best bed and furniture. Unto my daughter Hannah my meadow lying at the place called the Indian Hedge; Also, my meadow in the pitle, lying against John Lum's; Also, one half lot of meadow at Sebennuck. Unto my two daughters, Lydia Lane and Mary Smith, all my land and meadow lying at the Island. Unto my younger daughters, Eunice and Susannah, in equal shares, all my meadow lying at the place called Homes's Hill. The remaining two thirds of my moveable estate (after my debts are paid) to go to my five daughters, namely: Hannah Jennings, Lydia Lane, Mary Smith, Eunice Haines, and Susannah Haines, in equal shares. Unto my son-in-law, Zebulon Jennings, one half fifty of commonage from the Cannoe Place eastward. Unto my said five daughters, all my lands, meadows, and tenements, not above disposed of. I make my loving wife Mary, my son-in-law, Zebulon Jennings, and my friend, David Haines Foster, executors.

Dated January 12, 1778. Witnesses, Timothy Rierson, Stephen Rogers, of said county, yeoman, and Matthew Rogers. Proved, July 3, 1782.

Page 95.—In the name of God, Amen. I, THOMAS COOPER, of Southampton, Suffolk County, being in health of body. Those debts and duties that I do owe to be paid at some convenient time. I leave to my well-beloved wife Mary, as her right of dower, the one third part of all my lands, meadows, and buildings during her life; Also, one third part of my moveable estate after my debts and legacies are paid. Unto my son Elias all my lands, meadows, and buildings eastward of the "Criks" known by the names of Tyana and Red "Crik," excepting what is disposed of to my other sons hereafter; Also my sword, £1 in cash, and blacksmith's tools. Unto my son Thomas, £10. Unless my son Elias shall pay unto Thomas, within one year after my decease, £30, then Thomas to have six

acres of land at the west end of my home lot, next to
Jonah Halcey's land; unless my son Caleb shall pay,
within one year after my death, £10, to Thomas, then
Thomas to have my Cooper's Neck lot, about three
acres, more or less; Also my lot of land at Short
neck in Quag Purchase, except my son John shall pay
to Thomas, £10, within one year after my decease.
Unto my son John (on his paying the above £10 to
Thomas) all my buildings, lands, meadows, and commonage, westward of the "Criks" known by the
names of Tyana and Red "Criks," except three quarters of a lot of meadow at the long point lying with
Daniel Cook, also one half fifty of commonage is excepted.   Unto Caleb my house and lot, bought of
Jonah Howel, with the barn; Also my lower close,
about five acres, at Halsey's neck; Also the lot of
land I bought of Henry Pierson; my Cooper's neck
Close, about three acres; my orchard at Lebonock,
with the land adjoining to it, about ten acres; Also
two pieces of land in the lot adjoining on the south
side to Thomas Foster, and on the north by John .
Hains, about twelve acres; the other piece about three
acres near the Fish Cove adjoining to Hacchaliah
Foster on the east side; and one fifty in my lot at Ram
Pasture in Pog Quage, with one half fifty of commonage to Canoo Place, and one quarter in Quage Purchase; Also three quarters of a lot of meadow lying
within Daniel Cook at Long Point.   Unto my four
daughters, Mary, Hannah, Jane, and Mehetable, £1
each.   The remainder of my estate unto my sons, John
and Caleb.   I make my sons, Elias, John, and Caleb,
executors.

Dated January 1, 1771.   Witnesses, Henry Jessup.
yeoman, Jeremiah Jessup, Jane Jessup.   Proved,
July 3, 1782.

Page 97.—In the name of God, Amen.   I, Cornelius Halsey, of Southampton, in the County of Suffolk, yeoman, being in health of body.   I leave to my

son Timothy my now dwelling house at Potunk, with all my right of commonage in Southampton and one third of my right of lands in the Manor of Saint George or what is now called Halsey's Manor; Also, five shillings in cash. Unto my son William my dwelling house, barn, and out houses that standeth on Onouck Neck, together with all my lands and meadows in said Neck, that lyeth to the southward of my house (except what I hereafter give to my son Frederick); Also, all my upper land lying to the northward of my house, and on the west side of said Neck; Also, one third part of all my rights of commonage in Southampton; Also, one third of my right of lands in the Manor above mentioned; Also, five shillings in cash. Unto my son Frederick twelve acres of land and meadow as it lies promiscuously at the northeast corner of said Onuck Neck; Also, a piece of woodland in the upper Division containing, by estimation, about sixteen acres, bounded east by Lemuel Howell, south by William Stephens, west by Nehemiah Sayre, and north partly by William Stephens, and partly by myself; Also, another piece of woodland containing about eight acres, bounded, north by Timothy Bishop, east by William Stephens, south by myself, and west by Nehemiah Sayre; Also one third of my commonage running through the bounds of Southampton; Also, one third of my right of land in the Manor above mentioned; Also, five shillings in cash. Unto my two younger sons, Zopher and Solon, each £200 in cash, payable at the age of twenty-one years. Unto my five daughters, namely: Millescent, Martha, Cleopatra, Ruth, and Susanah, £50 each in cash, or an equivalent, payable at age or marriage state; Also, liberty to live in my houses so long as they remain unmarried. Unto my loving wife Millescent my negro girl called Dinah, and my negro boy called Jack; Also, £100 out of my moveable estate in such things as she shall choose, to be appraised to her by indifferent persons. The remainder of my estate to be equally divided between my two oldest sons, Timothy and William, whom I make executors.

Dated November 2, 1779. Witnesses, Timothy Parsons, miller, Stephen Rogers, yeoman, Matthew Rogers. Proved, July 3, 1782.

Page 99.—In the name of God, Amen. I, WALTER LONG, mariner, belonging to H. M. S. *Princessa*, Charles Knatchbull Esq., commander, being of sound mind and memory. All my wages, sums of money, lands, chattels, and estates, due, owing, or belonging to me at the time of my decease, I leave to my dear and well-beloved brother-in-law, Samuel Karkike, merchant in the City of New York; whom I make executor.

Dated February 9, 1782. Witnesses, John Pearse, Sarah Pearse, Charles Knatchbull. Proved, October 4, 1782.

[NOTE.—Samuel Kirk, the sole legatee and executor, identified the signature of the testator and witnesses.]

Page 100.—In the name of God, Amen. I, SAMUEL JAGGER, of the Town of Southampton, County of Suffolk, husbandman, being in a poor state of health. All my just debts to be paid out of my moveable estate. I leave to my son Joseph, all my right of land lying [in] Pongonguoge Neck. Unto my son James, one fifth right of land lying in the lot of Jonas Foster at the Canoe Place. Unto my son Samuel my now dwelling house, barn, and home lot; together with all my other lands, meadows, and commonage that I have in Southampton or elsewhere. In case he should die without male issue, then his portion to go to his three younger brothers, namely: Josiah, Joseph, and James. Also, my team (consisting of two horses and two oxen), and my team tackling, as cart, plow, harrows, etc.; Also, my loom and all my loom or weaver's tackling. Unto my loving wife Mary £5 out of my moveable estate. Unto my four daughters, namely: Hannah Jaggar, Phebe Jaggar, Eunice Coe, and Mehetable Goodale, five shillings each. The remainder of my moveable estate to be equally divided between my three sons, namely: Josiah, Joseph and James; who also with my wife shall have privilege to live in my now dwelling house one year after my decease. I make my son Samuel and my friend, Stephen Rogers, executors.

Dated September 18, 1771. Witnesses, Elias Peirson, weaver, Samuel Peirson, Mary Jaggar. Proved, July 3, 1782.

Page 102.—In the name of God, Amen. This 20th day of December, 1779, I, JAMES HAINES, of Southampton, Suffolk County, being sick and weak in body. I leave to my beloved wife Martha the west room in my house, bedroom and kitchen, the use of my oven and well, with the chamber over the west rooms; the third part of my barn, and the improvement of the third part of my lands and meadows, during her widowhood. After my just debts and legacies be fully satisfied, she to have half of my moveables, indoors and out. Unto my two daughters, Sarah and Elizabeth, £10 each, out of my moveable estate. Unto my son David the lot of land he now lives on, with all the buildings and improvements on the same; Also, Thedson's lot of land, about ten acres, and one half of my meadow at North Sea; one half fifty right of commonage, and one third part of my timberland in the lots Nos. 25 and 26; and one half of my North side lot No. 25; one half of the hay ground mendment. Unto my son Samuel my home lot, with the land I bought of the Town, and all the buildings and improvements on the same, and my lot of land, known by the name of the Lum Lot; and my new division lot at Calf Creek; and one third part of my woodland Nos. 25 and 26; and one half of my North side land; one half the hay ground mendment; one quarter of a fifty of commonage throughout the bounds, except Quague

Purchase; and one half of my meadow at North Sea. Unto my son Daniel my long pond land and orchard, about 17 acres, and a piece of woodland that I bought of Alexander King, about 9 or 10 acres, at the Brick Kilns. The remainder of my lands, buildings, meadows, and commonage to my son James. One half of my moveable estate to be divided equally between my four sons, James, Daniel, Samuel, and David. I make my two sons, James and Samuel, executors.

Witnesses, Abraham Rose, Abraham Rose, jr., Joseph Goldsmith, blacksmith. Proved, July 3, 1782.

Page 103.—In the name of God, Amen. I, MICEL OADELL, of Westchester County, being sick. I leave to my wife Elizabeth my one bed with the furniture, and half of my household goods. I make my sons, John, Isaac, and Henry, executors; they to sell all my estate and negroes, and after my lawful debts are paid to divide my estate equally between my wife, my three sons, and two daughters.

Dated July 22, 1782. Witnesses, Uzziel Fountain, yeoman, Thomas McCarthy, Benjamin Fowler. Proved, September 30, 1782.

Page 104.—I, PATRICK CAMPBELL, Major in his Majesty's Seventy-first Regiment of Foot, being of sound mind, memory, and understanding. All my funeral charges and just debts to be paid. I leave all the rest of my estate of every kind in Great Britain to my heir or heirs by my wife, and if she should not leave any heirs, or they should die under age and without lawful issue, in that case I give my said estate in Great Britain, to my brothers, Alexander, James, Collin, and Hugh, and to my nephew, Patrick Cameron, in equal shares. Unto my wife one third part of all my estate, both real and personal, in America (which I am now possessed of, or may hereafter receive from my father-in-law, Thomas Pearsall), at her own disposal; Also the use of one sixth part of my estate in America, during widowhood only; what I

have here given to be in lieu of her dower. Unto my
heir or heirs by my wife the remaining one half of
my estate in America; Also the one sixth part of my
estate, given to my wife during her widowhood, when
that may happen. In case my wife should have no
heir, then all my estate in America to my wife. I
make my father, Duncan Campbell, Esq., of Glenure,
in Scotland, and my brothers, Alexander Campbell
and Collin Campbell, executors to my estate in Great
Britain, and my father-in-law, Thomas Pearsall, of
the City of New York, merchant, and my wife, Sarah
Campbell, executors to my estate in America, my wife
to be an executrix only during her widowhood.

Dated June 8, 1781. Witnesses, John Glover, of the
City of New York, merchant, Thomas Clark, Quaker,
of the same city, merchant, and Nancy Pearsall.
Proved, September 30, 1782.

Page 106.—In the name of God, Amen. I, JOSHUA
VERMILYA, of the County of Westchester, yeoman,
being very weak in body. All my just debts and funeral charges to be paid and fully satisfied. I leave
to my dearly beloved wife as much of the household
furniture as she shall think proper; Also, my negro
wench Sarah; Also, £150, payable one month after my
decease by my executors, they also to pay unto her
as much money as will purchase her a decent suite of
mourning apparel. Unto my son Thomas £10 when
twenty-one. The lands and meadows that was left
between my brother Frederick Vermilya and myself,
by my father, to be divided as soon as possible and
the part falling to my estate be sold. In case it should
appear.to my executors that the monies arising from
the sale of my lands shall be better applied in pur-
chasing a place that may serve for the support and
bringing up my family and children better than putting the money to interest, they to do either they may
think best; should they purchase a place as aforesaid,
then the place so purchased to be sold when my son

Thomas becomes twenty-one years of age. My executors shall, immediately after my decease, dispose of my negro wench, Jane, my negro boys, Pomp, Yaff, and Squire, and my negro man, Jack, to the best advantage they can; likewise, my part of the crop of wheat I have sown on the farm of Mr. John De Lancey, when they shall think it most advantageous. I would wish and desire that my negro man John may remain with the family for the support and bringing up of my children as long as they keep a place or farm, and to be disposed of when the place or farm is disposed of. Unto my daughter Anna £25 when she becomes eighteen years of age. The remainder of my estate to be divided between my four children, vizt: Thomas, Isaac, Anna, and Polly, as follows: two thirds to my two sons, the remaining third between my two daughters. I make my trusty and loving friends, Abraham Volentine, and Gilbert Volentine, executors.

Dated October 3, 1782. Witnesses, Isaac Valintine, John Vermilya, and John Cregier, physician. Proved, October 14, 1782.

Page 108.—In the name of God, Amen. This 30th day of December, 1780, I, HENDERICK VANDERBILT, of Queens County. My wife Elizabeth shall have the full use of my farm in lieu of her dower, provided she brings up my children in a Christian, decent like manner, and yearly pays the interest upon the bonds that are against me, and if the money on bonds shall be demanded, my said wife shall pay off the bond and that money be refunded back as hereafter mentioned. Should my wife marry again my executors to raise money by the sale of such part of the estate, as they shall think best in order to refund that back to my wife that she has paid on my bonds. Should my wife die or marry my executors are to sell all my estate (except what my wife brought with her, that is of household goods, after I married her, that I give to her) and the proceeds to be equally divided between my three children, Fametie, Maregrite, and Elizabeth. I make my loving wife, Elizibett, and my friends, Andries Hegeman and Petrus Onderdonck, executors.

Witnesses, Daniel Rapalje, yeoman, Abraham Brinckerhoff, and Anne Rapalje. Proved, October 10, 1782.

Page 109.—In the name of God, Amen. I, DANIEL KISSAM, Esquire, of Cow Neck, in the Township of Hempstead, in Queens County, being in good health. All my just debts and funeral expenses to be paid. I leave to my dearly beloved wife Peggy £400; Also my riding chair, and my darkest brown chair horse; one of my best beds with the bedding and furniture belonging to it; my silver tankard, silver sugar-pot, silver teapot, my best dining-table, a tea table, the looking-glass used in the common room, six of my best chairs, and six silver teaspoons; Also, for her own use and residence, during widowhood (but not to be let or hired by her to any other person) the two western bedrooms in my dwelling house, and the cellar under them, and the use of one acre of ground annually, during her widowhood, for a garden or for planting, to be assigned to her annually by my executors, one year out of the lands devised to my son John, and another year out of the lands devised to my son Daniel, and so on alternately from year to year during her widowhood, with free ingress, egress, and regress to and from the same; Also, she to have pasturage for a horse and cow, and firewood for her own use of the land devised to my said two sons; all of which shall be in lieu of her dower. Unto my son John £400; my silver watch, library of books, all my wearing apparel, my negro man slave, Jacob, my black breeding mare, my new wagon, and new plow with their tackle; Also, my dwelling house and all that part of my farm on Cow Neck which formerly belonged to my father, together with a small piece of land adjoining the same. Whereas, there is a pond of water lying near about the center of my whole farm, surrounded with a considerable number of trees, which is a convenient watering place for each of the farms, given to my sons, I do hereby devise to my said son John all that piece of ground, extending from the southermost bounds of the said farm (devised to him), opposite to the said pond, three rods in breadth, east and west, so far southerly continuing the same breadth till it comes to the middle of the said pond, for the purpose of a watering place for his cattle. Unto my son Daniel my negro man slave, Will, and my negro child, Rebus, and my other wagon, plow, and tackle; Also that part of my farm on Cow Neck aforesaid, which I bought of Captain Samuel Cornell (except such parts thereof as are comprehended in the devise aforesaid to my son John). Unto my son, Benjamin Tredwell Kissam, £1,300, and my negro boy, James. Unto my daughter Phebe, wife of Richard Jackson, £200. Unto the said Richard Jackson a bond I have against him for £100. Unto my daughter Anne, wife of David Allen, £175, and my negro boy, Tom. Unto my daughter Sarah, wife of Elijah Allen, £200. Unto my daughter Elizabeth £500. The remainder of my lands and real estate to my said two sons, John and Daniel Kissam, in equal shares. The remainder of my personal estate, if any, as follows: one equal half to my said three sons; the other half to my said four daughters. I make Joseph Kissam, of Cow Neck, Daniel Kissam, Esquire, of Great Neck, my sons, John and Daniel Kissam, my sons-in-law, David and Elijah Allen, executors.

Dated October 17, 1781. Witnesses, William Thorne, of Hempstead, yeoman, Benjamin Kissam, John B. Kissam, of Hempstead, yeoman. Proved, September 13, 1782.

Page 112.—In the name of God, Amen. This 25th day of October, 1781, I, JOSEPH TOTTEN, of Hempsted.

Queens County, being of sound mind and memory. My executors to sell all my lands and Patent right in Hempsted, and the proceeds, together with my moveable estate, to be disposed of as follows: Unto Joseph Totten, my brother Samuel Totten's son, £20; unto my sister Mary Totten, £100; unto Samuel Eldard, the son of Israel Eldard, £50; the remainder to go to my two brothers Samuel and Daniel Totten, and my three sisters, Sarah Storm, Mary Totten, and Annar Eldard, in five equal shares. I make Israel Eldard, and my sister Mary Totten, executors.

Witnesses, Daniel Pettet and William Pettit, yeomen, Solomon Seaman.

Codicil. I now direct that my sister Mary shall have all the use, rents, issues, etc., of my dwelling house, out houses, lands and appurtenances, during her natural life; at her death to be sold and the proceeds disposed of as heretofore directed.

Dated August 23, 1782. Witnesses, Samuel Carman and Isaac Cromwell, yeoman, Richard Ellison. Proved, September 28, 1782.

Page 114.—In the name of God, Amen. I, BENJAMIN HEWLETT, of Great Neck, Hempstead, Queens County, yeoman, being sick and weak in body. All my just debts and funeral charges to be paid. I leave to my son Benjamin, all the Patent rights in the great plains of Hempstead and in the marshes at the south side of Hempstead, commonly called South (which are derived to me from and under my father). Unto my son George, all my rights of land in the great plains and marshes at South, which I purchased of John Carman and Thomas Tredwell, and all the lands and meadows which belong to me in virtue of said purchase. My executors to sell the residue of my lands and real estate, they to consult my wife and daughters, who now live at home with me. The proceeds of the sale to be disposed of as follows: Unto my dearly beloved wife Susannah, £280; unto my daughter Deborah, £280; a like sum to my daughters, Jane, Hannah, and Sarah; unto my daughter Rebecka, £60; which several legacies will make them equal to what I have already given to my daughter Susannah. Of the overplus of said proceeds, one seventh part to my wife, and each of my daughters, Rebecca, Deborah, Jane, Hannah, and Sarah; the remaining seventh part to my daughter Susannah and her two children, Elizabeth and Susannah, equally. My executors to put at interest the shares of my grandchildren for their benefit. Unto my son George, all my upland and meadow ground at the south side of Hempstead (which I now hold and occupy in common with him), he paying in consideration, £150. The use, profits, etc., of all the real estate, ordered to be sold, to go to my wife and four daughters, now living at home with me, for their common support, until the same shall be sold by my executors. What is herein given to my wife is in lieu of her Dower. I make Daniel Whitehead Kissam, of Cow Neck, and my two sons, Benjamin and George Hewlett, executors.

Dated August 13, 1782. Witnesses, Benjamin Kissam, Peter Bonnet, and Lawrence Hewlett, yeomen. Proved, October 3, 1782.

Page 116.—In the name of God, Amen. I, JOSIAH WHEELER, of Northfairfield, County of Fairfield, Colony of Connecticut, being in my perfect mind and understanding. I leave to my eldest son, Josiah, £25 out of my real estate; the remainder of my real estate to go to my two sons, Josiah and Zalmon in equal shares, provided they pay to my daughter Sarah, £25 each (as my free gift to her), provided my estate appear to be worth £500. Unto my dear and loving wife, all my moveable estate, to be at her will and pleasure. I make my loving wife, sole executrix.

Dated March 5, 1782. Witnesses, John Wallace, of City of New York, merchant, Chloe Wallace, Matthew Partleow. Proved, October 22, 1782.

Page 117.—In the name of God, Amen. The 13th day of November, 1781, I, WILLIAM EAMES, of New York, yeoman, being very sick and weak in body. All those debts and duties I owe in right or conscience to be well and truly paid in convenient time after my decease. I leave to my son Robert, one Spanish dollar for his birthright. Unto my son Henry, one Spanish dollar; my sons to be excluded from having any claim in my estate. Unto my dearly beloved wife, Margaret, and my two youngest sons, William and Jacob Eames, my two houses and lots (being leased estate), with all the buildings and household goods, money, now in my possession, or due to me, for their sole use. I make my dearly beloved wife, Margaret, and my trusty friend, David McConoughy, executors.

(Signed)   WILLIAM EMAS.

Witnesses, Abraham Bininger, and Thomas Dods, cordwainer, Peter Sparling, schoolmaster, both of the City of New York. Proved, October 27, 1782.

Page 119.—In the name of God, Amen. I, DAVID ROGERS, now of New York, pilot, being in bodily health, considering the perils and the dangers of the seas. I leave to my worthy friend, Jane Gregg, of the City of New York, inn-keeper, all my wages, sums of money, lands, tenements, goods, and chattels, as shall be anyways due, or belonging to me at the time of my decease; whom I make sole executrix.

Dated October 11, 1780.

(Signed)   DAVID RODGERS.

Witnesses, John Welsh, William Cumming. Signatures of testator and witnesses identified by William Edwards, Surgeon in His Majesty's Loyal American Regiment. Proved, November 4, 1782.

Page 120.—In the name of God, Amen. I, HENRY BREVOORT, of the City of New York, iron-monger, considering the uncertainty of this mortal life. All my just debts and funeral expenses to be paid. I leave to my eldest son, Abraham, £10. All my personal estate (not in this will bequeathed) to be disposed of by my executors to the best advantage; and the proceeds to be divided as follows: One fourth part unto my loving wife, Mary, in lieu of her Dower; the three remaining fourth parts unto my three children, Abraham, Hester, and Nicholas Brevoort; which shall be placed out by my executors, and the interest applied towards the support and education of my three children; the part of each to be paid as they respectively are twenty-one years old. Unto my wife, my negro wench named Bet, and all my beds, bedding, and household furniture. The house and lot of ground belonging to me, situate in Queens Street, adjoining the house of Christopher Robart, be rented out by my executors until the youngest child comes to majority; and the profits therefrom placed out at interest for their benefit. Likewise to her, the use of my new house and lot of ground situate on the east side of the above-mentioned house and lot, while my widow; should she marry again before the youngest child is twenty-one, then the said house and lot shall be rented out by my executors. Unto my son Abraham, my negro boy named Joe; to my daughter Hester, my negro girl called Cill; unto my youngest son, Nicholas, my negro girl named Diana. My negro man Harry to be sold with the rest of my personal estate. I make my loving wife Mary, my loving brothers-in-law, Theophilus Anthony, Peter Marcelis, and Theophilus Hardenbrook, all of the City of New York, executors.

Dated June 10, 1776. Witnesses, John Ray, Jr., Samuel Ray, John Cozine, Jr., of the City of New York, Esquire. Proved, November 4, 1782.

Page 122.—This is the last will and Testament of PRINCE HAWES, formerly of Redding, in the County of Fairfield, Colony of Connecticut, but now of the Township of Hempstead, Queens County, store-keeper. All my just debts and funeral expenses to be paid. I leave to my two brothers, Isaac and Samuel Hawes, now or late of " Kenk," in the County of Litchfield, Colony of Connecticut, all my wearing apparel, to be divided as near equal as possible between them. Whereas, I own a certain Block House, which I now occupy as a store, situate near the public house or tavern of James Poole, lying upon the Great Road, north side of Hempstead Plains, I require the same to be sold at the discretion of my executors for ready money. All my other goods, chattels or personal estate (except the above-mentioned wearing apparel) to be sold, and the proceeds, together with the ready money I die possessed of, to go to my two brothers, Isaac and Samuel, and unto my three sisters, Eunice, Zurviah, and Susannah Hawes, all now or late of " Kenk," in the County of Litchfield, Connecticut, in equal shares. I make my trusty and well-beloved friends, David Seabury, of the City of New York, merchant, and Richard Spragg, of the Township of Hempstead, Queens County, executors.

Dated April 22, 1782. Witnesses, Richard Spragg, David V. D. Water, of Hempstead, yeoman, John Dickson. Proved, October 12, 1782.

Page 123.—In the name of God, Amen. I, ANDREW BARRONS, of Sagg, in the Township of Southampton, in the County of Suffolk, merchant, being very sick and weak. After my just debts are satisfied, my wife Sarah and my son John have the sole disposal of all my lands, buildings, and moveable estate; my wife to remain in my dwelling house undisturbed till the children come of age; after that, to have the one half of the buildings and one third of the land, while my widow, to improve. My children, namely, Hannah, Matthew, Edmund, and Mary, to be paid £50 each by my executors. My son Matthew to have all my lands and buildings whenever his mother has done with it. Should my estate prove greater than I at present can see, the overplus to be given away at the discretion

of my executors to my child or children. My son John
to have £50 out of my estate. My wife to have all
the moveables belonging to the house. Unto my
daughter, Margaret Saterly, five shillings. I make
my wife Sarah and my son John, executors.

Dated March 3, 1782. Witnesses, Jedidiah Peirson,
and Caleb Peirson, yeomen, Joseph Gibbs. Proved,
September 9, 1782.

Page 125.—In the name of God, Amen. This 14th
day of December, 1776, I, ANDREW DEVOE, of New Rochel in the County of Westchester, yeoman, being of
sound mind and memory. All my just debts and funeral charges to be paid by my executors some short
time after my decease. I leave to my nephew, Daniel
Devoe, £5. Unto Mary Moss, the daughter of Samuel Moss, £10; unto Elizabeth Willis, daughter of
James Willis, £5. All the remainder of my estate,
real and personal, to be sold, and the proceeds of such
sale to be equally divided between my brother, Abel
" Devove's " children and my brother, Frederick " Devove's " children, and my sister, Magalene Schur-
man's children, in equal shares, and my nephew Daniel
his equal share with the rest. I make my brother,
Frederick Devove, my brother-in-law, Jeremiah Schur-
man, and my trusty friend, Peter Bonnet, of New
Rochel, executors.

         (Signed)   ANDREW DAVOVE.
Witnesses, John Stewart, Christian Schureman, of
the City of New York, spinster, Sarah Schureman.
Proved, November 12, 1782.

Page 126.—In the name of God, Amen. I, JACOBUS
VAN ORDEN, of the Out Ward of the City of New York,
yeoman, being of sound mind and body. My executors
to pay all my debts and funeral expenses out of my
personal estate. I leave to my well-beloved wife,
Christyntje, all the residue of my personal estate, and
all my real estate while my widow; to be in lieu of

dower; any claim of dower shall make this devise null and void. Should she so accept of the said devise, she may, while my widow, from time to time use and dispose of such necessary part of my personal estate for her maintenance and support, excepting, out of this bequest all such debts and sums of money which my daughter Jacomijntie and her husband, Isaac Schultz, shall owe me at the time of my decease, which I do hereby bequeath to them. Immediately after the decease or remarriage of my wife, unto my only son, Jacobus, £10, out of my personal estate, as an acknowledgment of his birthright. Unto my daughter Jacomijntie, all that lot of ground situate on the south side of and fronting Mulberry Street in the Out Ward of said City, and bounded in the rear by ground of Gerardus Hardenbrook; on the north-westerly side by ground of Isaac Schultz; on the south-east by ground of said Hardenbrook, and of David Malleshaw; 35 ft. x 102 ft. Unto my daughter Elizabeth, the wife of Richard Dawson, two pieces of land, situate in the said Out Ward, on the south-easterly side of the road leading from Greenwich to the Great Kills; bounded on the south-west by ground belonging to me in the Wyland Patent; on the north-east by land of John Leake; on the south-east by the road leading to Bloomingdale, or by the land belonging to the Corporation of the City of New York. Unto my daughter Magdelena, wife of Thomas Tibbot Warner, seventeen acres of land bounded north-westerly in front by the road leading from Greenwich to the Great Kills; on the north-westerly and south-westerly sides by land of John Morin Scott; and south-easterly in the rear by land late of Peter Van Orden. Also, that house and lot situate in Battoe or Dye Street in the West Ward of said City; bounded northeasterly in front on the said street; northwesterly by land of the widow Pulling; south-easterly by a lot of Paulus Banta; being 25 x 85 ft. All my salt meadow in the upper meadow near the Bull's on the west side of Hudson's River, in the County of Bergen and Province of New Jersey, unto my daughters, Elizabeth and Magdelena, in equal shares. No devise of real estate to my daughters herein before mentioned to take effect till after the decease or remarriage of my wife. The remainder of my real estate not herein disposed of unto my son, Jacobus Van Orden. All remaining personal estate unto my three daughters and son, in equal shares. I make my wife and son, and my son-in-law, Thomas Tibbot Warner, and my friend, William Vandewater, executors.

Dated October 8, 1772. Witnesses, John Morin Scott, John Graham, Peter Fountain, of the City of New York, barber. Proved, November 12, 1782.

Page 129.—In the name of God, Amen. I, WILLIAM PASMORE, being of sound mind and memory. My prize money and wages and effects and estate to be delivered into the hands of William Bollings, he being the only relative or friend that I have had in that place of my decease in the 4th Ward of the Parson's House on Long Island.

Dated, General Naval Hospital, May 12, 1782. Dr. William Pasmore. Witnesses, John Neville, of H. M. S. *Ceres,* Robert Taylor, Frances Green. Proved, June 10, 1782.

[NOTE.—Letters of administration granted to William Pye, H. M. S. *London,* mariner, assignee of William Bollings, sole legatee of William Passomore, deceased; dated September 6, 1782.]

Page 130.—I, JACOB VAN ORDEN, of the Out Ward of the City of New York, being weak in body. All my just debts and funeral expenses to be paid by my executors out of my estate within convenient time after my decease. My whole estate, real and personal, to be sold within six months. The proceeds to be divided into three parts as follows: One third part unto my loving sister, Magdelena Van Orden, the wife of Thomas Tibbot Warner; a like part to my loving sister, Jemima Van Orden, the wife of Isaac Schultz; the remaining third part to the children of my sister, Elizabeth Van Orden, deceased; by name, Charles and James Dawson; being the two children of Richard Dawson, deceased; and John Obrien, the son of Henry Obrien; said third part to be equally divided amongst them and paid when they come to age. Should any one of the three die before majority, then the survivors shall share the legacy. I make my loving brother-in-law, Thomas Tibbot Warner, and my friend, William Van de Water, baker, of the City of New York, executors.

Dated February 4, 1782.

(*Signed*)   JACOB VAN NORDEN.

Witnesses, Louis Andrew Gautier, David Mann, of City of N. Y., butcher, John Horn, of City of N. Y., yeoman. Proved, November 12, 1782.

Page 131.—In the name of God, Amen. I, DANIEL McSWAIN, of the County of Richmond, being weak in body. My fast and movable estate to remain as it is, until my son John is of age, for the purpose of bringing up the children. Unto my loving wife, the use of one third part of my fast estate during her natural life; Also, a room in the house during life; likewise to have a cow and feather bed, bedstead and bedding. Unto my son John, the northermost half of my land, to have an equal proportion of woodland with my son Vincent; also, to have one half of my moveables when he comes of age; he to pay to my daughter Catharine £60, and one cow; also to pay to my daughter Sarah £60 and one cow; also to pay to my daughter Mary £10. When Vincent is of age, my son John must pay one half of all my lawful debts. To my son John, 8 shillings. Unto my son Vincent, the southermost half of my land, including the house that I now live in; likewise, one half of my moveables when John comes of age. When Vincent comes of age, then the house is to be valued by two men, they each choosing one, and the one half of such valuation Vincent is to pay to his brother John. At his majority Vincent is to pay to my daughter Elizabeth £60 and one cow; to my daughter Mary £70 and one cow; likewise he must pay one half my lawful debts. Should any of the stock or moveables be stolen or taken away, then the heirs are to lose in proportion as the executors shall think proper to settle it. I make my loving wife and my true and loving friends, George Barns and Stephen Bedell, executors.

Dated February 9, 1782. Witnesses, Anthony Neill, farmer, David Day. Proved, November 11, 1782.

Page 133.—In the name of God, Amen. The twenty-fourth day of June, 1782, I, Bennajah Wiggins, of Hempstead, Queens County, being very sick and weak in body. All my just debts and funeral expenses to be paid. Unto my honoured mother, Elizabeth Skidmore, £20, to be levied out of my estate. Unto my well-beloved brother, Thomas Wiggins, my horse, saddle and bridle, and £20. Unto my beloved sisters, Martha Everitt and Kezia Betts, £10 each. Unto my beloved cousins, John Everitt, £20; Thomas Everitt, £10; Jane Everitt, £6; Richard Wiggins, the son of my brother Thomas, £10; John Wiggins, also son of said Thomas, a like sum. Unto my beloved cousin, Oliver Green, son of Richard Green, my young mare colt. The remainder of my estate, not herein before given, to be divided among the children of my brother, Daniel Wiggins, and the children of Keziah Betts, in equal shares. I make my brother, Thomas Wiggins, my cousins, John and James Everitt, executors.

(*Signed*) Benajah Wiggins.

Witnesses, Richard Everitt, John Cornell, of Hempstead, yeoman, James Everitt. Proved, October 25, 1782.

Page 134.—In the name of God, Amen. The third day of January, 1782, I, John Skidmore, of Hempstead in Queens County, yeoman, being now advanced

in years and very weak in body. All my just debts
and funeral charges to be paid. Unto Elizabeth, my
dearly beloved wife, one cow and all the household
furniture that she brought to me. The remainder of
my estate to be sold, the proceeds to be disposed of
as follows: Unto Elizabeth, my wife, £50 (to be in
lieu of her Dower); unto my well-beloved son, Whitehead, £5; unto my well-beloved daughter, Phebe Vannostrand, the now wife of Evert Vannostrand, £30;
unto my well-beloved son, Daniel, £100, if he shall be
living to receive it after my decease; should he die
before that time, then £50 only to go to his children
in equal shares, his wife to have the use of said sum
towards the support and bringing up of said children.
Unto my well-beloved son, Thomas, one bond or obligation which I have against him, conditioned for the
payment of £100. My executors shall not demand
the money. Unto my beloved granddaughter, Phebe
Skidmore, £10. The remainder of my estate not before given away to be equally divided among all my
children, that is: my daughter, Jane Smith, my son,
Whitehead Skidmore, my daughter, Phebe Vannostrand, my son, John Skidmore, my son, Thomas Skidmore, and my son, Daniel Skidmore. Whereas my
son, Samuel Skidmore, is now already dead, the part
or division that should have fallen to him to be
equally divided among his children. I make my son-
in-law, Evert Vannostrand, my cousins, Joseph Skidmore, and Benjamin Everit, executors. My granddaughter Phebe, herein mentioned, is the daughter of
my son, John Skidmore.

Witnesses, James Everit, Benjamin Everit, both of
Hempstead, yeomen, Abraham Hendrickson. Proved,
November 4, 1782.

Page 136.—In the name of God, Amen. September
15, 1782. I, DANIEL SMITH, of Hempstead, Queens
County, yeoman, being sick and weak. My just debts
and funeral charges first being satisfied. I leave to

my loving wife Phebe the use of all my estate, house, land, and meadow, together with all my moveable estate (except that otherwise disposed of) while my widow; or until my son Benjamin shall be twenty-one years of age; this to my wife towards the raising and edifying my children. Should my wife neglect or refuse to learn my children to read, write and cipher (that is to common learning), then my executors are to sell so much of my moveable estate as shall pay the expense of their learning. Should my wife marry before my son is twenty-one, she is to have no more than her father gave her when she and I were married. After such marriage my executors to sell all my estate, house, land, meadow and moveables. When my son is twenty-one, my executors to sell all my estate (except a certain part), and divide the proceeds according to the following: Whereas my wife is like to have a child, if that child lives and is a boy, then I give £200 to it; if a girl, it is not to have that sum. If it is a boy, then my son Benjamin is to have £200; if a girl, then £300 to him. The remainder equally to my loving wife Phebe, my son Benjamin, my daughters, Nancy, Catharine, Phebe, and Elizabeth Smith, and the child that my child is like to have. I make my loving brother, Richard Smith and my friend, Stephen Powel, executors.

Witnesses, James Wood, yeoman, Israel Carpenter, Elijah Wood, yeoman. `Proved, October 26, 1782.

Page 138.—In the name of God, Amen. I, THOMAS BROWN, Esquire, of Pamerpough (Pamrapo), in the Corporation and County of Bergen, in the State of New Jersey, being weak in body, do this twenty-first day of September, 1782, make this will. My funeral charges and my just debts, if any there be, to be fully satisfied. I leave to my grandson, Thomas Gutchear, all my lands and tenements in the City of New York, when twenty-one. Unto my other grandson, Daniel Gutchear, all my lands and tenements situate

in the State of New Jersey; Also, all my implements
of husbandry; together with all my horses and cattle,
and my negro Jack (if he has a mind to stay on my
farm in the State of New Jersey; when he arrives
at full age. If either of my grandsons should die
under age, then the surviving heir shall pay unto my
brother William's four children, to wit: William,
Thomas, Gitty, and Polly, £150 each; should both
grandsons die without issue and under age, then the
whole of my estate shall be equally divided among
my brother William's children. My cash, which is
between seven and eight hundred pounds (besides the
money which I have out at interest) to be put at interest at the discretion of my wife and executors; the
principal and interest to go to Thomas and Daniel
Gutchear, in equal shares, when they are of age, if
my wife and executors shall deem it expedient; but
should they find sufficient reasons to withhold the said
monies from my grandsons (thro' their irregularities
of behaviour or bad and prodigal conduct), they shall
have the privilege to withhold the same till my grandsons reform and lead honest and sober lives, and no
longer. If my wife and my executors should think
it convenient and profitable to repair the ferry, or
to repair or erect any other building on my said estates, then they shall have the privilege to make use
of said monies. Any of my other negroes which may
have a mind to be sold, I leave them to the discretion
of my wife and executors to dispose of. My wife to
have a right during her widowhood to remain on my
farm in New Jersey, or reside on my estate in New
York. I make my good friends, Peter Stoutenburgh,
cooper, and Samuel Stoutenburgh, merchant, both of
the City of New York, and my good friend, Abraham
Sickels, Clerk of the Reformed Dutch Church of Bergen, to be executors.

Witnesses, Zacharias Sickels, Barnaby Savage,
Thomas Cabberly, of East New Jersey, yeoman.
Proved, November 18, 1782.

Page 139.—In the name of God, Amen. I, WILLIAM CORBY, of the City of New York, being of sound mind and memory. After just debts be paid, I leave to my dearly beloved wife Ann, all my real and personal estate until my children, John and Elizabeth, shall be twenty-one years of age; who at their majority are to have equal shares of my real estate; every part of the personal estate at that time to become the sole property of my wife. Should both die in non-age, the whole real estate to go to my wife. She is to provide for the children until their coming of age. The mother of my wife, Mary Emett, shall remain on the estate and have a maintenance for the term of her natural life. I make my good friends, Richard Jenkins, and Jasper Ruckel, bakers, of the City of New York, jointly with my wife, Ann Corby, executors.

Dated August 15, 1782. Witnesses, William Walter, John Kirk, of City of N. Y., inn-keeper, William Bull. Proved, November 11, 1782.

Page 141.—These Presents witnesseth this twentieth day of May, 1782, that I, HANNAH BURTIS, of Hempstead, Queens County, widow, make this will. My estate, real and personal, to be sold by my executors (except what is herein given away). All my debts to be paid. I leave to my daughter, Marget Mott, all the provisions that I have in my house, or grain on the ground, or meat that may be fatting for my family's use. Unto my granddaughter, Elizabeth Mott, daughter of my daughter Marget, one chest; all the remainder of my estate unto my five daughters, Mary Weeks, Phebe Watts, Marget Mott, Jean Mott, and Martha Tattersall in equal shares; excepting £20, which is for Marget Mott. I make Samuel Titus, executor, and my daughter Marget, executrix.

Witnesses, Jehu Mott, Ruth Mott, Jehu Mott, 3d, of Hempstead, yeoman. Proved, November 10, 1782.

Page 142.—In the name of God, Amen. I, JOHN SMITH, of the City of New York, being of sound mind

and memory. After all my just debts be paid, I leave
to my lawful wedded wife, the part of the house she
lived in when I made my will; or, if she does not like
to live in the same, to an annual allowance of £30
during her natural life; as likewise the same liberty
as she always had of the whole garrat for her own
use. I make Jonathan Smith, Daniel Devo, and John
Noblit, executors. Unto John Smith, a grandson, 5
shillings sterling out of the estate more than the rest;
the remainder to be divided betwixt Jonathan, Mary,
and John Smith in equal shares; a small iron kettle
and trammel unto Mary, my daughter; the household
goods to be equally divided amongst them after my
loving wife's decease.

Dated March 11, 1782., Witnesses, James Nichols,
Samuel Stuart, of City of New York, tailor, Elizabeth
Stuart, his wife. Proved, November 25, 1782.

Page 143.—I, BENJAMIN BIRKETT, at present of the
City of New York, merchant, do make this will. I
leave to my honoured father, John Birkett, hat-maker,
at Hull in Yorkshire, five guineas; unto my dearly beloved sister, Jane Birkett, living with my father, five
guineas as a memorial of unimpaired fraternal affection. Whatever effects I have at my decease, as soon
as convenient after, to be turned into money. The
proceeds and other personal estate to be placed out
on good security on interest by my executors; the produce of which every quarter of a year they are to pay
to my honoured and dear Mother, Sarah Birkett, now
or lately dwelling at Kendal in Westmoreland, during
her natural life; such payments not to be liable to
the receipt or control of my father; her receipt alone
to be sufficient. After her decease, the whole of my estate unto my sister Jane; she paying to my aunt,
Hannah Satterthwaite, relict of my uncle, William
Satterthwaite of Kent Street Road, London, ten
guineas; unto my executors, nine guineas, as hereafter
expressed in confidence. Should she die without heirs,

and not have occasion to make use of more than her fortune's interest, she will at her decease leave to my worthy and dear friend, Esther Fisher, £40 sterling; unto Sarah, Miers, and Samuel Fisher, each £40; they being brothers and sisters to my deceased and dearly beloved friend, Jabez Maud Fisher, late of Philadelphia in North America, merchant. Should my effects not be sufficient to pay the last four legacies, then the legatees are to receive the same in proportionate shares; if there be any overplus, ten guineas, if so much remains, to be paid to the Monthly Meeting of Women Friends of Pine Street in Philadelphia, in remembrance of the memory of my valuable friend and mistress, Sarah Fisher, deceased. At the decease of my mother, unto my valuable and esteemed friends, Isaac Wilson and George Kendal, in Westmoreland, and Samuel Elam, of Leeds in Yorkshire (but now of New York), three guineas each, as a token of what I could wish to give them for the trouble they will have in executing the trusts in them reposed by this will appointing them executors.

Dated February 23, 1780. Witnesses, Abraham Duryee, Frances Duryee, of New Bushwick, Long Island, yeomen. Proved, November 26, 1782.

Page 144.—Know all men by these presents that I, WILLIAM FROST, of Matenecock in the Township of Oysterbay, Queens County, yeoman, being this twenty-sixth day of March, 1781, perfectly well in health of body, altho' I am far advanced in years. My executors to pay all my just debts and funeral charges that may arise. I leave to my son William, the one sixth part of my salt meadows in the Great Meadows, so called, at Metenecock, and the equal third part of my creek thatch and marshes at Pine Island; together with the equal third part of my plain land lying upon the great plains in Robert Williams' purchase and Patent. My executors to pay in money £100 to my said son William. Should he die and have no child,

then all that is given to him is to return to my other
two sons, Stephen Frost Charlton and Charles Frost
Charlton in equal shares, but the £100 to go to my
grandsons, Charles Thorne and Stephen Thorne, sons
of Daniel Thorne, deceased, in equal shares. Unto
my other two sons, Stephen Frost Charlton and
Charles Frost Charlton, all the remaining part of my
moveable estate, such as chattels, horses and stock
of all kinds, except £50, which is to go to my grandsons, Charles and Stephen Thorne. I make my two
sons, Stephen Frost Charlton and Charles Frost
Charlton; my two beloved friends, William Cock and
John Cock, executors; they to be reasonably paid for
their time, trouble and expense.

Witnesses, Penn Frost, Prior Townsend, Robert
Mitchill Baxter, all of Oysterbay. Proved, March 26,
1781.

Page 146.—In the name of God, Amen. This eighth
day of June, 1782, I, HEZEKIAH PARSALL, of Hempstead, Queens County, being sick in body. I leave to
Martha, my well-beloved wife, one room in my house
for her use as long as she remains my widow; likewise,
all my indoor moveables; the first choice of one of all
my cows. Unto my wife and daughter Mary, all my
fowls, geese, and turkeys, equally between them. My
out-door and moveable estate to be sold; the proceeds
to be equally divided between my wife and three
daughters, that is to my wife, Sucke Denton (wife of
Isaac Denton, Jr.), Martha Dorlon (wife of Joseph
Dorlon), and Mary " Parson," my youngest daughter.
Unto my three sons, namely Henry, Thomas, and Niah
Parsall, all my lands and buildings, lands lotted or
unlotted, with all my rights in lands divided or undivided, in equal shares. All my just and lawful debts
be paid out of my lands just mentioned; likewise,
my funeral charges. My three sons to provide for my
widow, sufficient bread and meat, and firewood brought
to the door, while she remains my widow. On the

death or marriage of my widow, the house I now live in and all the rooms thereof, to be sold; the proceeds to be equally divided amongst my three sons. I make Isaac Frost and Henry and Thomas Parsall, my sons, executors.

Dated June 8, 1782. Witnesses, Isaac Frost, Henry Pearsall, Daniel Pearsall, of Hempstead, yeoman. Proved, November 15, 1782.

Codicil. Out of my stock, within disposed of, unto my daughter, Mary Parsall, one three-year-old heifer.

Page 148.—In the name of God, Amen. I, WILLIAM ROE, of Flushing, Queens County, yeoman, this twenty-sixth day of December, 1780, being well in body. All my just and lawful debts and funeral charges be paid by my loving son John. I leave unto my dearly beloved wife Martha, my best bed and furniture, six of my best sitting chairs, six of my best pewter plates, two best pewter platters, my best iron pot, and kettle, my best cow (to be kept on my said farm), half a dozen knives and forks, my looking-glass, my riding chair and my black mare called the Chair Mare; all which is given in lieu of dower. Also, unto her, the interest of £200; to be paid her semi-annually by my son John; she to have the best room in my house, rent free; Also, the use of my black girl named Hannah. At my wife's death or second marriage, the said Hannah to go to my loving daughter, Elizabeth Roe. Should the said negro girl have a child or children while she is in my wife's possession, such child or children to go to my daughter Elizabeth. Unto my loving son Oliver, my lot of lands lying by Joseph Wright's; Also, a piece of salt meadow adjoining Samuel Cornell's and David Roe's salt meadow. Unto my loving daughter Ann, my second best bed and furniture called "her Bed," which she now has the use of; likewise, £25. Unto my loving son William, £100. Unto my loving son Thomas, £100, which is to draw interest to the day he is twenty-one years old. Also, my negro boy named Pompey. Unto my loving daughter Elizabeth, £100, to draw interest to the day she is eighteen years of age, or day of marriage; Also, my third best bed and furniture. Unto my daughter, Ann Cornell, my negro girl named Violet. Unto my loving son John, all my real and personal estate which I have in Flushing, excepting what I have herein given away. My executors as guardians of my two sons, John and Thomas, to put them to good trades, and let my house be a home for them when it may seem to be convenient for them to be at home, until their majority; and also keep and support my daughter Elizabeth with suitable food and raiment until she is eighteen years of age, or marry. Should my son John die and leave no issue, my son Thomas is to have the estate willed to his deceased brother. If my executors shall recover the one third part of 300 acres of land which I may have a right to in the West Jersey in Gloster.(Gloucester) County, near the De Laware River, it shall be valued, and if its valuation amounts to £400, then it shall go to my two sons, Oliver and William, if valued above that sum, the overplus to be divided between my sons, John and Thomas. My wife shall not take any person or persons into that part of the house that I allow her while my widow, without the consent of either of my sons, John or Thomas, whichever may possess the farm; but she shall be found with sufficiency of fuel for her fire at all times during her widowhood. I make my loving and trusty sons, John and Thomas, executors, at present under age. Should I die before they are of age, I make my trusty friends, David Haviland and Caleb Haviland, executors, or guardians over my said two sons until one or both arrive at the age of twenty-one years.

Witnesses, George Barwick, yeoman, Daniel Hitchcock, Abigail Haviland. Proved, November 5, 1782.

INDEX.